SO-BUG-269

Setting the Standard for the New Auditor's Report:
An Analysis of Attempts to Influence the Auditing Standards Board

STUDIES IN MANAGERIAL AND FINANCIAL ACCOUNTING, VOLUME 1

Editor: Marc J. Epstein, Graduate School of Business Administration, Harvard University

Studies in Managerial and Financial Accounting

Edited by
Marc J. Epstein
Graduate School of Business Administration,
Harvard University

Volume 1.
Setting the Standard for the New Auditor's Report:
An Analysis of Attempts to Influence the Auditing Standards Board
Marshall A. Geiger
Department of Accounting, University of Rhode Island

Volume 2.
The Shareholders Use of Corporate Annual Reports
Marc J. Epstein, *Graduate School of Business Administration, Harvard University*
and **Moses L. Pava,** *Sy Syms School of Business, Yeshiva University*

Setting the Standard for the New Auditor's Report:
An Analysis of Attempts to Influence the Auditing Standards Board

by **MARSHALL A. GEIGER**

Associate Professor of Accounting

University of Rhode Island

HF
5616
.U5
G44
1993
West

 **JAI PRESS INC.**

Greenwich, Connecticut   London, England

Geiger, Marshall A.
    Setting the standard for the new auditor's report : an analysis of
attempts to influence the Auditing Standards Board / by Marshall A.
Geiger.
        p.   cm. — (Studies in managerial and financial accounting ;
v. 1)
    Includes bibliographical references and index.
    ISBN 1-55938-561-8
    1. Auditing—United States—Standards. 2. Auditors' reports-
-United States.   3. American Institute of Certified Public
Accountants. Auditing Standards Board.   I. Title.   II. Series.
HF5616.U5G44   1993
657'.45'0973—dc20   93-1462
                                                              CIP

Copyright © 1993 JAI PRESS INC.
55 Old Post Road, No. 2
Greenwich, Connecticut 06836

JAI PRESS LTD.
The Courtyard
28 High Street
Hampton Hill, Middlesex TW12 1PD
England

All rights reserved. No part of this publication may be reproduced,
stored on a retrieval system, or transmitted in any form or by any
means, electronic, mechanical, photocopying, filming, recording, or
otherwise without prior permission in writing from the publisher.

ISBN: 1-55938-561-8

Library of Congress Catalog Card Number: 93-1462

Manufactured in the United States of America

CONTENTS

Foreword

The research presented in this monograph makes two rare and substantial contributions to auditing literature. One, it addresses a virtual void in research concerning the process by which authoritative auditing standards are established. Two, it employs and demonstrates an innovative research method that is eminently well-suited not only to research about audit standard-setting but about standard-setting in general.

This monograph is a comprehensive study of how a formal auditing standard was established for one of the most important and contentious areas of audit practice—audit reports. The monograph's literature review amply documents the controversies and milestones in the evolution of audit reporting and the rather sparse research efforts that have addressed that evolution. It is a rich source of history for both scholars and standard-setters.

A more prominent and special contribution, however, is the description and analysis of the most recent step in audit report evolution, the development of *SAS 58, Reports on Audited Financial Statements*. The research catalogs and examines the perspectives and influences of virtually all parties involved in establishing that standard: auditing standards board members, task force members, AICPA staff, regulatory agencies, and, perhaps most importantly, parties who submitted comment letters on the exposure draft of the proposed standard. The result is an extensive identification and rigorous analysis of the issues surrounding audit reports, the alternative solutions to those issues that were considered, and the rationale underlying the ultimate decisions embodied in the standard. These findings identify fertile subject matter for future research about audit reporting.

The research also deepens and enlarges our knowledge of the general process by which auditing standards are developed. The researcher had open access to both auditing standards board and task force meetings and the document drafts relevant to each, as well as the opportunity to discuss specific developments in the process with many of its participants. In addition, he had immediate access to comment letters. Thus, he was able to observe and examine virtually all of the steps in the standard-setting process as they occurred and analyze the causal relationship between inputs to that process and its product.

Another impressive and uncommon contribution is the two-phase research method employed. Phase one was a content analysis of comment letters on the exposure draft of the proposed standard. This analysis allowed the researcher to identify the significant issues likely to affect the auditing standards board's deliberations and to assess the level of agreement among types of commentators about these issues. The content analysis provided a major input into the second phase of the research, a longitudinal study of the development of an auditing standard. The longitudinal analysis was a study of the steps in the standard-setting process, including their interactions and iterations. Through this analysis, the researcher was able to monitor the sources and treatment of issues affecting the development of the auditing standard and diagnose their influence on the final standard.

This research method should be fruitful for research involving standard-setting in general. For example, the method could be used in research of the financial and governmental accounting standards processes and could also have applications in research on how standards are established by regulatory agencies.

For those interested in relevant research topics about audit reporting and standard-setting as a whole, as well as insights into a pioneering research method, this study is indispensable.

Alan J. Winters
Director of Auditing Research
American Institute of
Certified Public Accountants

Introduction

This monograph discusses two different but related subjects that affect virtually all practicing CPAs—standards for audit reports and how the AICPA's Auditing Standards Board (ASB) works. The issuance of *SAS 58, Reports on Audited Financial Statements*, is the latest event in the long and sometimes controversial history of audit reporting. This monograph traces that history and provides practitioners with insights into the political and practice issues that have shaped the evolution of audit reporting. Armed with these insights, practitioners will better appreciate changes in audit report language that have occurred over the last several decades and have a clearer understanding of why today's audit report reads as it does.

Practitioners will also obtain a detailed knowledge of the process that the ASB follows in establishing authoritative auditing standards. The author observed the process at work by attending meetings of the ASB and its task force as *SAS 58* was developed. In addition, the author discussed the process with individual board and task force members and AICPA staff. He also reviewed comment letters on the proposed reporting standard and was able to identify issues and monitor the deliberations of those issues at various ASB and task force meetings.

The result of this observation and analysis provides interesting and useful insights into the steps the ASB follows, the factors that influence standard-setting, and how practitioners' comments during the exposure period for a proposed standard affect the final standard.

For practitioners who seek a better understanding of audit reporting standards and the audit standard-setting process, this monograph is invaluable reading.

Dan M. Guy
Vice-President–Auditing
American Institute of
Certified Public Accountants

Overview

In 1988, the Auditing Standards Board (ASB) issued Statement on Auditing Standards (*SAS*) *58, Reports on Audited Financial Statements.* This monograph describes the ASB's procedures in establishing the final version of *SAS 58* and attempts to depict the salient influences on the board throughout the standard-setting process. The researcher was involved with the ASB during the entire process by attending the relevant ASB meetings and by conducting numerous interviews with ASB members and individuals at the AICPA involved with the project. The researcher also examined written responses to the Exposure Draft (ED) released for comment in 1987, proposing a new standard audit report wording. The project also examines the general evolution of the auditor's report in the United States, as well as the existing research on auditor's reports. The following summary presents the project's major conclusions.

• The majority of the influence on the ASB in arriving at the ED in 1987 was internal to the AICPA—ASB members and the AICPA's Auditor Communications Task Force (TF). The Securities and Exchange Commission (SEC), however, was also noted to affect the wording proposed in the ED by influencing the ASB to eliminate the contempted reference to "standards established by the AICPA" from the ED. In regard to the letters of comment to the ED, the general reaction to the need for a new audit report was largely positive. Some of the strong overall preferences indicated by commentors were: (1) eliminate from further consideration "intentionally or unintentionally," (2) retain a statement regarding management's role in financial reporting, (3) modify "materially misstated" in the scope paragraph, (4) continue not to mention client's system of internal control in the report, (5) retain additions of "independent" to the title, "reasonable assurance" to the scope paragraph and "in all material respects" to the opinion paragraph, (6) retain "fairly" in the opinion paragraph, (7) retain change from "examined" to "audited," and

(8) restructure the scope paragraph to make it easier to read and understand. Additionally, reaction was largely mixed on the deletion of the reference to consistency in the opinion paragraph. The respondents also noted a marginal agreement with the elimination of the "subject to" qualified report, but indicated that a new report on uncertainties should better emphasize the uncertainty and appropriate footnote disclosures contained in the financial statements.

- It was found that the TF was responsive to the concerns of the ED respondents and offered to the ASB a modified auditor's report that substantially addressed and potentially resolved these concerns. The exposure process was found to have worked as intended, in that the ASB actually listened to the respondents and gleaned new insight into the potential SAS based on the response letters.

- Outside influences such as the Treadway Commission, SEC, and Financial Executives Institute (FEI) were noted to have affected the board's discussions, and eventually affected the final wording of the standard report adopted in *SAS 58*.

- Early research on *SAS 58* has been generally favorable regarding the newly adopted report. However, continued research on user's behavior and perceptions of auditor responsibility is warranted. Research continues to be needed in regard to the SEC's concern with addressing consistent application of generally accepted accounting principles in the auditor's report, the elimination of the "subject to" report qualification for uncertainties, and how the new reports affect user understanding and the capital markets.

- Finally, more longitudinal studies similar to this one need to be performed in order to gain additional insight into the standard-setting process at the AICPA in particular, and in accounting in general.

Preface

This research examines the Auditing Standards Board in its process of developing and finalizing *Statement on Auditing Standards (SAS) 58, Reports on Audited Financial Statements*. Very little research has been conducted on how current standard-setters in accounting and auditing arrive at their final adopted standards. The intent of this study has been to present in detail the process of the Auditing Standards Board and the significant influences on the board in establishing this one SAS in the hope that a richer understanding of the standard-setting process would emerge.

Along with studying the standard-setting process, this monograph discusses the development of audit reporting in the United States, as well as provides a thorough review of the research conducted on the auditor's report. The chapter on the evolution of the audit report serves to frame *SAS 58* in its historical context. The literature review has been presented in annotated bibliography format and should serve as a resource for anyone interested in research conducted on audit reports.

I would like to express my appreciation to all of my colleagues in the Pennsylvania State University Ph.D. program for their assistance and willingness to serve on the panels as coders. I am also deeply indebted to Mark Dirsmith and Jim Thies at the Pennsylvania State University for their intellectual stimulation during the project and contributions on earlier drafts. In addition, I am grateful for the financial support provided by Price Waterhouse and Company. I would also like to thank the individuals at the American Institute of Certified Public Accountants, and especially Mimi Blaco-Best, Hank Jaenicke, David Landsittel and Jerry Sullivan for their time and candid participation. I am thankful to the American Accounting Association and American Institute of Certified Public Accountants for granting permission to use parts of this study that were previously published in summary form in *Auditing: A Journal of Practice & Theory* and the *Journal of Accountancy*, respectively. Finally, I want to thank my wife, Sue, for her enduring support and encouragement throughout the project.

Marshall A. Geiger

Chapter 1

Purpose and Nature of the Research

INTRODUCTION

After more than 20 years of debate, the auditing profession adopted a new standard audit report in *Statement on Auditing Standards* (*SAS*) *58*, "Reports on Audited Financial Statements" (AICPA 1988a). *SAS 58*, finalized by the American Institute of Certified Public Accountant's (AICPA) Auditing Standards Board (ASB) in early 1988, represents the culmination of documented dissatisfaction with the former standard audit report language in use since 1948 (AICPA 1978).

In response to a perceived need for change and to a belief that the time was right to again attempt a revision to the auditor's report, the ASB released an Exposure Draft (ED) on February 14, 1987, proposing a new standard audit report. This ED was the product of almost two years of work and was part of the ASB's "expectations gap" project, which included nine other EDs released for comment at the same time.

This ED proposed a modification to the standard audit report language that had remained essentially unchanged for 40 years. This longevity caused some commentors to argue that the audit report, because of its longstanding standard wording, had become more a symbol of the auditor's work than a substantive communication to report readers (Epstein 1975; Seidler 1976; AICPA 1978). Additionally, numerous authors had also indicated dissatisfaction with the standard report language itself (AICPA 1978, 1980; Augenbraun 1980; Chandler 1984; Estes 1982; Knoll 1976; Mednick 1986). Such a dissatisfaction caused Sale (1981, 82) to state that: "Since 1949 the [auditor's] opinion on financial statements has fossilized in esoteric language."

The research performed in this study has two primary purposes. First, the research is directed at examining the written comments submitted in response to the 1987 ED proposing a new audit report wording in an effort to understand the views of the various respondent groups regarding the auditor's report. Because seemingly similar audit report modifications were proposed earlier by the profession and later rescinded due to negative reaction, it is important to assess the level of respondent agreement with the successful proposal in 1987. This analysis is also an attempt to discern whether the ASB responded to the concerns identified in the response letters. As an institution representing and guiding auditors and audit practice, the ASB needs to be responsive to the concerns of its constituents. Second, this research is an endeavor to document the ASB's actual standard-setting process as it pertains to this particular SAS. The second research focus is an attempt to document the salient steps and significant influences that impacted the board during the course of establishing *SAS 58*.

This combination of cross-sectional and longitudinal approaches to studying the process of a standard-setting body is relatively unique to accounting. Several authors have analyzed respondents' views to the Financial Accounting Standards Board (FASB) EDs (Klein 1978; Brown 1981; Newmann 1981; Frazier et al. 1984; Puro 1984); however, no authors have adequately integrated this detailed cross-sectional work into the actual overall standard-setting process. Additionally, several researchers have applied various theoretical perspectives to the process and outcomes of standard setting bodies in accounting—primarily the FASB (Feroz 1987; Hussein and Ketz 1980, 1987; Hussein 1981; Newmann 1981; Tinker et al. 1982; Gorton 1991; for a review see Hussein and Ketz 1986). However, after their review of the literature, Hussein and Ketz (1986, 39) conclude that: "At this point in time little is known about the process called accounting standard-setting."

This conclusion is even more valid in regard to the setting of auditing standards. Relatively little empirical research has been conducted to document and evaluate the FASB's actual standard-setting process, and virtually none in regard to the ASB. With the possible exceptions of Kinney's (1986) analysis of ASB member voting patterns and Pearson et al.'s (1979) analysis of AudSEC voting patterns, there has been no detailed exploration of the ASB's standard-setting process.

In analyzing the adoption of accounting standards and the standard-setting process, the shortcomings of the existing research lead Hussein (1981) to conclude that:

> A longitudinal research project that takes an issue from the time of its inclusion in the (FASB) agenda through the final decision and implementation stages might be the most useful approach. Such a project can utilize several methods of field research, content analysis and interviews.

This research project has adopted such a longitudinal approach in regard to the new standard on the auditor's report. Accordingly, the purpose of this initial research is not to impose a preconceived theory of standard-setting (e.g., a power and domination or game theoretic perspective) onto the ASB, but to describe the standard-setting process and the various influences affecting the final adopted SAS, including a detailed analysis of letters responding to the ED. This research, then, may be viewed as an initial step in deriving a framework regarding the present auditing standard-setting process.

Additionally, Merino and Neimark (1982) indicate that to properly understand the standard-setting process and concluding resolutions, one needs to appreciate the historial and social contexts that have and do interact with the standard-setting body. To that end, and to frame this new SAS in its proper historical context, this research project will also discuss the general historical development of audit reporting in the United States, and the extant research on the auditor's report and reporting decision.

As a background for the procedures followed by the ASB, the next section will briefly summarize the formal steps in establishing current auditing standards at the AICPA.

THE FORMAL STEPS IN ESTABLISHING A STATEMENT ON AUDITING STANDARDS

The steps in the process of establishing an auditing standard are very similar to the well-documented series of steps undertaken by the FASB to establish a new accounting standard. However, the process established by the AICPA is not as well documented in the existing literature. The Auditing Standards Division Summary of Operating Policies, an AICPA in-house publication, summarizes the following procedures for preparing a Statement on Auditing Standards:

- Topic suggested by Board members, by other components of the AICPA, by the staff, by members of the public, or arising from a periodic review of existing standards.
- Topic considered for addition to the Board agenda by the ASB Planning Subcommittee, which will develop a proposed charge for a new component or develop a statement of issues to be addressed by an existing component.
- Addition of the topic to the agenda.
- Topic assigned to an existing or new component by the ASB Chairman.
- Preparation of a point outline by the component, with staff assistance.
- Discussion by the Board in open meetings of the component's point outline for purposes of providing general guidance to the component.
- Preparation of a preliminary draft(s) by the component, with staff assistance.
- Discussion by the Board in open meetings of the preliminary draft(s), concluding with instructions to the component to prepare a proposed SAS for purposes of balloting for exposure.
- Preparation of a ballot draft by the component, with staff assistance, and submission of such draft with a written ballot to the Board. Submission of a ballot draft to the Board requires the written authorization of the Board's chairman, the component chairman, outside counsel for the AICPA, and the Vice President-Auditing.

- Issuance of an exposure draft to all practice offices of CPA firms; state society presidents, executive directors and accounting and auditing committee chairmen; and individuals requesting copies. Issuance of an exposure draft also requires the written authorization of the Board's chairman, the component chairman, outside counsel for the AICPA and the Vice President-Auditing. Proposed SASs are ordinarily exposed for public comment for a period of 90 days, but in no event for a period less than 60 days.
- Consideration by the component of comment letters and preparation of a revised draft, if considered necessary.
- Discussion of the revised draft by the Board in open meetings.
- Preparation of a ballot draft of a final SAS by the component with staff assistance, and submission of such draft with a written ballot to the Board. Submission of a ballot draft to the Board requires written authorization of the Board's chairman, the component chairman, outside counsel for the AICPA, and the Vice President-Auditing.
- Issuance of a final SAS to all members of the AICPA and to certain specified individuals and organizations. Issuance of a final SAS requires written authorization of the Board's chairman, the component chairman, outside counsel for the AICPA, and the Vice President-Auditing (AICPA 1987, 108-10).

The ASB Planning Subcommittee, referred to above, is made up of the ASB chairman and four or five other ASB members selected by the chairman. This subcommittee additionally handles smaller issues regarding auditing standards that do not require the attention of the entire board. The "component" referred to above is typically a Task Force (TF), which is made up of both ASB members and other interested AICPA members, and is aided by the AICPA Auditing Standards Division staff. As indicated, the TF is established to more intensively identify and evaluate the issues involved in regard to the potential standard, and to assist the board in the establishment and wording of the final documents.

This process outlined by the AICPA differs from the FASB's "due process" in that the ASB does not require a Discussion Memorandum or public hearing. However, although not required to do so, the ASB may hold public hearings (meetings) at any time concerning issues they are presently addressing (AICPA 1987, 103). Non-members of the ASB are permitted to participate in these public hearings by expressing their specific positions or concerns regarding the issues addressed. The ASB did not hold a public hearing in arriving at the final SAS on the auditor's report in 1988. They did, however, employ such a mechanism earlier when the board was considering a modification to the audit report language in 1980.

Additionally, the ASB meets periodically with outside interested groups to inform them about the status of projects being addressed by the board. Groups that the ASB chairman met with throughout the process analyzed include the Securities and Exchange Commission (SEC), the General Accounting Office (GAO), the Financial Executives Institute (FEI), the American Bar Association (ABA) and the Commission on Fraudulent Financial Reporting (Treadway Commission). Even though not formally required, these meetings are regarded as part of the "process" and will be shown to have had an impact on establishing the final SAS. This established list of procedural steps and its actual implementation and final results will be the foundation for the remainder of the study.

ORGANIZATION OF THE STUDY

The next chapter will trace the development of audit reporting in the United States through the impetus that caused the ASB to once again examine the wording of the auditor's report which led to the 1987 ED. Chapter 3 will examine the research concerning the pre *SAS 58* audit reports. A discussion of the research methods utilized in this study will be presented in Chapter 4. Chapter 5 will discuss the establishment of the 1987 ED. Next, Chapter 6 will present and discuss the results of analyzing the letters of comment to the ED. A description of the salient influences affecting the ASB regarding the ED proposal and the eventual wording adopted in *SAS 58* will be presented and summarized in Chapter 7. Chapter 8 will discuss the research to date that has examined the *SAS 58* reports. A conclusion to the study, including implications for practice and future research, will be presented in the final chapter.

Chapter 2

Evolution of the Standard Auditor's Report in the United States

The fourth standard of reporting states that the auditor's report: . . . shall either contain an expression of opinion regarding the financial statements, taken as a whole, or an assertion to the effect that an opinion cannot be expressed. When an overall opinion cannot be expressed, the reasons therefor should be stated. In all cases where an auditor's name is associated with financial statements, the report should contain a clear-cut indication of the character of the auditor's examination, if any, and the degree of responsibility he is taking (AICPA 1986; AU 504.01).

This chapter will examine the development of the auditor's reports used by the profession in the United States in fulfillment of its reporting obligations. A historical perspective is warranted to better understand the nature and context of the current auditor's report and reporting obligation. This perspective will also add some richness in analyzing the significance of the 1987 report modification. The discussion will focus primarily on the standard unqualified auditor's report, but will also address issues pertinent to the development of alternate reporting categories.

EARLY BRITISH INFLUENCE

British auditing and reporting practices played an important role in influencing the early American auditor's report. A majority of early (mid- to late-1800s) audits in the United States were conducted by British auditors engaged by British investors in American enterprises (Flesher and Flesher 1980). As evidence of the pervasiveness of British auditors, Cochrane (1950, 449) notes that:

Until well after the end of the first world war there were practically no court decisions dealing with the duties and responsibilities of the auditor, other than British decisions, which later largely influenced the American accountant's thinking, and, consequently, his procedures.

The impact of British reporting requirements on U.S. reporting practices can be seen through the influence of the early British Companies Acts. These acts required an auditor's report on the accuracy of the balance sheet of the company. However, no specific form was prescribed by these early acts, and it was left to the auditor as to how best to convey the opinion to shareholders. This reporting freedom of the British auditors carried over to early U.S. auditor's reports. It is also important to note that the term "certificate" was used to reference the British auditor's report in the early Companies Acts. This term has been substantially deleted from the professional auditing literature since its early British use, as will be discussed, yet continues to be used today in the U.S. Securities Act of 1933 and Securities and Exchange Commission (SEC) regulations (Carmichael 1978).

The British Companies Act of 1900, along with subsequent acts, have since prescribed the content of the British auditor's report. Flesher and Flesher (1980) indicate that up until 1948, the British auditor was required to state whether, in his opinion, the balance sheet gave a "true and correct" view of the financial condition of the firm. Accordingly, in an attempt to attain this level of assurance, the British auditor had to make a detailed examination of the client's books and transactions. This high level of responsibility, and the relative availability in the United States of British auditors, along with the lack of a statutory requirement in the United States for audited financial statements, fostered slow early growth of the public accounting profession in this country. An early reliance on British practices can be readily identified as the auditing profession began to develop in the United States. The development of the auditor's report discussed in the next section clearly reflects this early British influence.

EARLY REPORTS

Early auditor's reports in the United States were also referred to as "certificates"—a direct reflection of the British influence—consistent with the use of the term "certify" adopted in most of the early audit reports. Due to the lack of statutory requirements and to the lack of explicit wording requirements on the part of the developing auditing profession, the auditor's report content and wording, as in Britain, were left entirely to the discretion of the individual auditor(s). There was no prescribed audit report, or designated reporting categories as there are today. However, Aranoff (1975, 4) offers the following report as one of the more commonly used "certificates" during the period from 1900 to after World War I:

> We have audited the books and accounts of the XYZ Company for the year ended December 31, 1915, and we certify that, in our opinion, the above balance sheet correctly

sets forth its position as of the termination of that year, and that the accompanying profit and loss account is correct.

Carmichael and Winters (1982, 2) offer the following Price Waterhouse & Co. report as another example of an early "certificate."

> We have examined the above accounts with the books and vouchers of the company, and find the same to be correct. We approve and certify that the above balance sheet correctly sets forth the position of the company.

These reports are examples of what was called a "short" certificate, or a short-form report. Jackson (1926, 46) states that a proper "short" certificate simply possesses three things: (1) a statement that an examination has been made, (2) the indication that the audit is for a specific period or given date, and (3) that the auditor "certifies that, in his opinion, the balance sheet as presented, though possibly subject to certain qualifications, fairly and correctly states the financial position of the business."

These "short" certificates were contrasted with "long" or "descriptive" certificates. A "descriptive" certificate would include the three basic elements incorporated in the "short" form, and would additionally include a brief description of the important points in the verification of the various assets and liabilities, as well as note significant events in which the business was involved during the period. Jackson (1926, 46-47) indicates that a typical "long" certificate would read something like the following:

> We have examined the books and accounts of The Blank Company for the year ended December 31, 1925, and find that the accompanying balance sheet as of that date and the relative profit and loss account are correctly prepared therefrom.
>
> During the year only actual additions have been charged to the property account, and the provision for depreciation is, in our opinion, fair and reasonable.
>
> The inventories of stocks on hand, certified by responsible officials as to quantities, have been valued at cost or market, whichever was lower at December 31, 1925. The accounts and notes receivable are, in our opinion, good and collectible, and we verified the cash and securities by actual inspection or by certificate from the depositaries. Full provision has been made for all ascertainable liabilities. The deferred charges represent expenditures reasonably and properly carried forward to the operations of subsequent years.
>
> We *certify that*, in our opinion, the accompanying balance sheet is properly drawn up and fairly sets forth the financial position of The Blank Company as of December 31, 1925, and the relative profit and loss statement correctly states the results of operations for the fiscal year ended at that date.

Even though these illustrations of early reports may have been "typical," they were by no means "uniform." In fact, auditors were faced with the dilemma of whether or not to write a completely different audit report for every engagement. Jackson (1926, 50-51) discusses this early dilemma.

There are some who maintain that unless each report is new and novel in its method of presentation the auditor has fallen into a rut and must expect to be shelved by those who are more progressive than he. It may be said, however, that the report prepared upon an audit is just as formal and important a document as is the ordinary brief prepared by the lawyer. Presumably it would not be maintained that each brief should not contain subject matter which is most applicable to the matter treated, even though the form be the same. Similarly, each audit report must carefully treat the matter under consideration, but there is no logical reason why the form of the report or the manner of presenting the material should be varied from period to period and assignment to assignment.

No intelligent auditor, on the other hand, would maintain that every report must follow the same form. It may not even follow the same general style or the same division into parts.

Hence, the conflict between innovation and standardization regarding the auditor's report was clearly an early concern. One logical explanation for the prevalent use of various report forms and wordings is that the auditor needed to both serve the client, especially in the early years of attempting to develop the auditing profession, as well as develop the firm's reputation. Without required audits, auditors were probably more apt to attempt to show the client that they were getting an adequate level of service for their money. Carmichael and Winters (1982, 2) call this concept the "service-to-the-client philosophy."

In his early article, Jackson (1926) continues by describing some items to be included in a "long" certificate. The description of these audit reports sounds very much like the management discussion and analysis, or management's report, found in today's financial statements. A discussion of significant transactions and events to which the client was a party seemingly forced the auditor using a "long" report to reword and possibly restructure the report for each engagement.

Chow (1982), in examining audits for the year 1926, found that proportionately more audits were conducted on "management-owned" firms than on firms owned by outside stockholders. This finding lends credence to the argument that auditors needed to demonstrate a high level of service (i.e., generating a different report for every client), because many audits were performed not for the benefit of outside owners, but for the owner/manager.

Flesher and Flesher (1980) also note that early American audit practice ranged from a complete examination to a partial balance sheet audit. This disparity in the level of examination certainly had an effect on the report's form and wording. Additionally, this wide disparity in actual practice and report form and content created difficulties for the early audit report reader. In some cases, the audit report was a relatively useless document. For example, Jackson (1926, 47-48) cites the following certificates:

I hereby certify that the above is a true and correct transcript of the Assets and Liabilities appearing on the books of The Blank Company on December 31, 1920.

We have made a superficial examination of the books of The Blank Company at the close of business December 31, 1922, and from the trial balance we prepared the above condensed balance sheet, which, in our opinion exhibits a correct view of the financial condition of the business at the date named according to the information and explanations given us and as shown by the books.

These examples are not necessarily representative of the average quality of audit reports issued by early auditors; however, they clearly evidence the disparity in care with which audit reports were prepared—and to some extent, the care with which "audits" were performed.

Another substantial problem of the early audit report was difficulty in differentiating the "descriptive" or "long" report from a report in which the auditor was highlighting qualifications or reservations regarding some aspect of the financial statements. Because there was no "standard" report for unqualified opinions against which to measure report variances, early report readers had to make their own determinations as to the intended level of assurance auditors were attempting to communicate. Consequently, distinguishing a "descriptive" certificate from a "qualified" certificate often was no simple task for the general report reader. A standard form of report was later seen as a necessary step in attempting to minimize this difficulty.

In retrospect, the use of the term "certify" in the American auditor's report was probably inappropriate in a majority of the cases in which it was used. Brown (1962) traces the objectives of auditing in the United States and notes that the detection of fraud was the primary audit objective up until around 1850. To attain this objective, early auditors detail tested, or "verified," most, if not all, of the client's transactions for the period. However, with the onset of larger firms engaging in far more and increasingly complex transactions, a detailed examination of substantially all the transactions was no longer an economically viable undertaking. In those earlier years, the term "certify" may have been more appropriately used, however, appropriate usage soon disappeared. Additionally, because the early U.S. audits were performed primarily for owner/managers, the use of the term was probably acceptable. With the growth in the size of clients and the number of transactions came a shift away from the emphasis on fraud detection and the verification of stewardship reports, to the provision of independent reports on the accuracy of financial statements for the benefit of third parties. This "new" objective was accomplished not by detailed examination of all transactions, but by selective testing. The shift toward testing of financial statements was a natural result of industrial expansion and increased demand for and reliance on financial statements by third parties. Brown (1962) indicates that the elimination of detail testing was substantially complete in the United States by the early 1930s, but had been well on its way to being eliminated by around 1900.

Additionally, Cochrane (1950) notes that the use of the term "correct" was also ill-advised due to the increasing need for making estimates in accounting, the probability of immaterial errors, and the increasing variety of acceptable accounting methods. Hence, even though the terms "certify" and "correct" were probably not appropriate, even for early audits, their use was still prevalent in the reports of early U.S. auditors. The service-to-the-client philosophy discussed earlier was a likely impetus for using these terms. If clients were going to pay for an audit that they were not required to undergo, then they would probably like to perceive the most assurance for their money—"certify" and "correct" provided them with that level of assurance. The next section will indicate that these terms, and phrases such as "accurately record conditions" and "represent the true financial position," were used in the auditor's report well into the twentieth century.

EVOLUTION OF A STANDARD REPORT

The evolution of audit report standardization began with early attempts to define accounting and auditing practice in the United States. The formation of the Federal Reserve Board (FRB) in 1913 and the Federal Trade Commission (FTC) in 1914 played an important role in the movement that fostered standardized audit reporting. Carmichael and Winters (1982) indicate that the FRB and FTC shared a strong dissatisfaction with financial statements audited by public accountants. A committee of the American Institute of Accountants (AIA), predecessor of the AICPA, conferred with the FRB and FTC and eventually convinced them that federal regulation of the accounting profession was not warranted, and that the AIA could provide adequate guidelines for independent accountants that would address their concerns. To meet this challenge, the AIA in 1912 developed a booklet titled *A Memorandum on Balance Sheet Audits*. This booklet was then published in 1917 by the FRB as a Federal Reserve Bulletin with the title *Uniform Accounting: A Tentative Proposal*. Cochrane (1950) indicates that this bulletin was widely distributed to the banking, manufacturing, accounting, and auditing communities. Even though the bulletin was titled *Uniform Accounting*, and the preface indicated that its purpose was to set forth a "proposal for a uniform system of accounting to be adopted by manufacturing and merchandising concerns" (FRB 1917, 3), the bulletin consisted mainly of recommended audit procedures, and only tangentially addressed uniform accounting systems. This booklet was later reissued in 1918 under the title, *Approved Methods for the Preparation of Balance Sheet Statements*.

In regard to the auditor's communication of audit results, the bulletin presented the first *suggested* form of the auditor's report (FRB 1917, 24):

I have audited the accounts of Blank & Company for the period from . . . to . . . and I certify that the above balance sheet and statement of profit and loss have been made in accordance with the plan suggested and advised by the Federal Reserve Board and in my opinion set forth the financial conditions of the firm at . . . and the results of its operations for the period.

Even though this recommended report was not required or universally adopted, it was the first step in the standardization of audit reports. It is interesting to note that the term "opinion" was also used in the bulletin's discussion, which suggests an awareness on the part of the AIA, as well as the FRB, that the term "certify," as used in the report, may not have been intended for literal interpretation. Carmichael and Winters (1982, 3) also point out that even though the impetus for this first step in the standardization process came from influences outside the profession, "[it] marked the beginning of the profession's exercise of self-discipline over the content of the auditor's report."

It is important to recognize that this suggested report refrained from the use of the terms "correctness" or "fair and correct view," which were prevalent in those days. These noticeable deletions provided a more accurate reflection of the increasing complexity of financial reporting alternatives and practices, and began to alert the report reader of the inexactness of the financial reporting process. Another disparity of this suggested report from reports of its day, is the inclusion of a detailed "statement of profit and loss" to be audited along with the balance sheet as a primary financial statement. Formerly, the profit and loss figure was typically included as one figure on the balance sheet without any supporting detail.

Hicks (1960, 61) indicates that reallocation, speculation, business expansion, and inflation following the end of World War I resulted in the growth of misleading financial reporting practices. To combat this problem, auditors in the 1920s began to object to such practices and qualify their opinions using the phrase "subject to." This reporting language was the forerunner of the "subject to" report qualification for unresolved uncertainties, although the application of the phrase "subject to" at this time was by no means limited to any particular type of qualification.

The next major step toward report standardization was the revision of the 1918 Federal Reserve Bulletin in May 1929. The AIA started the revision in 1928 in recognition of the growing size and complexity of transactions, mergers, issues of new securities, and diversity of financial reporting practices. Its final title was *Verification of Financial Statements*. The revised title more directly indicates that its subject matter was auditing, rather than accounting. This booklet stressed that tests of transactions, and not detailed examinations, were performed on the records of a company during an audit. This increased emphasis on testing reflects the changing economic conditions, as well as the switch in audit objectives away from fraud detection to financial statement accuracy as discussed earlier. However, the title, *Verification of Financial Statements*, does not, to this author, appear to adequately dispell the notion of *detailed* examination of all financial records that existed at this time.

The revised report presented in the 1929 booklet was still a suggested report, and was not required in any authoritative sense. The new report did make some substantial changes to the report included in the earlier bulletin. One of the major changes was the elimination of the reference to the plan suggested and advised by the Federal Reserve Board. The word "examined" was used instead of "audited" in the new report. Another substantial modification to the suggested auditor's report was the adoption of a two-paragraph format. The two paragraphs follow the format of the scope and opinion paragraphs of the former auditor's report.

The suggested report retained the term "certify," even though the bulletin itself stressed the use of testing during the conduct of an audit, and the auditor's inability to verify all transactions and amounts. However, with the report's ackward wording, the auditor's opinion was being certified rather than the fair presentation of the company's financial condition and the results of operations. Thus, the report retained the term "certify," but more prominently indicated that the auditor was expressing an opinion on the financial statements—not a declaration of correctness, as was done in the past.

This report form, like its predecessors, lacked mention of a title or addressee for the report. These vital omissions would soon plague the profession.

The next report revision was spurred by the prospect of legal liability stemming from the *Ultramares* decision in 1931 (Aranoff 1975). The *Ultramares* case introduced the public accounting profession to the term "gross negligence." Until this decision, accountants considered negligence and fraud to be two distinct phenomena. This court decision, however, proclaimed that auditors could be liable to third parties if their negligence was so great (i.e., gross) that it constituted what verged on fraud. The auditors' exposure to damages now extended beyond just their clients. That is, auditors were now liable for damages to third parties for this form of "constructive fraud."

This decision caused the profession to reconsider its position on a variety of issues, one of them being the auditor's report. A July 1931 editorial by A.P. Richardson, editor of the *Journal of Accountancy*, discussed the *Ultramares* case and its implications for the auditor and his report. The editorial offered the following suggestions (Richardson 1931, 5-6):

> it seems fairly clear that every accountant's report will be addressed to the client only . . . the accountant will divide his report into two sections, one dealing with fact [that is, scope of examination] and one with opinion.

The accountant perhaps should abandon certificates and merely make reports. . . . The word certificate, which has been used for many years, is quite inappropriate and should be abandoned, in any case, especially with reference to any opinion. It is absurd to speak of certifying an opinion. Perhaps the *Ultramares* case will be the means of bringing about a reform which will eliminate the words certify and certificate.

The editorial suggested a report form basically the same as that espoused in the 1929 bulletin, except for the elimination of the term "certify," which was already indicated to have been outdated and grammatically ackward, and the addition of a report title and addressee. With these few report modifications, the profession attempted to minimize its exposure to third-party liabilities.

Carmichael and Winters (1982) indicate that the *Ultramares* case decision and the editorial cited above did have an effect on the auditor's report. The term "certify" began to disappear from reports in an attempt to clarify that the report was an opinion and not a guarantee.

Like its predecessors, however, the 1931 report did not remain unaltered for long. The next report, suggested in 1934, was the culmination of years of work on the part of the AIA to combat financial reporting abuses that eventually contributed to the stock market crash in late 1929. Carmichael and Winters (1982) indicate that, as early as 1927, the AIA attempted, without success, to establish a working agenda with the New York Stock Exchange (NYSE) in an attempt to improve financial reporting practices. It was not until after the stock market crash of 1929 that the NYSE became interested in cooperating with the AIA to devise financial reporting reforms.

The Committee on Stock List of the NYSE and a Special Committee on Co-operation with Stock Exchanges of the AIA began meeting in late 1930. Their task was two-fold: (1) educate the public regarding the significance of financial statements, their limitations and usefulness, and (2) make the financial statements published by corporations more informative. A joint conference was held from September 1932 until January 1934 (Cochrane 1950).

One of the recommendations produced by these meetings was to require companies to select appropriate accounting methods within the limits of a broad set of accepted accounting principles. The methods adopted needed to be appropriate to the company and consistently applied. The NYSE considered the responsibility for assuring proper adoption and adherence to the acceptable accounting principles to be that of the auditor. Instead of making the user responsible for ensuring proper adherence to the espoused principles adopted, the auditor was to state in the audit report whether the company was properly following these broadly established principles.

In 1934, the AIA published a pamphlet titled *Audits of Corporate Accounts* that contained the written deliberations of the AIA and NYSE special committees. Included in this pamphlet was a revised audit report that attempted to address the concerns of the various groups, and made what Carmichael and

Winters (1982, 6) call an "evolutionary leap in audit report structure" that introduced reporting responsibilities that the profession would take another 15 years to formally recognize.

The report read (Cochrane 1950, 453):

> We have made an examination of the balance sheet of the XYZ Company at December 31, 1933, and of the statement of income and surplus for the year 1933. In connection therewith, we examined or tested accounting records of the company and other supporting evidence and obtained information and explanations from officers and employees of the company; we also made a general review of the accounting methods and of the operating and income accounts for the year, but we did not make a detailed audit of the transactions.
>
> In our opinion, based upon such examination, the accompanying balance sheet and related statements of income and surplus fairly present, in accordance with accepted principles of accounting consistently maintained by the company during the year under review, its position at December 31, 1933, and the results of its operations for the year.

A recommendation was made to address this report to the company's directors or stockholders, if they had appointed the auditor. This report retained the two-paragraph format suggested earlier, but was in marked contrast to all earlier report versions. The concept of testing was explicitly mentioned in the scope paragraph of the report, as were additional explanations of what an audit entails. The scope paragraph mentioned appropriateness of accounting methods adopted and of obtaining evidence from the company through officers and employees. Additionally, an important shift in report focus was made from examining the books or accounts of the company to examining the company's financial statements. The recommended report also allowed for the implementation of minor variations in the scope paragraph. Auditors could include, for example, any special forms of confirmations used during the audit. This relatively minor variation represented the only real flexibility in report wording.

As would be expected, the opinion paragraph continued to exclude the term "certify," in order to indicate that an opinion, and not a "guarantee" or "certificate" was given on the financial statements. The new wording also introduced to the opinion paragraph the controverisal phrase "fairly present, in accordance with accepted principles of accounting. . . position. . . and the results of its operations for the year." The intended meaning of this phrase has been a source of controversy within the profession ever since. Some discern its meaning to be composed of two distinct ideas: (1) fair presentation of the financial position and results of operations of the company, and (2) conformity with generally accepted principles of accounting. Others would consider the phrase to have one cohesive meaning—fair presentation through conformity with generally accepted accounting principles (GAAP).

Radoff (1975), for example, has argued convincingly that the original intent of the phrase was to use "fair presentation" as a separate and distinct criterion, apart from consistent adherence to GAAP as a requirement of financial statements. As partial support of this separation, Radoff (1975) cites a letter sent by Richard Whitney, the president of the NYSE in 1933, to presidents of corporations listed on the exchange, asking for audit reports and information on a list of points. This list included fair presentation and conformity with accepted accounting principles as two distinct items of interest. In the letters of reply, none of the recipients objected to these two items as separate points, and all responded to them individually (Radoff 1975, 18). Carmichael and Winters (1982, 6) use the 1934 report wording itself to argue for an alternate conclusion:

> In fact, the [1934] report would seem to resolve the rather recent debate over the meaning of the phrase "present fairly in conformity with generally accepted accounting principles." In the above [1934] report it is clear that the phrase "in accordance with accepted principles of accounting" modifies the term "fairly present," indicating that the committee was unwilling to use the phrase "fairly present" alone. This lends historical legitimacy to the contention that the phrase "present fairly in conformity with generaly accepted accounting principles" in the current standard report defines a *single* standard for judging accounting presentations (emphasis added).

From a historical perspective, however, the most significant attribute of the 1934 report was that it was the first report to have a *required* as opposed to a *suggested* report wording. The 1934 report revision was required for firms registered with the NYSE. Although the implementation of the report could be enforced only by the NYSE for listed companies, it certainly influenced the audit reports of unlisted companies as well. Cochrane (1950) indicates that deviations from this report, although not disallowed, came to be considered as deficient reports, and Radoff (1975) indicates that 95 percent all the annual reports to stockholders in 1935 included this report.

The special committee of the AIA recommended that the new report be adopted as the "standard" report. This committee believed that uniformity in report language was needed to rectify problems of report wording discussed earlier. The committee believed that a "standard" report would specifically accomplish two objectives: (1) institute uniform report language across firms, thus making reports more readily comparable and consequently reduce deficient report quality and misunderstandings due to ambiguous or vague wordings, and (2) make qualifications in audit reports more easily recognizable (Carmichael and Winters 1982, 6).

This basically inflexible "standard" report wording, essentially adopted by the entire profession, created a whole new era in auditor's reports. Once a "standard" report was utilized, any deviations from the standard would be readily apparent to report readers. Carmichael (1978), in the first AICPA *Auditing Research Monograph*, notes that this widely used standard report was the first step in developing distinct categories of report types. Qualifications of opinion in the auditor's report would become more differentiable from a "standard" unqualified report than they were previously—satisfying the second objective mentioned above. This easy identification of report qualifications, as well as other report types later adopted by the profession, was not without its drawbacks. Highly standardized wording in the auditor's report allows readers to perceive the report as a "symbol" of the auditor's work and not as a substantive communication made by the auditor as it was in earlier times. This dilemma would be identified and discussed by the Commision on Auditors' Responsibilities in 1978 as an undesirable attribute of the "standard" auditor's report, and will be discussed further in the next section of this chapter.

As part of the profession's response to the newly created Securities and Exchange Commission, and to the growing public criticism of the auditing profession and financial reporting community in general, the AIA revised the FRB Bulletin in 1936. The report adopted in 1934 remained unaltered in this revision titled *Examination of Financial Statements by Independent Public Accountants*. The revision, however, was an early attempt by the profession to begin developing separate accounting and auditing standards. One of the extensive discussions in the revised pamphlet was on internal control and its impact on audit tests and procedures (Carmichael and Winters 1982, 7). No mention of internal control, however, was allowed for in the auditor's report. The bulletin also recommended that the auditor's communication be exclusively referred to as a "report" and not as a "certificate," and the use of the term "verify" was consciously avoided in the new bulletin (Flesher and Flesher 1980, 63).

Not long after the adoption of this new bulletin, the McKesson & Robbins fraud was revealed. Surfacing in December 1938, this case became a source of embarrassment for the profession. The SEC held hearings on the case and released its report in 1940. That report primarily concluded that: (1) generally accepted auditing practices of the day regarding accounts receivable and their confirmation were inadequate, and (2) physical inspection of inventory should be required as a generally accepted auditing procedure.

In the meantime, however, the AIA had modified some of the positions espoused in the 1936 bulletin to incorporate these two projected findings of the SEC. A new pamphlet titled *Extension of Auditing Procedure*, was published in 1939 to disseminate the profession's newly adopted positions. This pamphlet was also approved by the membership of the AIA and reissued by the Committee on Auditing Procedure as the first Statements on Auditing Procedure (SAP). The report version included in *SAP 1* was as follows (AIA 1939, 12):

> We have examined the balance sheet of the XYZ Company as of December 31 1939, and the statements of income and surplus for the fiscal year then ended, have reviewed the system of internal control and the accounting procedures of the company, and without

making a detailed audit of the transactions, have examined or tested accounting records of the company and other supporting evidence, by methods and to the extent we deemed necessary.

In our opinion, the acompanying balance sheet and related statements of income and surplus present fairly the position of the XYZ Company at December 31, 1939, and the results of its operations for the fiscal year, in conformity with generally accepted accounting principles applied on a basis consistent with that of the preceding year.

This new report, for the first time, explicitly mentioned reviewing the client's system of internal control in the scope paragraph. Carmichael and Winters (1982) indicate that this reference to the use of internal control preceded any widespread use of control strengths by the profession to reduce the extent of substantive testing. Brown (1962) also indicates that reliance on internal controls was not fully implemented by practitioners in 1939. Hence, the new report not only attempted to clarify auditor responsibility and inform readers as to some of the processes of an audit, it also acted as the catalyst for modifying audit practice.

After considerable debate within the profession, the 1939 report changed "fairly present" to "present fairly" and repositioned the reference to conformity with accounting principles. The specific wording of the reference to these principles was, "generally accepted accounting principles," replacing the old reference "accepted principles of accounting." Thus, the phrase "generally accepted accounting principles" (GAAP) was introduced into the professional literature for the first time. This modification has remained in all later reports. It seems, however, that too many auditors formerly believed that "consistently maintained during the year" meant only intraperiod and not interperiod consistent application of GAAP. The new report wording attempted to dispel this misconception, but may have created confusion over the relationship of fair presentation and GAAP. Additionally, the reference to reliance on information and explanations provided by company personnel was misunderstood in practice (as evidenced by the McKesson & Robbins case) and was eliminated by the new report. The report also incorporated the concept of professional judgment when conducting an audit with the inclusion of the phrase "by methods and to the extent we deemed necessary."

SAP 1 also introduced a new reporting category to the growing repetoire of audit report types—the withheld opinion. Prior to the issuance of *SAP 1*, a typical practice was for the auditor to specify accounting deficiencies, scope limitations or omissions of auditing procedure and similar limitations encountered in conducting the audit in the audit report. The auditor, however, would go on to present an opinion on the financial statements by prefacing the opinion with a phrase something like "subject to the foregoing." This practice, however, left to the report reader the determination of the exact level of assurance provided by the auditor, and the extent to which the financial statements as a whole could be deemed reliable. *SAP 1* prohibited accountants from rendering an opinion on financial statements taken as a whole, if the exceptions were such as to negate their opinion, or if scope limitations rendered an overall opinion of the financial statements inappropriate.

SAP 1 did, however, allow the auditor an option to issue a report that indicated the work performed and results obtained, without expressing an opinion or explicitly disclaiming one. The specific allowance for such a report in *SAP 1* was made by the following statement on limitations in audit scope (AIA 1939, 4):

> the independent certified public accountant should limit his report to a statement of his findings, and, if appropriate, his reasons for omitting an expression of opinion.

For all practical purposes, the standard auditor's report included in *SAP 1*, with its separation of scope and opinion paragraphs and particular wording, can be considered the beginning of the modern audit report used by the profession. This 1939 report has formed the foundation on which all later modification attempts have been based.

The next report versions continued to stem from investigations of the McKesson & Robbins case. The auditing profession was under tremendous scrutiny in the wake of this highly publicized fraud. Accordingly, the SEC in conjunction with the Committee on Auditing Procedure (CAP) determined that a clearer distinction should be drawn between accounting principles and their application, and adequate auditing standards (Carmichael and Winters 1982, 9). The lack of adequate discrimination between accounting and auditing was indicated earlier in the discussion of the Federal Reserve Bulletins. It was also believed that SAPs had followed the same pattern and did not adequately separate the two areas. The AIA began work in the early 1940s to rectify this problem; however, efforts were suspended because of the demands World War II placed on the nation and the profession, and were not resumed until 1947.

The SEC, however, did not suspend efforts during this time and issued Accounting Series Release No. 21 soon after the conclusion of its lengthy investigation of the McKesson & Robbins case. Based on their findings, this 1941 release amended Regulation S-X to require changes in the auditor's report to indicate whether auditors conducted the audit "in accordance with generally accepted auditing standards applicable in the circumstances." This was the first reference to "generally accepted auditing standards" (GAAS). These "standards," however, would not be formally adopted by the profession until late 1948. Accordingly, after considerable debate, the AIA recommended that the following sentence be added to the scope paragraph of the 1939 report to comply with this new regulation (Carmichel and Winters 1982, 9):

Our examination was made in accordance with generally accepted auditing standards applicable in the circumstances and included all procedures we considered necessary.

Not long after this addition was made to the report, it was argued that the phrase "applicable in the circumstances" was inappropriate if auditing standards already had "general acceptance" within the profession. Accordingly, the sentence was modified later in 1941, and the following wording was adopted (Carmichael & Winters 1982, 10):

Our examination was made in accordance with generally accepted auditing standards and included all procedures which we considered necessary in the circumstances.

The final adoption of this report wording in 1941 again preceded practice and served, along with the SEC rulings, as a catalyst for the profession to identify and formally adopt appropriate "generally accepted auditing standards" (GAAS). After years of debate, the profession finally reached a general consensus on what should or should not have been considered part of GAAS in late 1948, and the AIA membership voted to approve the report titled *Tentative Statement of Auditing Standards, Their Generally Accepted Significance and Scope*. This long sought-after document led to a major revision of the auditor's two-paragraph report. The revised report in 1948 left the opinion paragraph unaltered, but instituted the following scope paragraph (AIA 1948, 2):

We have examined the balance sheet of ABC Company as of December 31, 19—, and the related statement(s) of income and surplus for the year then ended. Our examination was made in accordance with generally accepted auditing standards, and accordingly included such tests of the accounting records and such other auditing procedures as we considered necessary in the circumstances.

The scope paragraph of the auditor's report was considerably abbreviated— both in length and in its attempt to explain the auditing process. The new paragraph only retained part of the old first sentence that identified that an examination had been made on the financial statements prepared for a specific time period. The second sentence in the new paragraph, the sentence added in 1941, was modified to retain the reference to testing of the accounting records. The middle portion of the old scope paragraph explicitly mentioning audit attributes and procedures was eliminated. Reference to review of internal control, lack of "making a detailed audit of transactions," and "other supporting evidence" were all deleted in the new report. The overall communication of auditing procedures and of the audit process was considerably dampened by the new report. The new report, however, did maintain the same implicit assurance to readers through the retention of the reference to adherence to GAAS and the application of tests that were considered necessary in the circumstances, and the same opinion paragraph.

A deemphasis on explaining audit processes in the auditor's report was due to the profession's perception that the audit process was considerably better understood by readers and the public in 1948 than it had been in the past. Cochrane (1950, 456) offers the following reasoning for such an approach on the part of the profession:

> Auditing standards had now been established through issuance of the American Institute of Accountants' "tentative statements of auditing standards" and the auditor's report was required to state that the examination had been carried out in accordance with such standards.
>
> As it was now widely known and accepted that an auditor relied, and was entitled to rely, on the internal control in existence and on testing and sampling rather than detailed examination, reference to these facts in the report was no longer required.

An additional reason for deleting the explicit reference to the review of internal control was that in 1948 *SAP 24,* along with revising the auditor's report, proposed nine auditing standards. The fifth proposed standard referred to reviews of internal control. After creation of this standard, an explicit reference beyond GAAS was no longer considered necessary in the report (Flesher and Flesher 1980, 64).

The general supposition that the auditor's role was well understood in 1948 was not universally accepted. An editorial in the July 1947 *Journal of Accountancy* cites a public opinion survey indicating that only 53 percent surveyed believed that they could trust financial reports; and of that 53 percent, only 7 percent mentioned the independent auditor's report as a source of their confidence (Editorial 1947). Accordingly, the editor argued for a report modification quite different than that adopted in 1948 (Editorial 1947, 3-4):

> The short form of auditors' report or "certificate" now in general use was drafted in an effort to explain precisely what the auditor did and what he thought about the financial statements which he examined. Each word was selected with meticulous attention to its precise meaning and its connotations in relation to authoritative accounting literature and statutory and judicial concepts of the accountant's responsibility. Unhappily, the general public unfamiliar with this literature or these concepts, and perhaps even insensible to etymological refinements, does not always read into the auditor's certificate what he intends to put there. . . . There is undoubtedly a wider public interest in corporate financial statements then ever before, and it may be timely to reconsider the form of the auditors' "certificate" from the viewpoint of the lay consumer. A certificate is after all a form of communication to the reader of financial statements, and if it is not wholly intelligible to him it will fall short of achieving its full purpose, no matter how thorough and competent may be the audit which is its foundation.

The profession's perception of the level of general understanding regarding an audit would later turn out to be the cause of considerable debate, and fuel attempts to modify the abridged report form adopted in 1948.

The profession was also examining other auditor reporting requirements around this time. The *SAP 1* allowance for auditors' reports that described audit procedures performed but did not indicate whether an actual audit was performed and did not express an opinion on the financial statements, was no longer felt to be desirable. In order to correct for these types of "non-opinions," *SAP 23* was adopted in 1947. It eliminated this reporting uncertainty by specifically stating that the auditor had to either render an opinion on the financial statements taken as a whole, or explicitly indicate the reasons why an opinion could not be offered. *SAP 23* offered auditors three specific reporting alternatives: (1) unqualified opinion, (2) qualified opinion, and (3) disclaimer of opinion. The drawback of these three audit report categories was the inability of the auditor to state that the financial statements, in the auditor's opinion, did *not* represent a fair presentation of the financial position and results of operations of the client.

In 1961, *SAP 31* formally recognized this problem in the instance when a client changes a generally accepted accounting principle to one that lacks general acceptance. In these cases, when the change is sufficiently material, an adverse opinion was to be presented on the financial statements. This was the first time that the profession explicitly allowed the auditor to indicate that the financial statements were not fairly presented. In 1962, *SAP 32* further expanded the auditor's utilization of an adverse opinion with the following definition (AIA 1962, 4):

> An adverse opinion is required in any report where the exceptions as to fairness of presentation are so material that in the independent auditor's judgment a qualified opinion is not justified. In such circumstances a disclaimer of opinion is not considered appropriate since the independent auditor has sufficient information to form an opinion that the financial statements are not fairly presented.

Additionally, in 1954, the institute adopted the pronouncement *Generally Accepted Auditing Standards*. The auditor's reporting obligation, as set forth in this document (and earlier in *SAP 23*), was officially recognized as the fourth standard of reporting. Accordingly, *SAP 32* went on to differentiate the various report types, including the distinction between the "subject to" and the "except for" opinion qualifications. With the growth and adoption of these distinct report categories came a shift in emphasis from actually writing the report, as in earlier days, to deciding what type of report, including the prespecified report wording, was appropriate in light of the results of the audit. Thus, Carmichael (1978, 22) accurately indicates that "writing the audit report has changed from a literary to a coding activity," and that "professional latitude is far greater in the decision-making phase of reporting than in the writing phase."

Compatible with this "coding activity" concept, the standard report wording was not changed substantially from 1948 to 1988. In 1963 the report was modified to substitute "retained earnings" for the term "surplus," and in 1971 the statement of changes in financial position was added to the scope and opinion paragraphs to reflect its addition as a summary financial statement. Finally, *SAS 15* in 1976 modified the report to accommodate comparative financial statements for two or more years. Incorporating these three modifications, the standard short form auditor's report utilized until 1988 read as follows (AICPA 1986, AU §505.03):

> To ABC Corporation, its Directors, and Shareholders:
> We have examined the balance sheets of ABC Company as of [at] December 31, 19X2 and 19X1, and the related statements of income, retained earnings, and changes in financial position for the years then ended. Our examinations were made in accordance with generally accepted auditing standards and, accordingly, included such tests of the accounting records and such other auditing procedures as we considered necessary in the circumstances.
> In our opinion, the financial statements referred to above present fairly the financial position of ABC Company as of [at] December 31, 19X2 and 19X1, and the results of its operations and the changes in its financial position for the years then ended, in conformity with generally accepted accounting principles applied on a consistent basis.

The next section will discuss the profession's failed attempts to revise the basic report version adopted in 1948.

ATTEMPTS TO REVISE THE 1948 REPORT

In addition to the three minor report modifications discussed in the previous section, there have been several attempts by the profession to substantially revise the auditor's report since 1948. A primary area of debate is how users actually perceive the report and its intended messages. This topic of controversy is not new to the debate surrounding the auditor's report. In fact, this controversy was explicitly documented in the literature cited in the last section, when the profession was considering modifying the 1941 report version. The user's perception of an audit report is a critical determinant of what the audit report should state and how it should be stated. A confounding problem in assessing user perceptions is the existence of various types, or groups, of report "users," all with potentially different perceptions of the report. Because the auditor issues only one report per audit, it, by necessity, must cater to all these various user groups simultaneously. The debate over perceptions may continue with whatever report version may be used, and has certainly been evidenced in the more recent attempts to revise the auditor's report.

Interest in revising the 1948 report has seemed to largely coincide with increased criticism of the accounting profession due to widely publicized business failures and alleged auditor failures or increased litigation, usually culminating in heightened congressional scrutiny of the profession. Such was the case in 1964 when the AICPA's public relations counsel, as quoted in Carmichael and Winters (1982, 13), stated:

> Too many stockholders haven't the foggiest idea what your certificate means, and, if I may say so, I think the time is ripe for its revision in layman's language and in the light of changed circumstances in the past 30 years—particularly that of wide stock ownership.

In 1972, after seven years of debate, the AICPA Committee on Auditing Procedure (CAP) proposed a revised standard report. Aranoff (1975, 16-17) indicates that the committee attempted to devise a new report that would address four primary objectives:

1. Distinction between the responsibilities of the company management and the auditor.
2. The limitations of financial statements and the nature of generally accepted accounting principles. This includes the idea that amounts in the financial statements are reasonable approximations and not precise calculations.
3. Description of audit scope, i.e., the auditor's examination is performed in accordance with generally accepted auditing standards, and testing and sampling techniques are employed based on the auditor's evaluation of the client's system of internal control.
4. The meaning of "present fairly . . . in conformity with generally accepted accounting principles."

These four objectives indicate that CAP believed that the audit report needed to better communicate to users the roles and functions of the audit and the auditor in the financial reporting process. Clarity and delineation of audit responsibility were also sought in a revised report. Carmichael and Winters (1982) indicate that there was a concern over whether the nature and limitations of an audit were adequately described in the existing auditor's report, and whether the report adequately conveyed the distinction between the responsibilities of the auditor and of management in the scope paragraph. To meet these overall objectives, at least four different drafts of a modified report were contemplated between 1969 and 1972 (Aranoff 1975, 21). The final report draft considered by CAP in 1972 read as follows (Aranoff 1975, 31-32):

Report of the Independent Auditor:
To the Shareholders of XYZ Company

We have audited the accompanying balance sheet of XYZ Company as of December 31, 1972, and the related statements of income, shareholders' equity and changes in financial position for the year then ended. These statements are based on the company's records and other representations of the company management. Our audit was made in accordance with the generally accepted auditing standards of the American Institute of Certified Public Accountants. Accordingly, we applied auditing procedures to the financial statements and to the underlying data and transactions selected by us from the company's record; we consider the auditing procedures to be of a nature and to the extent sufficient to provide a basis for our opinion expressed below.

In our opinion, the financial statements mentioned above present in all material respects the financial position of XYZ Company at December 31, 1972, and the results of its operations and changes in financial position for the year then ended in accordance with generally accepted accounting principles applied on a consistent basis.

This proposed report version included several departures from the existing report. The term "audited" replaced "examined" to give the report more precision in describing the level of work performed. The phrase "of the American Institute of Certified Public Accountants" was inserted after the reference to GAAS in order to indicate to the readers the source of the standards to which the report referred. A reference to the fact that the financial statements are based on company records and management's representations was added in an attempt to indicate to readers that the financial statements are not the auditor's representations. The phrase "and accordingly included such tests of the accounting records and such other auditing procedures as we considered necessary in the circumstances" was considered too ambiguous. In order to stress the concepts of testing, audit evidence and auditor's use of professional judgment, the sentence beginning, "Accordingly, we . . .," was inserted into the report.

The opinion paragraph was modified to include the phrase "present in all material respects" in place of "present fairly." This modification was CAP's attempt to meet the objective of more adequately addressing the meaning of "present fairly . . . in conformity with GAAP." This issue was particularly important to CAP because of the recent 1969 court decision in the *United States* v. *Simon* (Continental Vending) case. The court's ultimate decision in this case was that the final test of whether or not financial statements were false or misleading was their fairness of presentation, and that presentation in conformity with GAAP alone does not necessarily assure a "fair presentation" of financial statements (Radoff 1975, 11).

Hence, CAP appears to have attempted to limit auditors' exposure to alternative interpretations and legal liability by eliminating the phrase "present fairly" from the auditor's report and by replacing it with "present in all material respects" (Carmichael and Winters 1982, 14). The 1987 ED deliberations by the Auditing Standards Board (ASB) have again addressed this concept of "fair presentation in conformity with GAAP," and have again changed the wording.

Although there was substantial agreement that the proposed report would have better communicated the role of the auditor, the revised report was withdrawn from further consideration in June 1972. Carmichael and Winters (1982, 15) indicate that many committee members believed that:

1. Proposed revisions, while technically correct, had unacceptable public relations implications for the public and regulatory agencies.
2. Legal interpretations of the auditor's function, role and responsibilities would probably not be altered by a more precise description of those attributes in an auditor's report.
3. The increasing effect of "consumerism" presented an unacceptable environment in which to attempt to describe limitations of the auditor's responsibilities in a revised report.

Concern about the revision's effect on various segments of the public overshadowed the belief that the report needed revision to increase its communicative value. The profession was experiencing increased public visibility and had to consider how the public might perceive revision of the report. Carmichael and Winters (1982) indicate that this concern outweighed the perceived increase in communicative value and stability of legal interpretations that would have resulted from report revision.

In an attempt to help clarify the unchanged auditor's report, and to partially address the recent *United States* vs. *Simon* case, the ASB in 1975 issued *SAS 5, The Meaning of "Present Fairly in Conformity with Generally Accepted Accounting Principles" in the Independent Auditor's Report.* This SAS states that an auditor is responsible for assessing (AICPA 1986, AU§411.01):

1. That the accounting principles used have general acceptance.
2. That the accounting principles selected are appropriate in the circumstances.
3. That the financial statements are informative of matters that may affect their use, understanding and interpretation.
4. That the information presented is summarized in a reasonable manner.
5. That the financial statements reflect the underlying events and transactions, within a range of limits that are reasonable and practicable to attain in financial statements.

Because numerous earlier attempts were unsuccessful in modifying this phrase, this SAS was issued to clarify its meaning and provide guidance for its application. Rosenfield and Lorensen (1974) suggest that the debate has been generated by three different interpretations of the phrase:

1. The presentation is in accordance with GAAP and therefore the presentation is fair.
2. The presentation is in confirmity with GAAP and GAAP have been fairly applied.
3. The presentation is in conformity with GAAP *and* the presentation is fair.

CAP, in its deliberations from 1965 to 1972, appeared to intend for the first interpretation to apply with its removal of "fairly" and insertion of "in all material respects." *SAS 5*, however, implies to this author that the highest level of assurance—the third interpretation—is currently the auditor's responsibility. *SAS 5* states:(AICPA 1991, AU §411.03):

> The independent auditor's judgment concerning the "fairness" of the overall presentation of financial statements should be applied within the framework of generally accepted accounting principles. Without that framework the auditor would have no uniform standard for judging the presentation of financial position, results of operations and changes in financial position in financial statements.

Hence, both conformity to GAAP and overall fairness of presentation are the auditor's attestation responsibility, which was also the earlier conclusion of the court in *United States* v. *Simon*. The varying interpretations of "present fairly in conformity with GAAP," however, still persist within the profession and will be shown to affect report revision attempts subsequent to 1975.

Additionally, *SAS 5* has served only as an extremely limited mechanism of informing report users as to the intent of "present fairly in conformity with GAAP" in the audit report. Although a debatable aid to auditors, it has been an ineffective tool in educating report readers, in large part because of its limited distribution and the use of technical language.

The climate in the early and mid-1970s surrounding the accounting and auditing professions did not substantially improve. Seidler (1976) indicates that by 1974, lawsuits against auditors were proliferating and articles critical of the profession were readily found in business publications and the popular press. In the wake of the Watergate investigations, the House Subcommittee on Oversight and Investigation, and the Senate Subcommittee on Reports, Accounting and Management began their investigations of the accounting and auditing professions.

These hearings became known as the Moss/Metcalf hearings, named after the respective chairs of the two subcommittees. The general intent of these hearings was to scrutinize segments of the financial reporting community as to their existing practice and fulfillment of responsibility. During this process, the auditing profession found itself faced with many probing questions regarding its actual responsibility in the financial reporting system, and its adequate fulfillment of that responsibility.

It was in this type of scrutinizing atmosphere that the AICPA appointed the Commission on Auditors' Responsibilities (CAR) to develop conclusions and recommendations regarding appropriate auditor responsibility for the betterment of the auditing profession. Seidler (1976), former Deputy Chairman of the CAR, indicated the commission's focus was originally viewed by commission members and the AICPA as relatively narrow. A "modest report," riddled with caveats about the various limitations of audits was the expected final output of the commission. However, the continued intense congressional and public scrutiny of the profession forced the commission to adopt a wider scope.

CAR's final report numbered some 195 pages and offered suggestions and recommended changes on a multitude of topics. One of the recommendations was for the profession to adopt a new auditor's report. To illustrate the direction, and not the exact wording, that CAR believed a new report should take, they offered the following example (AICPA 1978, 77-79):

<u>Report of Independent Auditors</u>

The accompanying financial statements and consolidated balance sheet of XYZ Company as of December 31, 1976, and the related statements of consolidated income and changes in consolidated financial position for the year then ended, including the notes, are the representations of XYZ Company's management, as explained by the report by management.

In our opinion those financial statements, in all material respects present the financial position of XYZ Company at December 31, 1976, and the results of its operations and changes in financial position for the year then ended in conformity with generally accepted accounting principles appropriate in the circumstances.

We audited the financial statements and the accounting records supporting them in conformity with generally accepted auditing standards. Our audit included a study and evaluation of the company's accounting system and the related controls, tests of details of selected balances and transactions, and an analytical review of the information presented in the statements. We believe our auditing procedures were adequate in the circumstances to support our opinion.

Other Financial Information

We reviewed the information appearing in the annual report [or other such document] in addition to the financial statements, and found nothing inconsistent in such other information with the statements or the knowledge obtained in the course of our audits. [Any other information reviewed, such as replacement cost data, would be identified.]

We reviewed the interim information released during the year. Our reviews were conducted each quarter [or at times as explained] and consisted primarily of making appropriate inquiries to obtain knowledge of the internal accounting control system, the process followed in preparing such information and of financial and operating developments during the periods, and determining that the information appeared reasonable in the light of the knowledge we obtained from our inquiries during the current year, from any procedures completed to the interim date in connection with our audit for each year, and from our audits for preceding years. Any adjustments or additional disclosures we recommended have been reflected in the information.

Internal Accounting Controls

Based on our study and evaluation of the accounting system and related controls, we concur with the description of the system and controls in the report by management [or, Based on our study and evaluation of the accounting system and controls over it, we believe the system and controls have the following uncorrected material weaknesses not described in the report by management. . .] [or other disagreements with the description of the system and controls in the report by management] [or a description of uncorrected material weaknesses found if there is no report by management]. Nevertheless, in the performance of most control procedures, errors can result from personal factors, and also control procedures can be circumvented by collusion or overridden. Projection of any evaluation of internal accounting control to future periods is subject to the risk that changes in conditions may cause procedures to become inadequate and that the degree of compliance with them may deteriorate.

Other Matters

We reviewed the company's policy statement on employee conduct, described in the report by management, and reviewed and tested the related controls and internal audit procedures. While no controls or procedures can prevent or detect all individual misconduct, we believe the controls and internal audit procedures have been appropriately designed and applied during the year.

We met with the audit committee [or the board of directors] of XYZ Company as often as we thought necessary to inform it of the scope of our audit and to discuss any significant accounting or auditing problems encountered and any other services provided to the company [or indication of failure to meet or insufficient meetings or failure to discuss pertinent problems].

Test & Check Co.
Certified Public Accountants

One of the primary concerns of CAR was that the existing auditor's report had largely become an unread symbol. It was felt that, because the report was standardized and remained unaltered, over time users of the report had disregarded the report's exact language and began to rely only on their impressions of what the report meant. The existing report was felt to have lost its communicative capability and was viewed solely as a symbol of the auditor's work and not as a substantive communication between the auditor and the report user. In an insightful research study noted by CAR, Epstein (1975) reaffirmed this view of the auditor's report. Epstein (1975, 3) concluded that report readers' impressions of the report match what the readers want from the auditor—a "seal of approval." In order for the auditor's report to once again become a substantive communication, CAR believed that the report needed to be considerably modified and expanded; thus, the rather lengthy suggested report. This report type, it was hoped, would better capture the reader's attention and would force users to relearn the report and decifer its intended messages. Also, once the reader's attention was captured, substantially more information could be communicated.

Another reason indicated by CAR for the need for a modified report was the apparent disparity of report wording and the existing auditor's responsibility, which had changed since the report was originally adopted in 1948. CAR's suggested report led the way for the auditor's report to begin incorporating additional attestation responsibilities. Items like supplemental replacement cost data, interim information, and information not a part of the annual financial statements were given recognition in the new "mold" of the auditor's report. The suggested report contained standardized wordings for the eight paragraphs; however, five of these referred to items of a supplemental nature and could be added or deleted depending on the particular audit services performed.

The CAR auditor's report also mentioned the client's system of internal control. This reflected the commission's evolving concept of an audit as a function to be performed over a period of time and not solely on a particular set of financial statements. This expanded audit concept was intended to incorporate all important elements of the financial reporting process, including intimate involvement with the client's system of internal control, as well as company policies governing such things as codes of conduct, meetings with audit committees, and the establishment and functioning of an internal audit function.

CAR's suggested report also reflected some of the ideas identified in the CAP deliberations and suggested in the 1972 report. For example, CAR also attempted to delineate the responsibilities of the auditor and of management by noting that financial statements "are the representation of XYZ Company's management, as explained in the report by management." This statement also indicates CAR's strong conviction that a management report should be included in the financial report, and that this report should also include an acknowledgment of management's responsibility for the financial statements. Also, the suggested report included the phrase "in all material respects" and eliminated "fairly" from the opinion paragraph as in 1972, indicating CAR's similar concern for the phrase "present fairly in conformity with GAAP." The commission concluded that "fair" conveys different messages to different readers and, to avoid possible confusion, it should be eliminated from the report (AICPA 1978).

Additionally, CAR noted that, with the 1971 adoption of APB Opinion No. 20, the reference to consistency in the auditor's report was redundant and should be eliminated (AICPA 1978).

The major focus of CAR's suggested report was on improved communication about the function of an audit with the intent to better educate audit readers as to what function an audit serves and what responsibilities an auditor assumes. The solution adopted was a considerable expansion of the audit report, and a more explicit description of the scope and limitations of an audit in the report to reduce reliance on readers' interpretations of the report's intended messages. This change in report focus and its wording was also a reflection of the commission's evolving view of the audit as a function that takes place over a period of time.

In 1979, the AICPA's Auditing Standards Board, based on the recommendations of CAR, decided to specifically examine the profession's standard audit report. The ASB, however, decided that a substantial departure from the existing report, as suggested by CAR, was not needed. After considerable deliberation, the following two-paragraph report was released in Exposure Draft form for comment in 1980 (AICPA 1980, 11):

Title to include the word "independent"

The accompanying balance sheet of X Company as of [at] December 31, 19XX, and the related statements of income, retained earnings and changes in financial position for the year then ended are management's representations. An audit is intended to provide reasonable, but not absolute, assurance as to whether the financial statements taken as a whole are free of material misstatements. We have audited the financial statements referred to above in accordance with generally accepted auditing standards. Application of those standards requires judgment in determining the nature, timing and extent of tests and other procedures and in evaluating the results of those procedures.

In our opinion, the financial statements referred to above present the financial position of X Company as of [at] December 31, 19XX, and the results of its operations and changes in its financial position for the year then ended in conformity with generally accepted accounting principles.

Carmichael and Winters (1982, 17-18) summarized the changes made in the proposed 1980 report as follows:

1. Add the word "independent" to the title.
2. Add an assertion that the financial statements are the representations of management.
3. Add a statement that "an audit is intended to provide reasonable but not absolute assurance as to whether the financial statements taken as a whole are free of material misstatements."
4. Replace the word "examined" with "audited."
5. Include in the scope paragraph that "application of (GAAS) requires judgment in determining the nature, timing and extent of tests and other procedures and in evaluating the results of those procedures."
6. Delete the word "fairly" from the opinion paragraph.
7. Delete the reference to consistency of application of GAAP.

An unprecedented 450 response letters were received on this exposure draft and after considering these responses, the ASB withdrew the revision attempt in March 1981. Douglas Carmichael, former AICPA vice president-auditing, indicated that despite CAR's mandate to revise the report, there seemed to be substantial feeling that the current auditor's report had served users well (*Journal of Accountancy* 1981, 3). James Leisenring, former ASB chairman, noted in the same announcement that public reaction to the ED was mixed, but that the total effect was "not seen as an improvement."

The next chapter will discuss in more detail the research performed on the letters of response to this ED. However, suffice it is to say that the majority of the respondents viewed the proposed report as being too negatively worded and believed that it gave the appearance that the auditing profession was trying to shirk legitimate responsibility. A majority of the suggested modifications in this report were the same ones considered in the 1972 version as well as in the example report suggested by CAR. The 1980 proposed report, however, far more clearly resembles the 1972 report than suggested by CAR. Because most of the proposed modifications were not entirely "new," it seems that there was some agreement that these aspects of the report needed revision. The majority of the respondents voiced their disagreement with how these modifications should be implemented and not with the need for change per se (Mitchell 1983, 40). However, the ASB was no more successful in 1980 than its predecessor, CAP, in reaching a consensus on the form the report revision should take.

Although many of the modifications faced opposition, the proposed change receiving the most disagreement, and commentary was the deletion of the word "fairly." The 1972 and CAR proposed report versions included the same deletion, however, these reports inserted the phrase "in all material respects" in order to retain the concept that the financial reporting process is not an exact endeavor, but one requiring auditor judgment. Without the term "fairly," and with no inclusion of an alternate phrase like "in all material respects," some respondents believed that the report seemed too much like an endorsement of the financial statements (Carmichael and Winters 1982, 18).

Carmichael and Winters (1982) indicate that many of those who favored the deletion of "fairly" believed that it was the main cause of confusion in the report, in that the term suggested that the auditor was, in effect, forming two opinions: one as to the fairness of presentation and one as to conformity with GAAP. They believed that the term placed more responsibility on the auditor than intended. However, *SAS 5*, as discussed earlier, seems to indicate that this dual responsibility is what the profession was presently fulfilling. Hence, the interpretation of the phrase "present fairly in conformity with GAAP" once again appears to have caused some confusion and sparked continued debate surrounding the auditor's report and auditor responsibilities.

The deciding factor on the report revision turned out to be the handling of the word "fairly." Some viewed this term as a "fatal flaw" in the report, while to others it was seen as an "irreplaceable virtue" (Carmichael and Winters 1982, 18). In 1981, the board eventually decided to retain the word "fairly" and deemed that if this was done, there would not be enough improvement to warrant changing the report.

Following this failed attempt at revision, the AICPA distributed a pamphlet aimed at educating users about the audit report and its intended messages. Because the standard report was not revised, yet still generally felt to poorly communicate the auditors' assumed responsibilities, and the audit procedure, the profession decided to approach the education of audit report users from a different direction. An AICPA pamphlet titled, *A User's Guide to Understanding Audits and Auditors' Reports*, was compiled in 1982, and represents a direct effort on the part of the auditing profession to try to educate audit report users. Carmichael (1978) notes that two earlier pamphlets were prepared by the profession in order to explain audit reports to nonaccountants: *Audits by Certified Public Accountants* in 1950 and *40 Questions and Answers*

About Audit Reports in 1965. An updated pamphlet containing the new SAS No. 58, auditors reports was also released in 1989 and is very similar to the 1982 pamphlet in intent and content (AICPA 1989b). By 1983, the profession had issued three documents, available to the public free of charge, that attempted to explain the auditor's report adopted by the profession in 1948.

The 1982 pamphlet, written by Winters, Academic Fellow of the AICPA Auditing Standards Division, discusses more than the standard auditor's report. For example, sections addressing financial statements and the accounting process, what an audit entails and modifications of the standard report, are also included in the pamphlet. However, the preface indicates that (AICPA 1982, i):

> The major objective of this booklet is to explain the contents and meaning of the auditor's report. It is intended for users of financial statements who want to better understand the meaning and significance of audit reports.

The pamphlet explains how the report user should interpret technical phrases in the standard short-form report and variations of this report. It is important to note that the pamphlet has a slightly different interpretation of "presents fairly in conformity with GAAP." It states that "present fairly" must always be joined with "in conformity with GAAP" to form a *single* concept of financial statement presentation. The booklet indicates that the reader should interpret the phrase to mean: "presents . . . based on reasonable accurate data portrayed in accordance with generally accepted accounting principles" (AICPA 1982, 11).

Communication/education efforts of this type do not seem to be reaching a large portion of the user population. Readers' knowledge of the audit function has been demonstrated to affect their perception of auditor responsibility (e.g., Bailey et al. 1983). However, education of this "voluntary" nature does not seem to have had a significant impact on users' level of audit awareness. Part of the dilemma is due to the fact that this, and the earlier booklets, have not been widely distributed to the groups that would potentially benefit from their insights. Also, Seidler (1976, 42) argues that "it is extremely difficult to explain to them (users) that the symbol means something else," and that "educational efforts such as these are probably not harmful; their effectiveness, however, is doubtful."

AUDITING STANDARDS BOARD'S LATEST ATTEMPT TO ALTER THE REPORT WORDING

In order to more directly address the problem of continuing public (user) misunderstanding of the standard auditor's report, the ASB in 1985 again began deliberations directed toward the modification of the standard auditor's report.

As in the past, this modification attempt came in the wake of congressional and public scrutiny of the accounting profession. After some tremendous business failures, in early 1985 the House Subcommittee on Oversight and Investigations of the Committee on Energy and Commerce, chaired by Rep. John Dingell, began hearings on the investigation into the accounting and auditing professions (U.S. Congress 1985). These congressional hearings continued sporadically for over three years into 1988. Rep. Dingel stated that the hearings had a purpose similar to the Moss/Metcalf hearings of the mid-1970s which was to "see how the accounting profession is functioning as a part of the federal regulatory system" (*Wall Street Journal*, 1985). Accordingly, Congress was again attempting to assess the existing practices of the auditing profession and determine if those practices were adequate to properly discharge the responsibilities assumed by the profession. In response to the onset of the hearings, the AICPA indicated that it looked forward to "the chance to update the Congress on the profession's progress" (*Wall Street Journal*, 1985).

These recent congressional investigations closely resembled the congressional scrutiny of the accounting and auditing professions a decade earlier, and coincided with the AICPA's appointment of the CAR, eventually culminating in the 1980 exposure draft. J. Michael Cook, AICPA President, in his inaugural speech in October 1986, said: "I was struck by the almost eerie similarities between the profession then [1976] and our circumstances today—truly deja-vu" (Cook looks ahead, 1986).

Cook was referring not only to the congressional hearings, but also to the similarities in the existence of independent commissions studying the role of accounting and auditing. In 1976, there was the Commission on Auditors' Responsibilities and an AICPA special committee to set the AICPA's agenda, and in 1986 there was the National Commission on Fraudulent Financial Reporting, chaired by James Treadway, and the AICPA special committee on standards of professional conduct for CPAs, chaired by George Anderson.

The National Commission on Fraudulent Financial Reporting (Treadway Commission) was established in October 1985, and was charged with the multidimensional task of identifying "causal factors that can lead to fraudulent financial reporting and steps to reduce its incidence" (*Report* 1987, 1). The final report issued in October 1987 recognized that fraudulent financial reporting was an extremely complex phenomenon and, accordingly, offered recommendations for public companies, the SEC and other regulatory and law enforcement agencies, accounting educators, and independent public accountants. Their report contained nine recommendations for the auditing profession; two of which address communicating the auditor's role to users of financial statements. The first recommendation regarding improved auditor communication is aimed at users of audited financial statements who "need to understand better the nature and scope of an audit and the limitation of the audit process" (*Report* 1987, 57). Their recommendation was to revise the standard auditor's report. Their specific recommendation was as follows (*Report* 1987, 57):

> The Auditing Standards Board should revise the auditor's standard report to state that the audit provides reasonable but not absolute assurance that the audited financial statemnets are free from material misstatements as a result of fraud or error.

The second recommendation suggested mentioning the client's system of internal control in the auditor's report, and read as follows (*Report* 1987, 57):

> The Auditing Standards Board should revise the auditor's standard report to describe the extent to which the independent public accountant has reviewed and evaluated the system of internal accounting control. The Auditing Standards Board should also provide explicit guidance to address the situation where, as a result of his knowledge of the company's internal accounting controls, the independent public accountant disagrees with management's assessment as stated in the proposed management's report.

This recommendation highlights the commission's emphasis on internal accounting control as a potential barrier to fraudulent financial reporting. The existing auditing literature required only a preliminary evaluation of a client's system of internal control in order to assess whether further evaluation may have lead the auditor to rely on the established internal controls and limit subsequent audit tests. The commission concluded that the public accountant should adopt a more active role, and explicitly indicated that they defer to the AICPA on the "determination of the appropriate extent of the independent public accountant's review of the system of internal accounting control" (*Report* 1987, 58).

The commission did not, however, suggest an alternate report, or even a specific report modification. They left the exact wording of any revision to the auditing profession. They did, however, indicate that the report should be modified to: (1) better communicate the responsibilities assumed by the auditor, (2) clearly explain the degree to which users can rely on an audit, (3) discuss the limitations of the audit process, and (4) explain that an audit does not guarantee or provide absolute assurance that the financial statements are reliable or accurate (*Report* 1987, 52).

In the midst of the congressional hearings, and almost simultaneously with the start of the Treadway Commission's deliberations, the AICPA announced in its July 1985 edition of "In our opinion. . .," the newsletter of the AICPA Auditing Standards Division, that it was going to reexamine auditor responsibilities in regard to fraud detection and the related "expectations gap" between auditors and financial statement users. This initial undertaking at the AICPA eventually culminated in the issuance of 10 exposure drafts in early 1987, including the proposed audit report revision. These projects were undertaken by the ASB in order to address the disparity in the beliefs of audit report users as to what the audit process entails with what professional standards actually require of auditors. In discussing these projects, Jerry Sullivan (1986, 1), chairman of the ASB, has stated that they were:

> spurred on not only by some sensational business failures and the congressional hearings that followed in their wake, but also by the belief that there is a crisis of confidence in the accounting profession; the ASB has begun several new projects that focus on issues that will have a broader impact on financial reporting than the previous SAS's did.

The ASB, in conjunction with recommendations from the task force, voted unanimously in their December 1986 meeting to expose the following proposed standard auditor's report for comment (AICPA 1987a, 7-8):

> Independent Auditor's Report
>
> We have audited the accompanying balance sheet of X Company as of December 31, 19XX, and the related statements of income, retained earnings, and changes in financial position for the year then ended. These financial statements are the representations of X Company's management.
>
> We performed our audit in accordance with generally accepted auditing standards. Those standards require that an audit be designed to evaluate whether the financial statements are materially misstated (intentionally or unintentionally). Reasonable assurance regarding that evaluation is achieved by examining evidence, on a test basis, that supports the amounts included in the financial statements, by assessing the appropriateness of the accounting principles used and the significant estimates made by management, and by assessing the appropriateness of the overall financial statement presentation and disclosures. We believe that our auditing procedures were appropriate in the circumstances to express our opinion presented below.
>
> In our opinion, the financial statements referred to above are, in all material respects, fairly presented in conformity with generally accepted accounting principles.

The exposure draft on the auditor's report was officially issued on February 14, 1987, along with nine other exposure drafts representing other "expectations gap" projects. The deliberations of the task force and the ASB leading up to the issuance of this report version will be discussed in Chapter 4.

SUMMARY

This chapter has depicted the evolution of the standard auditor's report in the United States. It has traced the report's evolution from early British influence, to the many report versions in the early twentieth century, to the latest attempt to revise the report version adopted by the profession in 1948. A summary of the more significant events is presented in Figure 2.1. In this process of evolution, it is not surprising to identify a host of influences affecting and guiding the use of the auditor's report and its wording. The auditor's report

Pre-1917	No prescribed audit report. Auditors wrote original reports for every engagement—typically using the term "certify."
1917	AIA presented the first suggested one paragraph report.
1929	AIA suggested a two-paragraph report form.
1931	The term "certify" was dropped from the auditor's report.
1934	First required audit report for SEC registrants, including an expanded scope paragraph that discussed attributes of an audit such as testing, evaluating the use of accounting principles and obtaining evidence from clients. Also the report was now to be addressed to the directors or stockholders.
1939	Report was revised to split scope and opinion paragraphs and to include client's system of internal control and the phrase "present fairly . . . in conformity with generally accepted accounting principles."
1941	Report was revised to mention "generally accepted auditing standards."
1948	Report was revised to eliminate reference to internal control and to substantially limit discussion of attributes on an audit.
1948-1976	Added the Statement of Changes in Financial Position to the report and made minor modifications to the terminology referring to the financial statements.
1965-1972	CAP deliberations on a report modification.
1978	CAR suggests a radical change in report form consisting of three standard paragraphs and five potential supplemental paragraphs.
1980	ASB proposes a modified two-paragraph report.
1981	ASB withdraws the 1980 proposal.
1985	AICPA begins deliberations regarding auditor's responsibility.
1987	ASB proposes a revised three-paragraph report which expands discussion of attributes of an audit and management's responsibility.

Figure 1. Summary of Significant Events

has been shown to have led the profession at times, and in other times it has been shown to have been affected by changes adopted by the profession, changes in the auditor's relationship with third parties, and changes identified with the evolving practice of financial reporting. All of these influences were incorporated into the auditor's report in an effort by the profession to effectively report to financial statement users.

In addition, this chapter has identified several recurring issues in regard to the standard auditor's report. One of the most fundamental issues is the determination of the audience of the audit reports. Is the audience only those individuals or groups possessing adequate knowledge regarding the audit function, like bankers and financial analysts, or does the audience include any potential "user" whether knowledgeable or not? Also, the question of "educating" users with the report must be addressed. Should the report attempt to educate those less knowledgeable users as to the function of an audit and the responsibility assumed by the auditor? If so, how much education can be reasonably achieved through the audit report? Several of these issues presuppose that an appropriate assessment can be made as to the level of user knowledge. However, this chapter has indicated that consensus on the level of user knowledge at any point in time has been difficult to attain.

Additionally, there have been several specific report modifications that have been consistently called for in proposals for change. These modifications are: (1) add "independent" to the report title, (2) change "examined" to "audited," (3) modify "presents fairly in conformity with GAAP," (4) include a phrase indicating that an audit provides reasonable assurance, (5) attempt to more explicitly identify that the financial statements are the responsibility of management and not of the auditor, and (6) delete the reference to consistency in the opinion paragraph. Although these particular modifications have consistently been proposed, implementation approaches have varied. Also, the issue of whether or not the report should refer to the client's system of internal controls is under continued debate. The ASB's current resolution of these issues will be discussed in subsequent chapters. The next chapter will examine some of the published research regarding the auditor's report prior to *SAS 58*.

Chapter 3

Review of the Research
on Auditors' Reports

This chapter provides a review of extant research on auditor's reports prior to *SAS 58* (see Estes 1982, Chap. 2, for a more comprehensive summary of the empirical research through 1981). Chapter 8 discusses the research to date regarding *SAS 58* reports and "updates" this review for the new report wordings. This review is presented in annotated bibliography fashion and incorporates studies performed on all audit report categories and is not intended to be restricted to studies only examining the standard unqualified report. To keep the literature covered by this review manageable, the large volume of opinion and argumentative pieces, as well as historical works, have been excluded. These omitted works, however, should not be considered trivial because they have made a valuable contribution to the body of literature on the auditor's report.

The research reviewed in this chapter has sometimes been "shoddy" and has often produced contradictory results, which might be expected from a stream of research that, particularly in the early years, was fragmented with no primary focus. Estes (1982, 29) reviewed the literature on auditors' reports through 1981 and concluded that: "If we have learned nothing else from the many research efforts during this period, we have learned that significant progress does not come so easily." An update of this literature has not altered this fundamental conclusion.

The literature in this chapter will be reviewed in several broad sections including: (1) readership of the auditor's report, (2) understanding of the auditor's report, (3) how the capital markets have reacted to various categories of reports, (4) laboratory and field experiments that have examined the reports' effect on individual behavior, (5) studies analyzing auditor reporting decisions, and (6) a final section on the studies that have examined the proposed audit report presented in the ASB's 1980 Exposure Draft.

READERSHIP OF THE AUDITOR'S REPORT

A number of researchers have assessed the extent to which the auditor's report is actually read. A diversity of audit report user groups have been examined through the use of survey instruments or interviews, resulting in mixed results.

Arthur Andersen & Company (1974). A study performed by Opinion Research Corporation for Arthur Andersen & Co. included a question about readership of the audit report. The following responses were obtained from the 404 shareholders asked the question, "How often do you read the auditor's report?"

All of the time	19%
Most of the time	31
Only sometimes	28
Rarely or never	21
No response	1

Barnett (1976). Barnett surveyed 110 professional and 277 nonprofessional investors from Texas. These two groups indicated the following readership patterns:

	Investors	
	Professional (%)	Nonprofessional (%)
Reports of Companies Currently Invested in		
Always	34.9	43.8
Usually	30.3	27.2
Sometimes	22.0	14.8
Rarely	11.9	11.8
Never	0.9	2.4
Reports of Companies Considered for Investment		
Always	34.9	38.0
Usually	24.5	29.7
Sometimes	24.5	13.3
Rarely	14.2	15.8
Never	1.9	3.1

Brenner (1971). This early study surveyed financial statement user groups to determine the extent to which annual reports were read, used and understood. The survey was sent to 1,000 bankers, 1,000 financial analysts, and 2,000 stockholders, and resulted in 340, 417, and 484 responses, respectively. Readership data were collected on seven annual report elements, with the following results obtained for the auditor's report:

	Bankers (%)	Financial Analysts (%)	Stockholders (%)
Read very carefully	43	32	14
Read somewhat carefully	27	29	24
Did not read carefully	20	26	27
Did not read	7	11	25
No answer	3	2	10

The study also ranked seven annual report elements as to importance, based on extent of readership. The auditor's report ranked sixth with the banker groups and seventh with the financial analyst and stockholder groups, indicating that the auditor's report was the least carefully read component of the annual report.

Epstein (1975). Epstein surveyed 432 stockholders nationwide and asked them to rank the usefulness of seven items in the annual report. The respondents indicated that the auditor's report is the least thoroughly read of the following items: income statement, balance sheet, statement of changes in financial position, footnotes, president's letter, essay and graphic material, and the auditor's report. In fact, the survey indicated that approximately one-third of the stockholders do not read the report at all, and that 56 percent indicated that the auditor's report was not at all useful to them.

Fess and Ziegler (1977). This study randomly surveyed 118 financial analysts, 214 bankers, and 188 individual stockholders to determine, in part, their respective levels of readership. The following responses were obtained:

	Bankers (%)	Financial Analysts (%)	Stockholders (%)
How often do you look for the auditor's report?			
Always	87.4	55.1	40.4
Often	7.5	23.7	22.9
Sometimes	3.7	16.1	21.8
Almost never	1.4	5.1	14.9
How carefully do you read the auditor's report?			
Carefully	69.2	28.0	27.3
Hurriedly	30.8	70.3	56.9
Note that it is there	—	1.7	15.8

Almost 30 percent of the stockholders indicated that they were only interested in making sure that an auditor's report was provided with the financial statements and were not particularly interested in what was said. By far the most cited reason for all three groups' low readership ratings was that they "are already familiar with it" and thus do not have to read it in every financial statement. Hence, these groups indicate an interest in ascertaining that an audit has been performed, but are not particularly concerned with the specific wording contained in the auditor's report.

Lee and Tweedie (1975). This study surveyed 374 United Kingdom stockholders of one company as to their level of readership of seven annual report items and found that the auditor's report was the least read and rated least important of all items. Other items included in the survey were the profit and loss statement, balance sheet, notes to the statements, chairman's report, director's report, and statistical data. Responses to this mail survey indicated the following readership pattern of the auditor's report in the annual financial statements:

Read thoroughly	17.4%
Read briefly for interest	39.0
Not at all	43.6

Lee and Tweedie (1977). This study was similar to their 1975 study, except that data were collected by interviewing 301 United Kingdom stockholders. Results similar to those obtained in 1975 indicated the following pattern of readership among stockholders:

Read thoroughly	16%
Read briefly for interest	36
Not at all	48

Stobie (1978). Stobie surveyed 91 investment analysts, 76 corporate managers, and 60 individual stockholders in South Africa. One question posed to these individuals was, "Do you always read the audit report when examining financial statements?" The following number of positive responses were received to this question:

Investment analysts	63%
Corporate managers	72
Individual stockholders	65

This study indicates a high level of interest by these individuals in the auditor's report, however, it did not attempt to assess how thoroughly the respondents read the report.

Summary

The studies reviewed in this section examine various audit report user groups from different areas of the United States and other countries. The results obtained are, therefore, hard to compare and may be considered somewhat fragmented. However, there is overall indication that more potential audit report users identify the existence of the auditor's report than actually read it thoroughly. This empirical phenomenon is clearly noted in the studies of Epstein (1975) and Fess and Ziegler (1977), and lends credence to the notion that the pre-*SAS 58* auditor's report was viewed by users as a symbol of the auditor's work and not as a substantive communication by the auditor to report readers.

UNDERSTANDING OF AUDIT REPORTS

A number of researchers have attempted to assess reader understanding of audit reports. The methodologies have ranged from questionnaire self-report items to field studies that attempt to capture users' "perceptual space" relating to various audit report forms. This section will present the research results across all methodologies employed.

Arthur Andersen & Company (1974). As part of their large opinion survey, Arthur Andersen & Company had Opinion Research Corporation gather data on the perceptions of the audit function and the assurances it provides. One question posed to the respondents was whether they agreed or disagreed with the statement, "the most important function of the public accounting firm's audit of a corporation is to detect significant fraud." The following percentages of agreement were obtained:

Respondent Group	
Business press	68%
Stockholders	66
Analysts/brokers	55
Institutional investors	39
Corporate executives	20
Securities lawyers	18
Government officials	16
Business professors	12
CPAs	6

These results clearly indicate the disparity between various groups' perceptions and the auditor's own perception of his responsibility for fraud detection. Principally, the groups of individuals most disparate from the auditors are those for whom an audit is primarily intended (shareholders, analysts, and investors). As a further illustration of their misunderstanding, the survey noted that 37 percent of the stockholders believed that auditors examined *all* the financial records of the company under audit. This study concluded that the groups surveyed largely misunderstood the purpose of an audit.

Barnett (1976). Barnett, in his survey of Texas investors, found that nonprofessional investors, on average, could correctly answer only 50 percent of test questions designed to assess their comprehension of the auditor's report. Professional investors did not have a much better understanding, with an average of only 51 percent. These results indicate that the investment community has an insufficient knowledge of the messages contained in the auditor's report.

Barnett, using communications theory, then goes on to formulate an audit report that he believes will produce a better understanding on the part of report readers. His suggested report is considerably longer than the former two-paragraph report. The report makes an attempt to eliminate "overly technical" terms, and includes a description of the nature of GAAS, a reference to the system of internal control, and eliminates the use of the controversial phrase "presents fairly in conformity with GAAP." Barnett concludes that the report needs to be considerably lengthened and modified in order for it to become an effective vehicle for improving user understanding of the audit function.

Beck (1973). Beck surveyed 711 Australian stockholders. The group showed significant misunderstanding of the auditor's role. This early work found that 93 percent of stockholders expect auditors to give assurance that no fraud has been committed by company management. He also found that 92 percent believed that an audit gave assurance that management had properly discharged all statutory duties, 71 percent believed that management was efficient, and, most disheartening, 81 percent believed that an audit gave an assurance that the company was financially sound.

Briloff (1966). In this early study, Briloff surveyed 72 members of the financial community and 64 accountants. He found that these groups were not in agreement on the form of opinion that would be issued when client management has selected a particular acceptable GAAP, but the auditor prefers another. He also noted that these two groups are not in agreement with one another, or among themselves, as to the meaning of "presents fairly in conformity with GAAP" in the auditor's report. The following positive responses were obtained in his survey:

	Report Users	Accountants
The statements are both fair and in conformity with GAAP	44%	34%
The statements are fair because they are in conformity with GAAP	22	30
The statements are fair only to the extent that GAAP are fair	28	20
None of the above	6	16
	100%	100%

These empirical results highlight the disparity of interpretations of the meaning of "present fairly in conformity with GAAP" as discussed in the preceding chapter.

Campbell and Muthcler (1988). These researchers assessed bankers' and auditors' perceptions about the auditor's role and the auditor's report when there is a going-concern uncertainty. Sixty-two Big Eight auditors and 41 commercial bank lenders from Ohio participated in the study. Subjects were asked to indicate which of the following statements most accurately describes why an auditor issues a going-concern audit report: (1) because failure is indicated, and therefore the financial statements cannot be fairly presented according to GAAP, (2) because failure is indicated, and it is the auditor's duty to provide a signal to the financial statement user, or (3) because failure is indicated, and the value of assets reported does not indicate recoverable value. Subjects were also asked to respond to 14 semantic differentials regarding the meaning and usefulness of the going-concern opinion.

Most of the bankers (49%) favored option 2 above, while most of the auditors (42%) favored option 3—both as expected. However, a large portion of auditors (39%) also believed the auditor's primary role in issuing the going-concern report was to send a signal (option 2) to financial statement users. Additionally, on most of the semantic differentials, the two groups responded similarly. The largest differences were on the clear/unclear and used/unused dimensions with lenders indicating the report was less clear and used less than indicated by the auditors. In general, however, the going-concern report was viewed in a "positive" light by both groups.

Dillard, Murdock, and Shank (1978); Shank, Dillard, and Murdock (1978 and 1979); Shank, Dillard, and Bylinski (1979). These four studies represent a series of investigations of auditors' and various users' perceptions and attitudes toward "subject to" audit opinions. The same survey methodology was used with the following four groups:

	# mailed	# responding	Response rate (%)
Partners in international CPA firms	500	232	46
Bank loan officers	500	304	61
Corporate financial officers	500	307	61
Financial analysts	790	207	26

Each study presented the subjects with eight separate contingency scenarios taken from actual financial reports and provided them with five possible disclosure options: (1) nondisclosure, (2) disclose information in unaudited section of the annual report, (3) disclose only in a footnote, (4) disclose in a footnote and in a "subject to" qualified report, and (5) disclose in a disclaimer of opinion report that discusses the reason for the disclaimer. For each scenario, the subjects were asked to indicate: (1) the level of disclosure they believed best communicated the contingency described, and (2) the level of disclosure they believed would be provided by the company's actual annual report. A table summarizing the congruence between the level of disclosure the respondents believe should be presented and the actual disclosures in the annual report follows:

	CPA Partners (%)	Bank Loan Officers (%)	Corporate Financial Officers (%)	Financial Analysts (%)
Respondents preferred level of disclosure agreed with actual disclosure	52.7	39.3	48.1	44.2
Respondents preferred level of disclosure was lower than the actual level of disclosure	17.3	14.4	20.4	15.7
Respondents preferred level of disclosure was higher than the actual level of disclosure	30.0	46.3	31.5	40.1

These results suggest that there was no consensus regarding the level of disclosure among auditors or across these surveyed user groups. The results do indicate, however, that a large number of auditors and users of financial statements would prefer a higher level of disclosure (i.e., "subject to" and disclaimer reports) regarding unresolved contingencies than was being exhibited in actual annual reports. Additionally, the authors conclude, based on responses from all four groups, that the "subject to" audit opinion does provide useful information to these various groups and that such usage should be retained.

Epstein (1975). His survey of 432 stockholders disclosed that 22 percent had difficulty understanding the auditor's report, and ranked it fourth in difficulty of seven financial report items presented. The auditor's report was ranked harder to understand than the income statement. Additionally, 13.9 percent of the stockholders responding expressed a desire for additional information about audit reports. This finding evidences that some stockholders admit lack of total comprehension of the auditor's report and the messages contained in it.

Fess and Ziegler (1977). This research surveyed 118 financial analysts, 214 bankers and 188 individual stockholders selected at random. The following responses were obtained to the question, "How well do you believe you understand the auditor's report?":

	Financial Analysts (%)	Bankers (%)	Stockholders (%)
Completely	41.9	49.3	33.3
Most of it	53.0	49.3	52.0
Much of it	4.3	1.4	12.6
Do not understand it	.8	—	2.1

These self-assessment results indicate that whether or not these groups actually do properly understand the auditor's report, they *think* they understand it.

Fiebelkorn (1977). Fiebelkorn surveyed sophisticated users of corporate financial reports and obtained responses from 47 loan/investment officers of commercial banks, 92 trust officers of commercial banks, 59 investment officers of insurance companies, and 34 investment officers of investment counseling firms. An analysis of the responses of these groups to the mail survey indicated that the CPA's opinion on the financial statements not only made them more believable, but also was the vital component for user reliance on the financial statements. This result was consistent across all groups surveyed.

This study also found that these sophisticated report users viewed the responsibility for preparing the financial statements as shared between the CPA and the company's management. This perception was also found to be stable across groups. This perception of the auditor's responsibility is in stark contrast to the auditor's view that their role is that of independently attesting to the accuracy and fair presentation of *management's* financial statements.

Houghton (1987). This study attempts to assess three different meanings of the concept "true and fair view" indicated in the standard audit reports of various countries (e.g., Australia, United Kingdom, and South Africa). This concept is very similar to the U.S. reporting concept of "present fairly." The three meanings assessed were: (1) the accountants' own meaning, (2) the accountants' perception of shareholders meaning, and (3) the shareholders' own meaning. The subjects were 22 Chartered Accountants and 28 private shareholders. Twenty-two semantic differentials developed by Haried (1973) were used to derive the respective meanings.

Houghton found that accountants held markedly different meanings than did the shareholders. However, the accountants perceived the shareholders' views to be very similar to their own. Additionally, the accountants cognitive structures relating to this concept were considerably more complex than those held by the shareholders. These results depict a considerable, unrecognized difference between accountants and shareholders on a concept central to the financial and audit reporting process.

Lee and Tweedie (1975). This survey of 374 United Kingdom stockholders revealed that approximately 10 percent of the respondents believed that the legal responsibility for the company's financial statements belonged to the auditor. This erroneous view of auditor/management responsibility would be further explored by these two researchers in 1977.

Lee and Tweedie (1977). This extension of their earlier work involved interviews of 301 United Kingdom stockholders. Through these interviews, the authors determined that the stockholders level of audit report knowledge could be summarized as follows:

Reasonable	41%
Vague	20
None	39

Hence, almost 60 percent of those stockholders interviewed were assessed to have little or no knowledge of the auditor's report. This result is strikingly below the level of understanding demonstrated by the more "sophisticated" report readers, as determined in other research efforts.

Libby (1979a). This field experiment attempted to assess the perceptions of sophisticated report users and auditors as to the relative similarities of audit report types. Thirty Big Eight audit firm partners and 28 commercial loan officers from large banks were selected from the Chicago area. These subjects were selected for their higher probability of exposure to various audit report forms. The task involved 10 audit reports, including unqualified, various scope qualifications, GAAP departure qualifications, an adverse opinion and an unaudited disclaimer report. The subjects were asked to rate the similarity of these 10 reports given two at a time. The subjects were then supplied with 13 descriptive phrases to use in rating each report.

The author used multidimensional scaling to assess the two group's perceptions of the 10 reports. The two-dimensional perceptual plots presented almost identical results for both the bankers and auditors, leading Libby to the conclusion that "the fears of miscommunication of the messages intended by audit reports to more sophisticated users may not be justified" (p. 118).

Louis Harris and Associates, Inc. (1986). This study was conducted by Louis Harris and Associates, Inc. specifically for and under the direction of the AICPA. The study is described as "a comprehensive survey of the principal publics which make up the universe in which Certified Public Accountants and the public accounting profession operate" (p. 1). To this end, a telephone survey covered the following sample groups:

General Publics

A national cross-section of adults	1,200
Individuals deemed "knowledgeable" about accountants	681
Individual stockholders	550

Specific Publics

Owners or managers of small business	232
Owners or managers of medium-sized business	232
CEOs and CFOs of large corporations	101
Audit committee members of large corporations	60
Key state and federal officials dealing with financial related topics	60
Key aids to members of Congress	63
Senior bank lending officers	60
Lawyers knowledgeable about financial affairs	60
Members of the financial media	40
Leading accounting academics	61
Top security analysts	67
	3,402

This study attempted to extend and update the Peat, Marwick, Mitchell and Co. (1983) survey, discussed later in this section, by maintaining some of the identical questions utilized in that study. Accordingly, the same statement regarding fraud detection was also posed in 1986, "The most important function of an independent auditing firm is to detect management fraud and dishonesty." The following affirmative responses were received:

General public	70%
"Knowledgeable" public	67
Stockholders	64
Small business executives	46
Medium-sized business executives	25
Large corporate executives	16
Audit committee members	28
State and federal officials	40
Key congressional aides	48
Bank lending officers	25
Lawyers	42
Financial media	50
Accounting academics	25
Security analysts	36

A detailed comparison of these percentages with those attained in 1983 indicates that, in general, more respondents agreed with this statement in 1986. This observation led Louis Harris, Inc. to state:

> there is a sore temptation on the part of many to expect that accounting and CPAs can and do perform beyond reasonable expectations. A real problem centers on the view that the most important function of an independent audit is to detect management fraud and dishonesty (p. 10).

The survey also asked the question, "To whom is an independent CPA firm responsible to on an audit?" A majority of all groups indicated the stockholders or owners. The question was then asked, "who has the basic responsibility for preparing the financial statements to be audited?" The percentages of respondents attributing responsibility to management had decreased compared to the earlier 1983 survey, and those attributing responsibility to the auditors had increased. Overall, however, management was usually assigned this responsibility. As in earlier studies, the groups most likely to attribute responsibility to the auditors were the "general publics." The indicated responses of the general public groups were as follows:

	Top Management (%)	*Board of Directors* (%)	*Auditors* (%)	*Not Sure* (%)
"Knowledgeable" public	27	15	45	7
Individual stockholders	29	16	42	6

This compares to 56 percent attributing responsibility to top management, 29 percent to the board of directors, 15 percent to the auditors, and 2 percent unsure as a response pattern for stockholders surveyed in the 1983 Peat Marwick study. A similar trend was also seen in all comparable "special public" groups surveyed in 1983 and 1986. However, in 1986, the average response to this question was that responsibility rested clearly with management (68%) and not with the audit firm (18%). This deteriorating trend of attributed financial statement responsibility is unsettling and indicates that the level of user knowledge of auditing and the financial reporting process may have declined in the past few years.

The final observation of Louis Harris, Inc. fairly well sums up the results of this extensive survey:

> These results are at one and the same time both reassuring to the accounting profession and yet also illustrative of the enormous job that remains to be done in explaining and in educating the broad public about just what an independent auditing firm does and does not do and what its audit really can be taken to mean.
>
> . . . it is equally clear that relatively articulate segments of the general public do not have any clear notion of what that kind of rendering ["clean" opinion] really is.
>
> . . . it comes as a solitary result to find that . . . there is overwhelming support for the proposition that *the accounting and auditing profession needs to be better understood* (pp. 38-39, emphasis in original).

Lynn and Gaffney (1990). This tangential study examines the perceptions of auditors toward different municipal audit reports. Similar to research on private sector reports, this study presented 62 CPAs involved in municipal audits a set of eight audit reports (i.e., two unqualified, four qualified, one disclaimer, and one adverse) and asked them to rate sets of two reports as to similarity, as well as rate each report according to nine adjective scales measuring the messages communicated. The authors manipulated the reporting responsibility of the auditor (i.e., reporting on either the general purpose accounts or individual fund financial statements only; or both together), as well as report type and reason for unqualified report (e.g., omission of fixed asset records, use of nonactuarial reporting methods for pensions, and scope limitations).

The results of the similarity ratings indicate that auditors pereived differences in audit report type, but not level of responsibility assumed. Results of the adjective statement analysis indicates auditors did not differ as to reason for an unqualified report. However, they believed that: (1) auditors are more responsible for information accompanied by an unqualified opinion, (2) the auditor performs a more complete inspection if financial statements are accompanied by an unqualified opinion, (3) unqualified opinins provide higher levels of assurance that financial statements are in accordance with GAAP, (4) analysts need more information to make loan decisions if statements are not accompanied by an unqualified opinion, (5) loans are riskier to a city when the city does not receive an unqualified opinion, and (6) unqualified opinions provide higher levels of guarantee that the financial statements are not misleading. Additionally, auditors also placed more credence in the financial statements when the auditor takes responsibility for both general purpose and individual fund financial statements (rather than only the general purpose financial statements).

Mutchler (1984).   In a study not directly related to the auditor's report, this research probed 16 partners of Big Eight accounting firms about their perception of the auditor's role in the presence of going-concern uncertainties. Mutchler interviewed each of the 16 subjects in order to obtain a more robust understanding of the auditor's decision-making and information-gathering processes when a going-concern uncertainty arises. These interview responses were then utilized to formulate a 35-item questionnaire intended to assess auditors' perceptions of the severity of a going-concern uncertainty, and identify crucial circumstances that should be evaluated in these instances.

Of relevance to this study is Muthcler's observation, based on her interviews, that *SAS 34*, "The Auditor's Considerations when a Question Arises About an Entity's Continued Existence," is not interpreted consistently among auditors. This disagreement on the auditor's role, it was noted, "may contribute to the inability of the ASB to remove successfully the 'subject to' option" (p. 24). However, at the same time, she noted general auditor dissatisfaction that

> the example of an audit report given in paragraph 12 (*SAS 34*) gives the impression that this is the way the audit report *should* be written. Most respondents argued that going-concern problem situations were often unique and flexibility had to be built into the form of the audit report (p. 21, emphasis in the original).

These empirical observations are germane to the ASB's deliberations in 1987 regarding elimination of the "subject to" audit report, and the auditor's reporting responsibility in instances when a client's ability to continue as a going-concern is of question, and will be more fully addressed in subsequent chapters.

Nair and Rittenberg (1987).   This study extended the works of Libby (1979a) and Bailey, Bylinski, and Shields (1983) to CPAs and bankers of both large and small organizations. The study involved 40 bankers and 40 CPAs selected to represent a cross-section of large and small organizations operating in the Chicago and Milwaukee areas. Nine reports were used in this field study: (1) eight report types modeled after the existing authoritative literature consisting of five audit reports, two review reports, and a compilation report, (2) the ninth report utilized was the required three paragraphs of the audit report suggested by CAR.

This study concluded that, in the aggregate, CPAs and bankers had fairly consistent perceptions of auditor's reports. The study also noted that, as would be expected given earlier research results, "bankers place less responsibility for the correctness of the financial statements on management and more on the auditor than do the CPAs" (p. 25). This disparity was reduced, however, by the report recommended by CAR that explicitly states that management has primary responsibility for the financial statements. The research results also suggest that both large-firm and small-firm CPAs perceive auditor's reports similarly. These two groups of CPAs were most inconsistent in their perceptions of compilation and disclaimer reports.

When the responses of small-firm CPAs were compared to those of small-firm bankers (primary issuers and users of nonaudit reports), the apparent similarities of the groups disappear. The authors note that the difference "between the two groups relate largely to their differing assessments of compilations and reviews" (p. 21). Disclaimers were also noted to have caused considerable discrepancy between these two subgroups of CPAs and bankers. In general, bankers from smaller banks were noted to have the most disparate perceptions of auditor's reports. Differences in assessments across groups, however, were primarily due to nonaudit reports rather than to audit reports (excluding disclaimer reports), indicating that educational efforts should also be directed toward users of nonaudit reports (Strawser 1991).

Peat, Marwick, Mitchell and Company (1983). This large survey was conducted for Peat, Marwick, Mitchell and Company jointly by Research Strategies Corporation and Opinion Research Corporation. A total of 2,024 persons participated in this survey, 1,573 by mail and 451 by telephone.

	Number	*Response Rate (%)*
Mail Response		
Chief executive officers	731	30
Security analysts	145	29
Portfolio managers	124	26
Lawyers	162	33
Regulatory officials	100	26
Congressional administrative assistants	65	12
Accounting professors	246	62
Telephone Response		
News media staff	151	
Stockholders	300	

In general, the survey found an adequate understanding of the auditor's role and of the auditor's report. The survey did note, however, that those individuals that assessed themselves to have more knowledge of the auditing profession and its duties also rated the profession's performance more favorably. Ninety-eight and 96 percent of the corporate executives and accounting professors, respectively, assessed themselves to understand the profession "very well" or "fairly well." This contrasted with only 16 percent of the stockholders, 56 percent of the regulatory officials, and 58 percent of the congressional administrative assistants. The survey found that, overall, 84 percent of the respondents attributed the responsibility for financial statement preparation to management, 7 percent to the board of directors, and 6 percent to the auditors. Stockholders showed the most misunderstanding of financial statement preparation responsibility. Only 56 percent of this group attributed responsibility to management, 15 percent attributed responsibility to auditors, and 5 percent were not sure who had responsibility.

In asking what a "clean opinion" means, the following responses were obtained.

	Means "Reasonably Reliable" Financial Statements (%)	Means All Figures are Completely Accurate (%)
Total survey	73	19
Corporate executives	89	9
Accounting professors	86	0
Portfolio managers	80	14
Security analysts	77	16
Lawyers	61	36
Regulatory officials	53	36
Congressional assistants	52	37
Media representatives	52	36
Stockholders	45	34

These figures indicate that there are substantial numbers of audit report users who perceive that an unqualified audit report provides more assurance on the accuracy of the financial statements than is attainable.

When asked how responsible the auditor is for detecting fraud or dishonesty in the company, it was the opinion of roughly 70 percent of all groups that auditors had responsibility only with regard to material financial statement misstatements. Thirteen percent said auditors had complete responsibility for fraud detection, and roughly the same number believed that they had no responsibility for detecting fraud.

Stobie (1978). Stobie surveyed 91 investment analysts, 76 corporate managers, and 60 individual stockholders in South Africa. Consistent with prior research, this survey found that of these three groups, stockholders had the worst understanding of an audit and financial analysts had the best understanding. However, even within the financial analyst group there were approximately 15 percent with distorted perceptions of an audit.

This survey found that almost one-quarter of the corporate managers and one-third of the stockholders believed that an auditor examines *all* financial records during the course of an audit. Approximately one-third of all groups expected the unqualified audit report to provide assurance as to the effectiveness of the company's system of internal control. Many respondents perceive that an unqualified audit report provides assurance that management is efficient, that no frauds have occurred and that the company is financially sound. Similarly, the following positive responses were obtained to the statement, "An unqualified audit report guarantees the accuracy of the amounts:"

Investment analysts	16%
Corporate managers	33
Individual stockholders	27

Surprisingly, the corporate managers most often had this erroneous view of the audit function. The responses received in this survey often reflected considerable misunderstanding on the part of all three groups regarding the nature of an audit and the intended messages in the auditor's report.

Winters (1975). This article presents the results of a study not directly related to the auditor's report, but describes a questionnaire mailed to bank lending officers that attempts to assess perceptions of unaudited financial statements verses financial statements with auditor association—auditor review. Five-hundred and sixty-six usable responses were obtained, representing a 47 percent response rate. A majority of the bankers (95%) indicted that they do use unaudited financial statements in their loan review process. However, most indicated that they would prefer to use financial statements with some type of auditor association. When asked whether auditor association (i.e., review) would increase the reliability of and reliance on the financial statements they utilize, the following responses were received:

Increases reliance greatly	17%
Increases reliance somewhat	61
No effect	18
Decreases reliance somewhat	4
Decreases reliance greatly	0
	100%

This study also found that a majority of bank loan officers (86%) believe that the likelihood of conformity with GAAP is also increased as a result of auditor association with financial statements presented with loan applications.

Summary

These studies indicate that user understanding of audit reports may have increased slightly over the past decade. The general picture presented is that the more sophisticated user groups, such as bankers and security analysts, demonstrate a better understanding of the auditor's role than do stockholders and similar nonsophisticated user groups. However, agreement on the auditor's responsibilities is still relatively poor—even among auditors and "knowledgeable" users. A large majority of those intended to be direct beneficiaries of the audit process and the auditor's report—stockholders and investors—have demonstrated a considerable lack of understanding of the audit process and of the resulting auditor's report. A complicating factor in this multi-dimensional "understanding" problem is indicated in the results of Fess and Ziegler (1977) which document that the vast majority of *all* major groups *think* they understand the messages behind the auditor's report. Hence, any knowledge or communication problem that exists will be heightened by user overconfidence in their perceived "knowledge."

Almost all the studies in this section support the conclusion cited earlier by Louis Harris, Inc. (1986, 39, emphasis in original) that the "*auditing profession needs to be better understood.*"

EFFECT ON CAPITAL MARKETS

This section will present the literature examining the effect of various audit report forms on the securities markets. The primary investigation vehicle employed in these studies has been the market model.[1] The market model, as employed by these studies, in essence attempts to capture the aggregate impact of the audit report on the market price of the firm's common stock, adjusted for dividend distributions. Various audit report types have been examined and differing event periods have been utilized by these researchers in attempting to assess the impact of auditor's reports on the capital markets.

Alderman (1977, 1979). These articles report on a study that utilizes the market model to attempt to evaluate the effect of uncertainty-qualified audit reports on the capital market's assessment of firm risk. Monthly returns were utilized and the time period selected for analysis was 36 months before and after the month of qualification. Twenty firms included in *Accounting Trends and Techniques* were identified with "subject to" qualifications starting with the period from 1968 to 1971, along with 20 others receiving unqualified reports during the same period.

The results suggest that the uncertainty-qualified report has little or no impact on the market's assessment of both systematic and unsystematic risk as compared to the control group of firms receiving unqualified reports. A cross-sectional analysis, however, did indicate that firms receiving uncertainty qualifications consistently exhibited higher levels of unsystematic risk than those firms receiving unqualified reports. The author indicates that, based on the results of this study, elimination of the "subject to" report qualification may be warranted.

Ameen, Chan, and Guffey (1992). This study extends analysis of the information content of qualified audit opinions to over-the-counter (OTC) firms. The auditors contend that reports issued to smaller OTC firms carry substantially more information due to the relative lack alternative information sources compared to NYSE and ASE traded firms. Accordingly, they examine a sample of 51 first-time qualifications for OTC firms from 1977 to 1988. No distinction as to reason or type of qualification was made. Similar to earlier researchers, they employed a market model methodology to generate expected returns in order to assess the information content of the audit qualifications. Several estimation and event windows were analyzed around the qualifications announcement date.

The traditional test for a negative market reaction to the qualified audit report ("bad news" scenario) evidenced little, if any, information content. However when the qualified report was not restricted to signalling a "bad news" scenario, and the standardized squared abnormal returns evaluated, there was a significant reaction to the qualification announcement. These findings indicate that the qualified audit report may provide information to the OTC markets for both "bad news" and "good news" disclosures.

Ball, Walker, and Whittred (1979). An examination of the effect of a qualified audit report on the security prices of publicly traded Australian firms was undertaken for the period from 1961 to 1972. A final sample of 117 qualified reports issued to 101 companies were included in the analysis. Weekly share prices were used in a market model to assess the effects of audit report qualification. The audit report qualifications were classified into the following eight categories:

(1) Depreciation on buildings 46
(2) Valuation of shares in or amounts due from subsidiaries 10
(3) Valuation of other assets 12
(4) Provision for bad debts 2
(5) Provision for deferred taxes 5

(6) Accounting treatments (capitalization vs. expensing items)   12
(7) Miscellaneous   12
(8) Multiple qualifications   18
     ———
     117

Almost 82 percent of the report qualifications in the sample relate to years ending in 1971 and 1972. Most of the 117 qualifications would be considered "except for" qualifications in the United States because they relate mainly to noncompliance with prescribed accounting principles. The most common qualification was for failure to record depreciation expense on buildings, due to the newly instituted ruling in 1970 by the Institute of Chartered Accountants in Australia that effectively initiated the practice of depreciation.

Overall, the combined sample of qualified audit reports produced no significant effect on security prices of the 101 firms. However, the firms with qualifications for failure to institute proper depreciation recognition (Category 1) produced a significant ($p < .05$) *positive* abnormal return for the week of the audit report release. Similarly, a subgroup of Categories 7 and 8 ("other" qualifications) combined produced a significant ($p < .05$) positive abnormal return for the week immediately following the release of the annual report. All other estimated abnormal security price effects were found to be insignificantly different from zero. The authors conclude that "certain types of audit qualifications are associated with changes in shareholders' assessments of the value of securities" (p. 33), but offer no further rationale or explanation for the results obtained.

Banks and Kinney (1982). This study used the market model to analyze the impact of uncertainty disclosures on stock price performance. Three levels of uncertainty disclosure were used in this study:

1. No footnote disclosure, unqualified opinion;
2. Footnote disclosure, unqualified opinion;
3. Footnote disclosure, qualified opinion.

The analysis was performed on firms listed in *Accounting Trends and Techniques* that were exposed to a new loss contingency which was disclosed in the footnotes for the period from 1969 to 1975. This procedure produced 92 sample firms, 16 of which received qualified audit reports. Additionally, these firms were matched to control firms from the same industry and with the same sign of unexpected earnings for the year. Cumulative abnormal returns (CARs) were calculated for the contingency firms and for a portfolio of firms to which they could be matched. The differences in these two CARs were used to assess the impact of the uncertainty reporting on stock price performance.

The relevant results from this study to the present discussion are the differences in CARs for unqualified and qualified audit opinions to their control groups of -.037 and -.149, respectively. The qualified report results are significantly different from the control group at the .067 level. The differences between the unmatched means of the unqualified and qualified groups is significant at only the .141 level. The empirical results lead the authors to conclude that:

> The presence of loss contingencies which were required to be footnoted under GAAP led to performance which was worse than that of firms without such a requirement. The presence of contingencies which were required to be accompanied by a qualified opinion under GAAS led to performance which was worse than that of firms which require only footnote disclosure. Without this association, it would, of course, be very difficult to argue that qualified opinions should be continued (p. 253).

Hence, this study did note some association between a qualified audit report and firm stock performance.

Baskin (1972).   Although several researchers have addressed similiarities of companies making accounting changes, this early study attempts to discern if the former consistency qualification presented incremental information to the capital markets. Baskin identified 128 companies from *Accounting Trends and Techniques* that reported principle changes and received qualified audit reports during the period 1965 to 1968. A control group of firms consistently applying principles was identified. Market reactions were captured via the market model.

The results present no significant price reaction to the qualified reports compared to the control groups and suggest "that the consistency opinion does not apepar to have information content for most investors" (p. 50).

Chow and Rice (1982a).   This study used a sample of 90 qualified-opinion firms and 90 unqualified-opinion firms for the years 1973 to 1975 matched on the basis of sales, SIC code, and auditor. Asset realization qualifications were rendered to 26 firms, uncertainty qualifications were rendered to 54 firms, and 10 firms had an uncertainty qualification coupled with another type of qualification. These last 10 firms were assigned to the uncertainty group for analysis. The market model with an industry component was used to calculate twelve- and three-month firm-specific stock returns. The impact of earnings reports and other information releases were controlled for using four earnings prediction models.

The three-month model was determined to be more appropriate analytically because it was found to contain less "noise" than the twelve-month model. The results indicate that the unqualified opinion sample had significantly higher stock returns then the qualified opinion sample across all four earnings prediction models. Thus, these findings evidence that a qualified audit report does have a stock price impact. Although not tested for specifically, the authors note that the asset realization qualified firms demonstrated consistently larger negative stock price impacts than uncertainty-qualified firms. This result suggests that varying forms of audit report qualification do differ in their impact on stock prices.

Davis (1982). The author attempts to assess the security price impact of the "subject to" audit opinion qualification issued for the first time to corporations during the period from 1968 to 1975. A total of 147 firms were identified in this period for which suitable security price return data could be obtained. These firms were individually matched to a control firm based on industry membership, earnings forecast errors, and beta. Daily security returns and the market model were used to address differences in abnormal returns for the sample groups for two time periods—the period surrounding the earnings announcement date and the period surrounding the release of the annual report—and two event periods—10 days before and after the event and the period -224 to +10 days surrounding the event. Additionally, the group of firms was further partitioned as to the projected sign (positive and negative) of the firms' earnings forecast error.

The results suggest that there were no significant differences in abnormal returns around the earnings announcement date. This test was used to ensure that any differences in returns around the annual report release date were due to the existence of the "subject to" report qualification and not due to earnings information.

There were also no significant differences found for the period surrounding the report release date. The author then analyzes the "subject to" group by type of report qualification and finds no significant difference in the returns based on reason for report qualification. Based on these results, the author concludes that the auditor's uncertainty qualification "does not contain new information for the average investor" (p. 30).

Dodd, Dopuch, Holthausen, and Leftwich (1984). This market study examines the effect of announcements of "subject to" audit opinions and disclaimers of opinion on stock prices. A sample of 604 first-year audit qualifications were identified for companies whose securities were traded on the New York or American Stock Exchange for the period from 1969 to 1980. The *Disclosure Index* and the NAARS system were used to identify the sample firms. The market model was utilized to estimate the impact of these audit reports on daily security returns.

Of the 604 sample reports, only 26 were disclaimers of opinion and the remaining 578 were "subject to" qualifications. The "subject to" reports were further classified into four categories based on type of uncertainty: litigation, asset realization, future financing, and multiple uncertainties. A five-day event period (-2 to +2) was selected for the major portion of analysis. The results suggest that public announcements of "subject to" audit opinion qualifications do not have a statistically significant impact on stock prices in general. These results are also consistent across all subcategories of "subject to" reports. However, there is a significant negative impact on stock prices when disclaimers of opinion are publically reported. The authors stress that caution should be exercised when formulating conclusions relating to disclaimers of opinion due to the limited sample size.

Abnormal price effects were also analyzed for periods prior to the public announcement of the audit opinion qualifications or disclaimers. These results indicate that many of the sample firms experience negative abnormal performance (average of -8.9%) for the 125-day period prior to release of the audit report. This significant result, however, vanishes as the event period is shortened to any period less than 60 days prior to the report release date. The authors attribute this phenomenon to "the economic events that culminate in the qualification" (p. 22) and warn that the preannouncement performance "illustrates the dangers of using long event windows to capture the information effects of the qualification" (p. 23).

Dopuch, Holthausen, and Leftwich (1986). This study examines stock price reactions to media (*Wall Street Journal* and *Broad Tape*) disclosures of "subject to" report qualifications. A total of 114 observations of media disclosures were identified from 1970 to 1982. The market model was used to assess abnormal returns on these stocks. Using a three-day event period, the average abnormal return was -4.7 percent, which is statistically less than zero. These findings differ significantly from other studies which were unable to detect price effects associated with disclosure of qualified audit opinions.

The authors note that media disclosures of "subject to" qualifications prior to 10-K filings or financial statement release dates are rare, but when they occur, their negative stock price effects are significant. They also attempt to reconcile their results with those of other researchers without success and note that "strong" inferences cannot be drawn from their study because of the selection process that produces only a sample of media disclosures of "subject to" qualifications. However, at a minimum, the authors observe that "the results of this paper call into question the argument that qualified opinions have no effect on stock prices" (p. 94).

Elliott (1982). The author assesses the association between abnormal security price returns and "subject to" audit report qualifications. The National Automated Accounting Research System (NAARS) was used to identify companies that received "subject to" audit report qualifications during the years

1973 through 1978. The 145 usable "subject to" qualifications were divided into five categories: going-concern, asset-realization, litigation, utility rate case, and "favorable" potential changes in cash flows due to the uncertainty.

The majority of the tests implemented were made on abnormal returns using weekly security price return data in the market model. Sample firms were also matched to other firms receiving unqualified audit reports by industry and unexpected earnings changes.

Primary conclusions of the study are:

1. Significant negative abnormal returns are observed in the 45-week period before the "subject to" report is released.
2. Whether the "subject to" report itself has information content is unresolved in this study.
3. Issuance of a "subject to" opinion, however, does have implications for security prices.
4. "Subject to" opinions receive little attention in the financial press.
5. Communication channels for "subject to" opinions are not formalized or easily predictable.
6. When "subject to" opinions are issued, release of earnings data is significantly delayed.
7. Once a company receives a "subject to" opinion qualification, several successive years of qualification are likely.

In analyzing the five categories of "subject to" qualifications separately, it was concluded that going-concern and asset-realization categories exhibited -30 and -24 percent CARs, respectively. Other instances of "subject to" qualifications exhibited no statistically significant abnormal returns in the aggregate when compared to their control groups. Elliott also used varying event periods and sources for release information on report qualifications. A subset of 14 explicit dislosures in the *Wall Street Journal* of "subject to" report qualifications exhibited a negative average difference of 4.8 percent for days -1 and 0 combined. However, Elliott notes that this test was a joint test of the "auditor's decision to qualify, the *WSJ* editor's evaluation of the newsworthiness of the qualification, and other potentially informative disclosures in the article" (p. 636).

Fields and Wilkins (1991). This study examines the stock price reactions of 52 public companies that had their "subject to" qualified reports rescinded during 1978 to 1987. Share price reaction was measured around the announcement dates of the withdrawn qualifications. Care was taken to identify only announcements of the withdrawn qualification and not joint announcements with other firm-specific information. The market model was used to estimate abnormal returns around the announcement date.

The results indicate a significant positive abnormal stock price reaction (mean of 2.298%) to the announcement of the withdrawn qualification for this group, with 61.54 percent of the firms experiencing positive abnormal returns. The sample firms were then analyzed by reason for the "subject to" qualification. In the second analysis, firms receiving original qualifications due to asset realization and going-concern uncertainties had the largest positive abnormal returns (3.08% and 5.79%, respectively), Additionally, a subset of 28 firms that publically announced the withdrawals prior to any other potential information source (i.e., 10-K or annual report releases) were separately analyzed. The results of this subset are very similar to the overall set of 52 firms.

The authors conclude that the 52 withdrawn "subject to" opinions were valuable information signals to investors and that *SAS 58*, in its elimination of the "subject to" report, underestimates the value of the former qualification.

Firth (1978). Firth attempted to measure the information content of qualified audit reports in the United Kingdom for the period from 1974 to 1975 using the market model.

The major types of opinion qualifications in the United Kingdom are:

1. *True and fair view*—similar to an adverse opinion in the United States.
2. *Going concern*—similar to a "subject to" or disclaimer of opinion in the United States.
3. *Asset values*—similar to an "except for" qualification in the United States.
4. *Subsidiary audit*—reports qualified because either a subsidiary has not been audited, or it was audited by another firm.
5. *Statements of Standard Accounting Practice* (SSAP)—similar to a GAAP departure in the United States.
6. SSAP and concur—similar to a consistency modification in the United States.
7. *Continuing audit qualifications.*

The largest 1,500 traded firms in the United Kingdom were studied, and 247 qualified audit reports were identified for the years 1974 and 1975. Firth used a matched-pairs design and matched the qualified report companies by size and industry to those with an unqualified report. A 41-day event period was selected and was believed to "be more than sufficient to capture the information impact" (p. 645).

The analysis revealed that only the "true and fair view," going-concern, and asset-valuation qualifications seemed to produce significantly lower cumulative average residuals via the market model employed. The other report qualifications produced only small price movements. These results led Firth to conclude that "clearly, investors were using the audit qualification information to alter their opinions of these securities" (p. 648). It also demonstrates that different types of audit opinion qualification have varying effects on the securities markets.

Frishkoff and Rogowski (1978). This study examined the relationship between a disclaimer of opinion report and abnormal security returns for the years 1972 and 1973. Twenty-two firms received disclaimers, however, only 10 were included due to data collection restrictions. Relative weekly and monthly returns were calculated for varying time intervals spanning three months prior and subsequent to the announcement of the disclaimer report. In all, 16 time periods were analyzed. The comparison of company and industry price change indexes produced no significant differences in any of the periods analyzed. The authors conclude that either: (1) securities markets are able to impound information about disclaimers well in advance of the disclaimer report announcement date, or (2) the information content of a disclaimer is "irrelevant" (p. 57).

Frost (1991). This research updates and replicates the Banks and Kinney (1982) study that investigated 92 loss contingency reports and stock prices from 1969 to 1975. The sample used in this study combined these 92 firms with 72 additional firms that experienced loss contingency reports from 1976 to 1984.

In general, the results support the earlier conclusions that firms receiving the former loss contingency qualified reports experienced significantly lower cumulative abnormal returns than firms receiving unqualified reports. The research also found that auditors rank as most serious those loss contingencies receiving *Wall Street Journal* coverage, those occurring in a stagnant economy, and those in firms with relatively low earnings and stock returns. Lastly, auditors appeared more apt to issue qualified reports on smaller clients than on similarly larger clients.

Frost (1992). In this study, Frost analyzed the incremental information content of initial uncertainty qualified audit reports issued to 183 publicly traded firms for the years 1983 to 1987. She compared the firm's actual earnings with predicted earnings (using a random walk model) one and two years after the initial qualification. She also divided her sample firms based on the degree to which news of the qualification was released concurrent with news of annual earnings and/or nonearnings news.

Her results indicate that for companies which reported positive earnings in the initial years, an uncertainty qualified report signaled a reduction in actual future earnings and also elicited significant negative stock price responses. However, companies that reported negative earnings in the year of qualification exhibited increased earnings one year out, and had no significant stock price response to the report announcement. She attributes these findings to the hypothesis that the market expects auditors to issue qualifications to these latter companies, but not the former companies.

Keller and Davidson (1983). This research analyzed market reaction to the former "subject to" qualified audit reports by examining trading share volume. The researchers obtained 64 matched pairs of firms from 1972 through 1977.

The results indicate that trading volume was significantly greater for firms receiving initially qualified reports than for the control group. Additionally, significant differences in trading volume were found when previously rendered "subject to" qualifications were removed due to the resolution of the uncertainty. Accordingly, the authors conclude that "there is information content in the qualification itself" (p. 16).

Loudder, Khurana, Sawyers, Cordery, Johnson, Lowe, and Wunderle (1992). This study analyzes the information content of the pre-*SAS 58* "subject to" report qualifications. A sample of firms receiving 83 first-time subject to qualifications from 1983 to 1986 was analyzed.

The study also used the methodological refinements developed by Dopuch, et al. (1987) to incorporate a variable that identifies the market's assessment of whether a qualified audit report will be announced. The authors additionally incorporated an unexpected earnings variable and an audit report "lateness" variable to control for these two potential effects on security prices.

The study found that the returns around the qualification date for firms with "expected" qualifications was not different than zero, but that the returns for those in the "unexpected" group were significantly negative. Also, delaying disclosure of an expected qualification resulted in negative market reaction. These results indicate that the market does react when it receives unexpected "bad news" in the form of an unanticipated audit qualification or delay of an expected qualification. Contrary to earlier studies, these findings suggest that the subject to audit qualification does provide information content to the securities markets, especially if the qualification is unexpected or is expected but delayed.

Mittelstaedt, Regier, Chewning, and Pany (1992). This study examines whether the pre-*SAS 58* consistency qualification provided information to the equity markets. A sample of 293 firms that early adopted *SFAS 87 (Employers' Accounting for Pensions)* was selected. One hundred and fifty of these firms did not receive a consistency qualification, while 143 did. The market model was used to estimate abnormal returns and three accumulation periods from 1 to 10, -1, to 1, and day 0 (representing 12-, 3- and 1-day windows) around the release of the audit report. Additionally, numerous multiple regressions were run that included 31 financial statement and pension variables in order to control for the concurrent release of the financial information that could effect security prices..

Results of the times series tests for all three event windows do not evidence any information content of the consistency qualification. Firms receiving consistency qualifications did not differ in average cumulative abnormal returns (CARs) or normalized average CARs from the control group. The multiple regression analysis, which employed the most explanatory of the 31 independent variables, did not provide any evidence that the consistency qualification provided any information to the market. An additional regression excluded firms whose qualification/nonqualification was easily predicted based on prior information releases (i.e., those with income effects of less than 2.5% or greater than 7.5% due to the accounting change), and again no information content of the qualification was evident.

These results are consistent with those of Baskin (1972) and indicate no significant additional information is provided by the consistency qualified report to the equity markets.

Summary

The effect of audit reports on security prices is still not resolved by the extant literature. The literature reviewed in this section has often arrived at conflicting results primarily due to the use of different announcement dates of audit reports, different event periods used to attempt to capture abnormal performance associated with announcements, and the numerous confounding effects of other information released during the period or along with the annual report for which abnormal performance is measured. Inconsistent results, then, may be partially attributed to differences in methodologies. Many of the articles reviewed (e.g., Elliott 1982; Dodd et al. 1984) provide excellent discussions of these potential differences and some expected effects across studies. Also, Bailey (1982) provides a critical analysis of utilizing security prices to attempt to capture the "information content" of auditor's reports and concludes that security price research methodologies may not be at all appropriate in this endeavor. However, regardless of any conclusions we may make from the various results, none of these studies necessarily implies that audit reports and their qualifications are unimportant, or that auditors' opinions should be eliminated. More studies than not have concluded that the auditor's "subject to" report qualification contains questionable information content for those publicly traded firms analyzed. However, more recent research (i.e., Fields and Wilkins 1991; Frost 1991; Loudder et al., 1992) has found a more definitive association; but no clear consensus has emerged. Additionally, the methodology employed by these studies cannot address the question of whether an audit report qualification has an impact on smaller, nonpublicly traded companies. These shortcomings of methodology are addressed by the literature examined in the next section.

EFFECT ON BEHAVIOR

This section will review the literature attempting to determine if, and to what extent, varying types of audit reports affect decision making and alter behavior. Many research methodologies have been employed and various types of audit reports have been subjected to empirical analysis. The vast majority of studies have utilized an experimental approach in which the only item of information changed across subjects has been the type of audit report presented. This methodology has attempted to isolate individual behavioral effects, as well as control for many of the confounding effects noted in the methodological approach adopted by researchers in the last section.

Abdel-khalik, Graul, and Newton (1985). This experiment examined risk assessments by 64 commercial bank loan officers of seven large banks in Canada. These subjects were selected because the "subject to" report qualification was eliminated in 1980 for Canadian auditors. The study is an extension of Libby (1979b), and used a manipulation of three audit report disclosure types: (1) unqualified opinion, (2) "subject to" opinion, and (3) a two-sided opinion (unqualified report for Canadian stockholders and immediately below it a "subject to" opinion for U.S. readers); and two loss contingency types: (1) tax assessment, and (2) litigation. These manipulations were varied across three hypothetical, similar companies, with loss contingencies always disclosed in the footnotes of the financial statements.

The results indicated that the type of loss contingency did not affect the bankers' assessments of risk, as reflected in the loan premium they would have charged the company. The experimental results also indicated the following:

1. The disclosure of the contingency and not the audit report qualification was the important factor in assessing risk.
2. When the contingencies were settled, bankers significantly reduced the level of the interest rate premium so that is was comparable to companies that were not involved in loss contingency situations.
3. Bankers reported that the audit report was not very important to their evaluation of the client's uncertainty.

These results are consistent with those of Libby (1979b) and indicate that there is no incremental information content in a "subject to" opinion once management has made the proper disclosure in the footnotes to the financial statements.

Ashton, Willingham, and Elliott (1987). This study reports on some of the determinants of "audit delay," that is, the length of time between the company's fiscal year-end and the date of the audit report. A sample of 488, Peat, Marwick,

Mitchell and Co. audits for 1982 was selected and data obtained from the respective partner in charge of the audit. Data was obtained on various client specific variables such as industry classificattion, whether the client was publicly traded, the quality of the companies' system of internal control, complexity of their operations, and type of audit report rendered (qualified or unqualified).

Of interest to this study is their finding that qualified audit reports (excluding consistency reports) were strongly associated with dealys in audit report releases. These findings support those of Whittred (1980) who found similar delays for qualified audit reports in Australia, and indicate potential differences in auditor behavior / action due to rendering different audit opinions.

Chow and Rice (1982b). This study attempts to determine if a qualified audit opinion affects a firm's tendency to switch auditors. Data on audit opinions rendered and firms switching auditors were collected for the years 1973 and 1974. A total of 1,132 qualified reports were identified along with 8,328 unqualified audit reports for the period. Firm switches for the period totaled 418 (141 with qualified and 277 with unqualified reports, respectively). A chi-sqaure test for independence clearly supports the hypothesis that changing auditors is *not* independent of receiving a qualified audit report. To further analyze switching tendency, a logistic regression was run which included as independent variables the following potential reasons for auditor switching:

1. Receiving a qualified report.
2. Change in company management.
3. Merger activity.
4. New financing arrangements.
5. Any other explicit reason given for switching.

The dependent variable was whether or not auditors were switched. All variables were scored dichotomously as a 1 or a 0.

The results of the logistic regression indicate that only the auditor report qualification variable is statistically significant in predicting audit firm switches. The authors also assess the tendencies of the Big Eight and all other firms combined to issue qualified audit opinions, and note that switching companies do not tend to switch to auditors that render fewer qualified reports than their former auditor. The results also indicate that companies switching auditors after a qualified opinion, compared to companies receiving qualified reports that do not switch, are not more likely to receive an unqualified report in the following year. Hence, the results are partially contradictory and indicate the need for future analysis of the effects of qualified audit reports on firms' auditor-switching behavior and on the auditor-switching phenomenon itself.

Estes (1982). This research used a post test-only-control-group experimental design to examine the effects of unqualified, "except for," "subject to," adverse, and disclaimer of opinion audit report forms on investor behavior. Three groups of investors were selected to take part in the study: professional investors, shareholders, and general business persons. General business persons were obtained from graduate-level evening business courses. These groups were selected to reflect the wide range of sophistication among financial statement users. A hypothetical company was developed based on average actual data from manufacturing firms. A packet of financial statements and other materials was given to all subjects, the only variation being the type of audit report that accompanied the information. One of the following report types was randomly selected and given to the subjects:

1. No auditor's opinion.
2. Standard unqualified report.
3. Unqualified report with an explanatory middle paragraph.
4. "Except for" qualified opinion.
5. "Subject to" qualified opinion.
6. Adverse opinion.
7. Disclaimer of opinion.

All the explanatory middle paragraphs (Reports 3 through 7) were identically worded and dealt with the company's lack of provision in the financial statements for a pending patent-infringement lawsuit. The opinion paragraphs were appropriately modified, if necessary, to properly conform to prescribed report wording. All footnote disclosures were identical across report forms. Subjects were then asked to:

1. Estimate the company's net income for next year.
2. Estimate a fair price per share for the company's common stock.
3. Indicate whether the company was "successful."
4. Indicate whether the company's management was "well qualified."
5. Decide how much of a $100,000 fund should be invested in the company.
6. Give a self-assessment of confidence in the investment decision.
7. Indicate amount of agreement with the statement, "It appears that the risk of fraud in J company is low."

Unfortunately, this study suffers from a relatively low response rate:

Group	# mailed	# received	Response Rate (%)
Professional investors			
Institutional investors	1,500	224	15
Security analysts	1,500	179	12
Shareholders	3,500	405	12
General business persons	551	551	100
(evening graduate students)			

Thirty-five null hypotheses were formulated and can be summarized as follows:

H_{0-1}:   The addition of a standard audit report will have no significant effect on (*one of the seven dependent variables*).

H_{0-2}:   Replacement of a standard audit report with (*one of four nonunqualified audit reports*) will have no significant effect on (*one of the seven dependent variables*).

H_{0-1} produces seven hypotheses, while H_{0-2} produces another 28 (4 x 7). Using an alpha of .10, the null is not rejected in any case for the disclaimer of opinion or "subject to" report. The standard and "except for" reports produce only one rejection each, while the adverse opinion had four rejections of the null hypotheses (including company and management evaluations, investment decision and assessment of fraud).

These results lead the author to conclude, that in general, "the audit report has little effect on investor decisions and attitudes" (p. 87). He also espouses that the results obtained are due to the *standardized* wording of the auditor's report and calls for a major shift in the profession's approach to the auditor's report: "All standardized wording should be dropped; the auditor's report should be composed anew, 'from scratch,' for each audit" (p. 93).

Estes and Reimer (1977).   This study attempted to assess the impact of a qualified audit report on bankers' lending behavior. A mail survey instrument was sent to randomly selected bank loan officers and included a description of a hypothetical company, a set of three-year financial statements, including footnotes, and an auditor's report. The control group was given an unqualified report while the experimental group received an "except for" qualified opinion due to the company's use of the cost rather than the equity method of accounting for certain investments (i.e., an APB Opinion 18 exception). All other information remained identical between the groups, including the footnote disclosures discussing the GAAP depature for accounting for these investments. The bankers were asked to indicate the maximum amount that they would loan to the company at 1-1/2 percent over the prevailing prime rate.

A 22 percent response rate was achieved, with 120 usable responses received from the experimental group and 102 from the control group. The results indicate that the mean maximum loan of both groups was not statistically different, and both ranged from $0-150 million. The authors conclude that the surveyed bank loan officers "were not affected significantly by an "except for" opinion on "financial statements when the basis for the exception is otherwise fully disclosed in a footnote" (p. 254).

Estes and Reimer (1979). In this similar study, the authors attempt to analyze the effect of the auditor's opinions on financial analysts' decisions. The same methodology and test instrument utilized in 1977 was also implemented in this study. One thousand financial analysts were randomly selected. Half were sent packets with an unqualified audit report; the other half were sent identical packets with an "except for" qualified audit report. Subjects were asked to indicate the price at which the company stock would represent an attractive investment.

One hundred and six responses were received from the control group and 92 from the experimental group, representing 21 and 18 percent response rates, respectively. The results indicated that those subjects receiving the "except for" qualified opinion indicated significantly lower share prices as being an attractive investment in the hypothetical company. These results suggest differences in share prices due to the type ("except for" versus unqualified) of auditor report rendered, and lead the authors to conclude that the audit report is "a separate stimulus in the decision models of informed investment-oriented users of financial statements" (p. 161).

Firth (1979). This study examined U.K. bankers' perceptions of a standard audit opinion, two versions of uncertainty qualifications (going concern and asset valuation), and an opinion-qualified report because of nonconformity with acceptable accounting principles (use of base stock inventory accounting). A set of financial statements was derived from a hypothetical company and sent to 1,500 randomly selected U.K. bankers. Seven hundred bankers were sent the financial statements and all four audit report versions, while the remaining 800 were sent just one of the report versions. The bankers were asked to state how much they would lend to the hypothetical company at 2 percent above the going prime rate. Bankers receiving all four reports were asked to respond to this question for each of the different audit report states.

The results indicate that, in the aggregate, the subjects receiving and responding separately to all four audit reports responded similarly to the subjects receiving only one form of auditor opinion. The audit reports qualified for uncertainties both exhibited significant differences when compared to the unqualified report; and the report qualified for noncompliance with accepted accounting principles produced no significant difference compared to the unqualified report, but did result in a significant difference when compared to the two uncertainty qualifications. Hence, the more "serious" qualifications did elicit a different response from the bankers.

Gul (1990). This study examines the effects of unqualified versus "except for" qualified audit reports on Australian banker's share price estimates. Additionally, this is the first study analyzing the effects of cognitive style on users of audit reports. Thirty-four subjects were given identical financial information on a hypothetical company, except half received unqualified opinions and the other half received an "except for" qualified report due to the lack of a provision for depreciation. They were then asked to indicate their opinion as to the most appropriate price for the company's shares. Subjects also completed the Embedded Figures Test in order to determine their cognitive style (i.e., field dependent or field independent).

The results indicate that the subjects receiving qualified reports presented significantly lower share price estimates. However, when cognitive style is introduced, the significant audit report effect is better explained by the interactions of report type and cognitive style. Field independent subjects did not show significantly different price estimates across report types; however, field dependent subjects showed drastically reduced share price estimates when presented a qualified report. These findings give strong evidence that individual cognitive characteristics should be addressed in future research involving the effects of audit reporting on the behavior and perceptions of financial statement users.

Houghton (1983). This experiment was designed to assess the loan decisions and decision processes of 173 responding Australian lending bankers on a set of hypothetical financial statements and a loan application. The loan officers were asked to approve or decline the loan application in its entirety ($60,000) and were also asked to state their procedural steps in arriving at their decision, and to state the single most important reason and other reasons for making their decision. They were also asked to give certain biographical and work details. The financial statements and loan applications were identical across subjects, except that three different audit report scenarios were presented to the lending officers: (1) no audit report, (2) unqualified audit report, and (3) "subject to" audit report qualification (due to unsettled litigation).

The results of this experiment indicated that the existence of a qualified audit report does not necessarily have a significant impact on the decision to approve or deny a loan, however, it did have an impact on the banker's loan-decision process. This experiment also noted no significant relationship between the "any opinion/no opinion" report and loan approval. This result was attributed to the fact that "the provision of no audit report, as well as the provision of a clean opinion, might be seen as unexceptional by Western Australian bankers" (p. 19). These results on the audit report qualified "subject to" resolving existing litigation appear to be consistent with the earlier research results of Firth (1979) and Estes and Reimer (1977).

Johnson and Pany (1984). This study provides information on whether auditor association with financial forecasts affects the judgments of CPAs and bank loan officers. A random selection of bank loan officers and CPAs were mailed a packet of case materials, including historical data, on an average men's retail clothing store. The cases were identical except for the form of auditor association with the forecast information (none or reviewed) and the level of earnings forecast (conservative or optimistic), providing a total of four scenarios. Subjects were asked to indicate their confidence that the forecasted data were free from material clerical errors, whether they believed forecasted net income would deviate materially from actual income. Additionally, the loan officers were asked to make recommendations regarding a loan request by the company.

Thirty percent (119) of the bank loan officers and 26 percent (104) of the CPAs responded to the instrument. The results of MANOVA and ANOVA tests suggest that auditor association increased the confidence of both groups that the forecast data were free of clerical errors and that net income projections would be materially accurate. The bank loan officer subjects, however, had lower confidence in clerical accuracy, and a lower increase in confidence compared to CPAs on the accuracy of forecasted net income as auditor association increased. These results were said to evidence the existence of an "expectation gap" between CPAs and loan officers regarding confidence in auditor association with forecast financial information. Consequently, auditor association with forecast data had no impact on the loan officers' final loan decisions.

Johnson, Pany, and White (1983). This study examines the differences of perception and action among 98 bank loan officers across four forms of auditor association—none, compilation, review, and audit—using a nonrepeated measure design. All subjects were given the same set of loan application materials for a fictitious company demonstrating a marginal borrowing capacity, with the exception of auditor association. They were then asked to accept or reject the loan application, and if accepted, to specify an interest rate premium that would be assessed on the loan. They were then asked to indicate their confidence rating as to whether the presented statements were: (1) in conformity with GAAP, (2) free from the effects of fraud, and (3) free from the effects of clerical error.

The experimental results indicate that neither the decision to grant the loan, nor the decision on the interest rate premium was significantly affected by the form of auditor association. However, all three of the confidence variables were significantly affected by the form of auditor association, with an audit providing the most perceived assurance. The authors are quick to point out that a potential explanation for not finding a significant relationship between auditor association and loan decisions could be the relatively low response rate of 16.3 percent, and that overall generalizations may not be warranted due to the small sample size.

Libby (1979b). This experiment was designed to assess the effect of the "subject to" report qualification on bank lending officers' evaluation of perceived risk and use of additional information to estimate the outcome of the uncertainty. The study utilized 34 bank officers from four banks located in one city. The subjects were presented with information regarding a fictitious company that was currently involved in a pending litigation uncertainty. All subjects were given a case that varied in financial statements themselves, management's evaluation and the uncertainty disclosures and supplemental information. Three uncertainty disclosure scenarios were presented: (1) no uncertainty disclosure combined with an unqualified audit report, (2) a footnote disclosure of the uncertainty coupled with an unqualified audit report, and (3) a footnote disclosure and "subject to" report qualification highlighting the litigation uncertainty. Subjects were asked to respond as to: (1) whether or not they would approve the loan, (2) the interest rate premium they would require on the loan, (3) if no approval was made, what interest rate premium they believed other banks would charge on the loan.

An ANOVA analysis revealed that a disclosure of a major uncertainty, combined with supplemental nonaccounting information regarding the uncertainty, had a major impact on the bankers' risk assessments. However, this risk assessment was not affected by the addition of the auditor's "subject to" report qualification. Libby concludes that, of the most plausible explanations of this result, "the redundancy explanation appears the most likely alternative" (p. 52). The author concludes that the qualified report has no incremental information content once other sources (footnotes or supplemental information) have already identified the existing uncertainty.

Pany and Smith (1982). This study examines financial analysts' perceptions of the reliability of quarterly information given alternate degrees of auditor involvement. Fifty-seven financial analysts from five commercial banks in a large midwestern city participated in the study. A repeated measures design was employed and each subject replied six times to sets of information that varied as to the past accuracy and consistency of the presented company data. Four separate questionnaires were used for the four levels of auditor association tested: none, limited review at year-end, limited review at quarter-end, and audited quarterly.

The results suggest that the subjects generally did not perceive a different level of reliability on the first three levels of auditor association, however, a significant increase in reliability is obtained when the quarterly information is audited. Thus, the subjects did not generally differentiate limited auditor association from no auditor association. Auditor association was found to be a significant variable only for those firms which previously released inaccurate quarterly financial information.

Robertson (1988). A single case was used wherein a disguised investment company was depicted as having 47 percent of its net assets in securities having no quoted market value. In this type of situation, auditors could render any one of six different reports—disclaimer (unaudited), unqualified, qualified "subject to," qualified "except for," modified "except for," and disclaimer (due to uncertainty). A random sample of 1,000 financial analysts was sent a set of case materials with one of the six possible audit report types or a report by management. Subjects were asked to indicate responses ("Yes," "no," or "don't know") to these three questions: (1) whether the auditor's report added credibility to the financial statements, (2) whether they could rely on the financial statements for an investment decision, and (3) if they believed the auditor's report satisified their investment analysis needs insofar as the auditor's association with the financial statements.

An analysis of the 176 usuable responses indicated that on all three questions the subjects did not make any distinctions among the qualified "except for," modified "except for," and the unqualified opinions. A predicted adverse reaction to the "except for" qualification as compared to the "subject-to" qualification was not found. The "except for" reports ranked highest for all three research questions. Additionally, the analysts appeared to properly perceive the disclaimer reports and the reports by management as different than the other audit reports.

Stobie (1978). In his survey of Australian financial statement users, the following question was posed: "Does a qualified audit report have a significant effect on your willingness to invest in a particular company?" The following responses were obtained:

	Yes (%)	*No* (%)
Stockholders	85	15
Directors	82	18
Investment analysts	88	12

Those respondents answering "Yes" indicated that they did so because the qualified report:

	Shareholders (%)	Directors (%)	Investment Analysts (%)
Effects share prices	27	22	14
Reflects management's ability	45	50	45
Affects potential funding sources	22	25	23
Other effects	13	13	25

Whittred (1980). This paper examines the effect that qualified audit reports have on the timeliness of information released in Australian annual reports. The study compares the reporting behavior of 100 firms receiving a "subject to" qualification, 16 firms receiving an "unable to form an opinion" report (similar to a disclaimer of opinion report in the United States), and 9 firms receiving a "not true and fair" report (similar to an adverse opinion report in the United States) to 120 randomly selected firms receiving an unqualified report for the period from 1965 to 1974. The reporting behavior of the firms receiving "qualifications" is also analyzed for the years preceding the qualification.

The results indicate that the occurrence of a "qualification" does delay the release of the preliminary profit report (required by the Australian Associated Stock Exchanges) and the release of the final annual accounts. The results also indicate that the more serious the "qualification," the greater is the delay; with "subject to" and a combined cateogry for the "unable to form an opinion" and "not true and fair" reports evidencing an average additional total lag of 17 and 62 days, respectively, compared to the firms receiving unqualified reports. The author considered various explanations for this phenomenon and concludes that the most likely explanations are an increase in both the time to complete the extended year-end audit procedures and the additional time spent in auditor-client negotiations at the close of the audit.

Summary

The research examined in this section has produced diverse and sometimes contradictory results regarding the audit report's effect on behavior. A majority of the studies used bank lending officers and auditors as subjects, to the exclusion of many other audit report user groups. This was primarily due to the higher probability of bank lending officers' exposure to various audit report types and to their availability as experimental subjects. An additional commonality is the research result that once financial information has been included in the data set of the subjects, either by inclusion in the footnotes or as supplemental information (i.e., Libby 1979b), the form of audit report takes on much less significance. This general result lends some support to the ASB's elimination of the "subject to" audit report form in 1988.

STUDIES OF AUDITOR REPORTING DECISIONS

While several researchers have analyzed characteristics of firms that have received qualified audit reports (Altman 1982; Altman and McGough 1974; Bremser 1975; Cushing and Deakin 1974; Gosman 1973; Neumann 1969; and Warren 1977), the research reviewed in this section attempts to assess the auditors' final reporting decision. Included in this literature is a growing body of recent research that has attempted to model the auditors' reporting decision with various publicly available information. Although there are numerous related studies, this section will present studies that focus primarily on the auditors' rendering of a specific report type.

Bell and Tabor (1991). This is one of the latest studies that assess auditor reporting decision behavior and attempts to model the initial uncertainty qualification decision. Bell and Tabor analyzed 131 manufacturing and retail companies receiving an initial uncertainty qualified report (excluding specific litigation and tax uncertainty qualifications) and 1,217 companies receiving an unqualified report during the period 1971 to 1984. The authors used seven financial factors measured three different ways (i.e., ratio-level, rate of change, and industry-standardized) and three additional measures of size, growth, and return variability. Both univariate and multivariate logit models were employed.

The univariate models indicate that firms receiving first-time qualifications differ in terms of short-term liquidity, return on investment, financial leverage, capital intensiveness, and firm size; with more levered, less capital intense and smaller firms receiving higher rates of qualification. Although several multivariate models were run, the final model incorporated five of the seven financial factors—return on investment, inventory intensiveness, receivable intensiveness, short-term liquidity, and financial leverage. They found their model predicted probabilities of qualification that were significantly greater for the qualified than unqualified companies. Also, several relative costs of Type I and Type II errors were imposed on the model, with a 20:1 ratio resulting in the highest percentage reduction in misclassification costs of 73.0 percent and a .5:1 ratio resulting in a reduction of misclassification costs of 40.2 percent. Hence, the authors were able to demonstrate that the initial uncertainty qualified reporting decisions of auditors could be fairly accurately modeled using financial variables.

Chen and Church (1992). This study builds on earlier going-concern opinion-modeling research (i.e., Mutchler 1985; Bell and Tabor 1991) by incorporating default on debt and restructing of debt agreements with the financial statement variables into the decision model. The study examined 127 firms receiving first-time going-concern opinnions from 1982 to 1986 along with a matched set of 127 frims from the same period not receiving a similar opinion.

The results of the logit analyses indicate that the expected cost of misclassification using six different relative cost ratios was minimized in each case by using the decision model that included both financial variables and debt default status. The authors also found that a majority of the firms receiving a going-concern report that did *not* file for bankruptcy in the succeeding year were in default or were restructuring debt agreements at the time of the opinion. Yet, almost all the subsequently failed firms that did not receive a going-concern report were not in default nor in the process of renegotiating debt arrangements. Thus, these findings suggest that while the default status of a firm may be viewed by auditors as substantial evidence of going-concern difficulties, it should not be used as the sole determination of impending firm failure.

Chewing, Pany, and Wheeler (1989). In this related study the authors examine audit reports for 71 firms changing principles from 1980 to 1983 in order to ascertain how auditors interpret the materiality concept. Three changes were analyzed: (1) FIFO to LIFO, (2) adoption of *SFAS 43* on compensated absences, and (3) adoption of *SFAS 52* on foreign currency translation. Of relevance to the present study is their finding that auditors issued consistency reports for relatively small effects on operating income (i.e., 4% and above), and that when holding the income effects constant, more qualifications were given for discretionary changes (e.g., FIFO to LIFO) than required changes (e.g., adopting *SFAS 43* or *SFAS 52*). Additionally, there is some evidence that Big Eight firms had higher materiality thresholds and thus issued fewer qualified reports than non-Big Eight auditors.

Chewing, Pany, and Wheeler (1992). The study extends their earlier work and examines large accounting firms' propensity to modifying pre-*SAS 58* opinions for consistency. Five hundred and sixty-two firms making one of the three changes analyzed in their 1989 study for the period 1980 to 1983 were identified on the NAARS data base. Of these firms, 267 received unqualified opinions and 195 received consistency qualified opinion. The authors attempted to incorporate measures of audit firm structure and, audit quality, as well as relative size of the accounting change (as a percentage of income) in assessing the tendency of opinion qualification.

As expected, all firms had the same tendency to qualify opinions for accounting changes resulting in large income effects. However, the results indicate significant differences between Big Eight firms and non-Big Eight firms, as well as among Big Eight firms, for smaller accounting changes. The non-Big Eight firms had a greater tendency to qualify their reports than Big Eight firms for smaller income effect changes (0-4%). Also, Ernst and Whinney and Deloitte, Haskins, and Sells had lower tendencies to qualify their reports than the other Big Eight firms when the financial statements specifically stated that the change was immaterial. Additionally, audit firm structure was not able to explain audit opinins qualification. However, audit firm quality, in terms of relative litigation frequencies, did help in explaining firm's opinion-qualification propensities. Higher litigation experiences were associated with higher tendencies to qualify the audit reports for firms making 0-4 percent changes, and for firms indicating the change was immaterial in the footnotes.

Cushing (1974). This study analyzed, in part, the reporting of accounting changes required to be disclosed by APB No. 20 and *SAS 1*. Annual reports of 100 of the *Fortune 500* companies for a four-year fiscal period ending around July 1973 were examined for the presence of consistency qualifications.

Of importance to this study, Cushing found that 23 percent of the consistency reports issued the first year after APB No. 20 and *SAS 1* took effect did not indicate agreement or disagreement with the accounting change in the report as required. Additionally, he found that a substantial number of reports were improperly worded in the attempt to qualify their "except-for" opinion. In general, this study demonstrates a lack of adherence to the newly adopted professional reporting standards in the early 1970s.

Dopuch, Holthausen, and Leftwich (1987). The authors attempt to use financial and stock market variables to model the auditor's decision to issue qualified audit reports in situations involving contingencies and uncertainties. A sample of 275 publicly traded companies receiving first-time subject to qualifications and 441 traded companies receiving unqualified opinions for the period 1969 to 1980 were identified. For each company the probability of receiving a qualified opinion is estimated with a probit model including nine financial statement and stock market variables. Each firm's modeled opinion is then classified as either unqualified or qualified based on the models probability scores. The authors also analyzed the expected cost of misclassification for alternative costs of Type I and Type II errors.

The results indicate that the auditor's qualification decision can be accurately modeled with the financial and stock market variables and that the expected misclassification costs of the model outcomes are significantly lower than those of the naive benchmarks of issuing all unqualified reports. Additionally, they found that the predictive ability of the model varies across types of qualifications. Going-concern qualifications were most accurately predicted while litigation qualifications proved more difficult to predict.

Frishkoff (1970). This early study examines the auditors' utilization of the materiality concept in reporting on changes in accounting principle. From his sample of 2,218 annual reports in 1963, he ascertained whether the respective firm received a consistency qualified report, whether there was indication of an accounting change, and financial information to derive 17 other independent variables (i.e., the effect of any change on net income, total reported stockholders' equity, etc.)

He found that 217 companies had accounting changes for the year, yet only 136 received a qualified report. His stepwise discriminate analysis indicated that three variables—(1) the absolute effect of the change divided by net income, (2) the net worth of the company, and (3) whether the change was a reclassification—were the only variables significant in discriminating firms receiving/not receiving qualified reports at the .10 level. However, he goes on to argue that because the magnitude of the change could not properly classify firms by itself, there was no necessary relationship between the materiality of the change and the auditors' rendering of a qualified opinion.

Garsomke and Choi (1989). This study examined the relationship between the failure rates of companies receiving a going-concern qualification or going-concern disclaimer report and firms in the same industry and having the same propensity to fail receiving unqualified reports from 1982 to 1985. For the 183 firms examined receiving going-concern qualified or going-concern disclaimer reports, the failure rate was significantly greater (23.1% and 37.7%, respectively) than for firms getting an unqualified report (1.6%), even when firms were matched by industry and propensity to fail (i.e., z-scores). The authors conclude that their results could be interpreted as being consistent with both the "self-fulfilling prophecy" hypothesis and the claim that going-concern reports do provide incremental information to financial statement users.

Hopwood, McKeown, and Mutchler (1989). This study examines the association between audit report qualifications and eventual financial failure. The authors examine a sample of large bankrupt and nonbankrupt companies for the years 1974 to 1981, and a holdout sample for the period 1982 to 1985. Three types of qualified reports were identified: (1) going-concern, (2) other "subject to," and (3) consistency. The authors use a log-linear approach and investigate one univariate and two multivariate models.

Results of the univariate models indicate associations between all three types of qualification and bankruptcy for the year preceding bankruptcy. For the multivariate models, they found significant associations only for the going-concern and other subject-to qualifications. Additionally, when the audit reports were tested jointly with a set of bankruptcy prediction ratios, the consistency and going-concern qualifications were still associated with bankrupt firms. In testing the models in conjunction with varying costs of Type

I and Type II errors, they conclude that the model with just the audit opinion was the most cost effective in the last three years prior to bankruptcy, and that the prediction of no bankruptcies is as accurate as any of the models in the fourth and fifth years prior to bankruptcy. Their overall results led them to conclude that "the qualified opinion has the ability to serve as an early warning signal for entity failure" (p. 4).

Kida (1980).   In this study Kida examined partners of national CPA firms and their judgments involving going-concern companies. First, 40 manufacturing companies were identified as being "problem" firms or "nonproblem" firms based on criteria provided by the auditors as indicative of firms with going-concern problems. Next, a discriminate model consisting of financial statement ratios was developed which properly classified 36 of the 40 companies. Financial data from these companies was then presented to the auditors who, in turn, were asked to indicate whether the respective company was or was not a going-concern problem. The average number of correct classifications was 33.2 out of 40. The auditors were then asked to indicate what type of audit report they would render for the company. Results indicate that even if problems were felt to exist, a "clean" opinion was issued in 24.6 percent of the cases.

Kida also elicited responses to 20 questions regarding the auditor's belief about the effects of the qualified report on the company and the audit firm. In general, the results indicate that the auditors qualifying the least number of times had stronger beliefs that they would lose the client, that the client would sue and that deteriorated relations with the client would occur. The auditors qualifying most often had stronger beliefs that the clients' creditors would sue, that the accounting firm's reputation would be diminished and that the accountant's responsibility would not be fulfilled if the opinion were not qualified.

Taken together, these results indicate that the auditors were fairly accurate in identifying the problem firms, but that this identification alone would not necessarily result in a decision to qualify the audit report. The analysis shows that auditors look for mitigating evidence and weigh factors related to qualifying or not qualifying before rendering a final audit opinion.

May and Schneider (1988).   This study, in essence, updates the earlier work of Cushing (1974) on the practice and reporting of accounting changes. These authors examined 156 companies available on the LEXIS/NAARS data base receiving a consistency qualified audit report from 1980 to 1985.

Auditor reporting on consistency was found to have improved since the Cushing (1974) study. Overall, they found that in only approximately 5 percent of the time did the auditor's report neglect to state approval of or exception to the change, as prescribed by professional standards. This study indicates that auditors were more closely adhering to promulgated guidelines than found in the earler study on auditors' reporting of consistency.

McKeown, Mutchler, and Hopwood (1991). This research examines auditor reporting decisions for companies that subsequently go bankrupt. The research attempts to identify factors associated with the auditor's decision to issue a going-concern report and develops a decision model that incorporates financial stress, auditor factors and client factors as well as a "hidden fraud" variable (a fraud publicly reported after the audit report date). One-hundred and thirty-four bankrupt NYSE and ASE companies from 1974 to 1985 were identified. Of these, only 54 received a qualified audit opinion. Additionally, a sample of 160 nonbankrupt companies from the same period were selected. The samples were divided into financially stressed and nonstressed groups based on the six financial statement stress indicators presented by Hopwood et al. (1989). Also company size (in terms of sales) and timing of the audit report were also incorporated into the models.

The findings suggest that a hidden fraud variable has explanatory power in the nonstressed group but not the stressed group. It was also found that bankrupt companies that did not receive qualifications were more likely to have ambiguous bankruptcy stress probabilities, were more likely to be larger, and were more likely to have short time periods between the financial statements and audit report dates than those receiving a qualified report.

Menon and Schwartz (1987). Eighty-nine companies that filed for bankruptcy from 1974 to 1980 were utilized in developing a logistic regression model to predict whether a going-concern qualification would be issued to the company. Two validation samples were constructed: (1) 39 companies filing for bankruptcy between 1981 and 1983, and (2) 46 nonfinancial firms with accumulated deficits in retained earnings and net losses for 1981 that did not file for bankruptcy through 1985. Five financial statement ratios and two other financial statement items were used in the development of the model.

The model development phase found that the variables "change in current ratio" and "recurring operating losses" were significant ($p > .05$) by themselves, and that the full model had an index of correlation between predictions and actual results of .76. The two validation samples were found to be fairly accurately depicted by the respective predicted probabilities produced by the model, with the second sample somewhat less accurately predicted. These overall results indicate a fairly strong correspondence of financial statement data and eventual audit report qualification.

Morris and Nichols (1988). This study examined auditors' materiality judgments concerning the implementation of *SFAS 34* on interest capitalization leading to consistency qualified audit reports. As in Mutchler

(1985), this study attempts to discern whether the ensuing qualified audit report can be predicted by publicly available financial information and knowledge of audit firm structure. Their sample consisted of 334 publicly traded companies audited by a Big Eight auditor and referring to *SFAS 34* in their annual report. Audit reports were qualified for the new interest capitalization for 127 companies, while the remaining 207 companies received no such qualification.

Using logit regression the authors found that they could accurately predict the qualified audit report companies between 75 to 100 percent of the time with the publicly available information. They also found that judgment consensus, as measured by dispersion from the logit model, for these consistency qualifications varied between Big Eight firms. The more structured firms exhibited high consensus and the less structured firms exhibited the least consensus.

However, the results of this study have been subsequently criticized by Stone and Ingram (1988) as being statistical artifacts of small sammple sizes per firm (sizes ranged from 12 to 48), coupled with a relatively large number of independent variables.

Mutchler (1985). This landmark prediction study examined auditors' going-concern opinion reporting. Mutchler identified 119 manufacturing companies in the Disclosure II Database that received a going-concern qualification in 1981 and matched them with 119 manufacturing companies that had similar financial problems but did not receive a going-concern qualification. Publicly available signals of financial distress discussed in Mutchler (1984) were used to identify the firms, and included items such as negative net worth, negative cash flow, negative income from operations, and so forth. Her discriminate model variables included: (1) a good news/bad news variable derived from items found in management's discussion, (2) financial statement ratios, (3) an improvement variable (the change in net income divided by ending total assets), and (4) whether the firm received a qualified report the year before.

The results of various discriminate analyses using combinations of the independent variables showed that between 80.2 percent to 89.9 percent of the qualified/nonqualified companies could be properly classified, with the model using ratios and the prior audit report variable performing best. Overall, the models accurately distinguished between the qualified/nonqualified firms. This result leads the author to conclude that for most firms the auditor's report does not provide additional information beyond what is publicly available, referring to the report as redundant.

Mutchler (1986). In this study, Mutchler used the 119 manufacturing companies identified in her 1985 study as receiving a going-concern opinion, along with the characteristics indicative of a going-concern problem company from her 1984 study. She then added to the sample another 119 companies that exhibited going-concern problems but did not receive a going-concern report and 238 nonproblem companies that received unqualified reports. She then analyzed the type and frequency of problem characteristics, the existence of "good news" or "bad news" in the 8-K or annual report, the level of financial distress of the company, the company size, and type of auditor (Big Eight vs. non-Big Eight).

She found that companies exhibiting eight or more of the problem characteristics typically received a going-concern report, while those meeting five or less characteristics typically did not receive a going-concern report. Companies meeting six or seven problem characteristics appeared to present auditors with situations calling for more judgment before the audit report was issued. Discriminate analysis indicated that companies meeting five or fewer problem characteristics, who did not receive a going-concern report, exhibited lower financial stress scores than those receiving a going-concern report. Companies meeting six or seven, and eight or more characteristics that did not receive a going-concern report exhibited significantly more "good news" than "bad news" items. These findings suggest that for companies meeting numerous problem characteristices, auditors assessed contrary and mitigating factors, as described in *SAS 34*, before rendering an opinion. Additionally, evidence suggests that auditors were more likely to issue going-concern reports for larger companies, and that, overall, non-Big Eight firms were more likely than Big Eight firms to issue a going-concern opinion.

Mutchler and Williams (1990). This study examined the relationship between audit technology, client risk profiles, and the auditor's decision to issue the former going-concern qualified opinion. Big Eight audit firms were analyzed according to their degree of audit structure as espoused in Kinney (1986). A sample of 1,870 manufacturing firms with Big Eight auditors was identified for 1985 to 1986 and divided into three groups: (1) nonfinancially distressed, (2) financially distressed without going-concern opinions, and (3) financially distressed with going-concern opinions. The authors tested for, among other things, the correlation between going-concern opinions and audit firm structure, and used logit to assess going-concern opinion decision differences across the Big Eight firms.

Results indicate that unstructured audit firms issued a significantly lower proportion of going-concern reports than more structured firms. However, once differences in the respective firm's client risk profiles were accounted for, no significant differences were found to exist for the tendency to issue a going-concern report across audit technologies.

This leads the authors to conclude that any apparent differences across Big Eight firms in their tendency to issue going-concern reports is driven more by the audit firm's client risk profile than by the adoption of audit technology.

Neumann (1968). This early study examines auditors' materiality thresholds and the reporting of potential accounting changes for 300 companies. The two potential changes examined were: (1) the newly allowed use of accelerated depreciation as a tax deduction in 1954, and (2) the accounting for the investment tax credit in 1964.

In essence, Neumann found that these two changes were inadequately reported in financial statements and auditors' reports according to prevailing professional requirements. His findings lead to his conclusion that more guidelines are needed on dimensions of materiality in order to achieve consensus of when consistency qualified audit reports are needed, and thus make them more useful to financial statement users.

Noglar and Schwartz (1989). This research examined auditors' reporting diversity on companies that undergo a voluntlary liquidation. The researchers identified 40 companies from the Compustat Industrial Research File that undertook a voluntary liquidation during 1986 and examined firm specific data like their basis for accounting, footnote disclosures and the resultant audit report.

The analysis found that 31 of the liquidating firms continued to use historical cost as a basis for accounting and that 19 of these 31 firms received an unqualified audit report. Of these 19, only 12 provided a supplemental middle paragraph indicating that the company was in the process of liquidating.

Wilkerson (1987). This study analyzed firms receiving the former uncertainty qualified report by comparing them with similar firms not receiving the qualified report. Wilkerson attempted to identify firms in very similar circumstances that did and did not receive qualified reports. In order to accomplish this, his sample consisted of 49 firms involved in nine different antitrust (price-fixing) investigations from 1972 to 1981. Unlike earlier studies, his sample selection procedures held the type of uncertainty constant across the firms. Sixteen firms received initial uncertainty qualified reports, while the remaining 33 did not receive a similar qualification, and all were audited by one of the Big Eight. In order to assess differences in the two types of firms, he used three independent variables in a logit model. The independent variables were: (1) the firms' financial statement exposure from litigation—defined as intraindustry sales divided by stockholders' equity, (2) cumulative abnormal returns for event windows around the announcement of the threat of litigation, and (3) a measure of downside return variables—defined as the return semivariance of the firm before announcement.

The results of the logit analyses found that firms with high intraindustry sales ratios received more qualifications, that downside return variability was greater for the qualified firms, and that negative prediction errors were found for both qualified and nonqualified firms, but that there was no significant difference between the two groups. These overall results, coupled with earlier market studies, indicate that the stock price reaction was to the litigation and not the qualified report, per se. Also, these results evidence differences in the characteristics of the firms that may cause auditors to qualify their reports more often.

Summary

The studies reviewed in this section focused primarily on assessing the auditor's reporting decision. Typically, studies have analyzed the qualified report decision with firms that received or could have received qualified reports. A majority of these studies have been able to accurately predict or model the auditor's final report decision, usually with financial statement ratios and/or other publicly available information. Although useful analysis, these studies do not necesarily purport that since the reporting decision can be modeled that auditor judgment, or the report is not informative. In fact, Kida (1980) warns against such a conclusion and argues that auditor's are faced with a multitude of simultaneous assessments before rendering a report. Additionally, Mutchler (1985) notes that even though she was able to predict between 80 to 90 percent of the qualified and nonqualified reports in her sample, the qualified auditor's report can still be a useful reinforcing signal to report readers.

1980 PROPOSED AUDITOR'S REPORT

This final section will review research on the audit report proposed in the ASB's 1980 exposure draft that was subsequently withdrawn in early 1981.

Bailey, Bylinski, and Shields (1983). This study examines the differences in subjects' perceptions of the proposed reworded audit reports included in the 1980 exposure draft and the existing report language. The study involved a relative difference experiment and an absolute difference experiment on two groups of subjects with different levels of audit report knowledge. The ASB's 1980 exposure draft indicated that an absolute difference due to the proposed wording was desired, however, no relative difference between the various audit reports was intended by the proposed wording changes of the audit reports.

The subjects for the relative difference experiment were 44 advanced accounting undergraduate students who had not yet taken an auditing class, and 27 individuals recently graduated from accounting programs who had recently taken the CPA examination. These two groups were identified as having low and high levels of report knowledge, respectively. In this experiment, the authors employed Libby's (1979a) fictitious company and 10 audit reports, to which were added 10 other audit reports modeled after the wording outlined in the 1980 proposal. Similar to Libby (1979a), subjects were given pairs of either of the sets of 10 reports and asked to rate their similiarity. Subjects were also asked to rate each of the 10 reports on 12 attribute phrases. This experiment produced multi-dimensional scaling results similar to Libby's (1979a) and indicated no relative difference in the perception of the reports based on report wording.

Subjects for the absolute difference experiment included 24 recent graduates who had taken the CPA exam and 38 advanced accounting students. These two groups were given combinations of the 20 audit reports described earlier, exposing them to both existing and proposed report wordings. However, no subject was exposed to alternate wordings for the same report. Subjects were asked to rate the reports on the same 12 attributes as in the earlier experiment. The results of this experiment indicate that there was an absolute shift in perceptions of the wordings of the reports. Subjects rated the proposed reports as attributing more responsibility to management. This experiment also noted a statistically significant knowledge effect, in that the more knowledgeable subjects rated management as influencing the auditor less in the choice of audit report type, rated management as being more responsible for the financial statements, and rated the auditor as using greater discretion when interpreting the results of an audit.

These experimental results support the hypothesis that the proposed wording in 1980 would have accomplished the ASB's expressed objectives of having no relative differences in perceptions between the new reports, but creating an absolute difference in report readers' perceptions as compared to the existing audit report language.

Dillard and Jensen (1983). These researchers performed a gross form of content analysis on 388 of the 453 responses to the 1980 exposure draft. An attempt was made to understand the views of the various groups responding in order to help explain the withdrawal of the proposal. The analysis was performed on three of the groups responding to the exposure draft: public accounting firms (256), industrial firms (101), and financial institutions (31).

This analysis noted that only 26.5 percent of public accounting firms expressed an unfavorable reaction to the overall proposal. This, however, compares to 60.3 percent and 51.6 percent unfavorable reaction by industrial firms and financial institutions, respectively. Each respondent's reaction to the exposure draft was also assessed in terms of the six major changes proposed in the exposure draft (as discussed in Chapter 2), and group profiles were developed accordingly. These six changes, along with the percentage of individuals responding to these proposed changes, were depicted using a three-dimensional analysis.

The proposed change receiving the most disagreement was the deletion of the word "fairly" from the report. This change also received the most comments.

Overall, public accounting firms agreed with all proposals except the "fairly" proposal. In general, industrial firms agreed with adding the word "independent" to the report title and, financial institutions didn't agree with any revisions, but were indifferent to the "independent" and "judgment" proposals. The dominant reason for the unfavorable reaction to the proposed changes was that the revision would weaken the opinion, that is, reduce the auditor's implied responsibility regarding the financial statements. The documented response pattern showed that these three groups did not respond identically to this proposed revision of the auditor's report.

One troubling aspect of this study is the aggregation of all auditors into one response group. The research conducted by Mitchell (1983) did not suffer from the same aggregation problem and noted that there were differences in the responses of small and large CPA firms.

Mitchell (1983). This study analyzed the response letters to the ASB's 1980 exposure draft and used a more detailed content analysis approach than Dillard and Jensen (1983), and also separated responses of large and small CPA firms. The patterns of responses submitted by the nonauditor response groups were generally consistent with that of Dillard and Jensen (1983); however, differences in response patterns between size of CPA firms were noted.

In general, financial statement issuers rejected most of the proposed modifications by a wide margin, while the smaller CPA firms and, to a lesser extent, individual CPAs strongly supported most of the proposals. On the issue of whether the existing report was in need of modification, the largest support for modification came from individual CPAs and smaller CPA firms, while a majority (56%) of the largest CPA firms indicated that the existing report should be maintained and the proposed report withdrawn. Overall, the author also discerned that the general feeling in the response letters toward the proposed report was that it was too negative in tone and that it should either be withdrawn or substantially modified to correct its shortcomings. The primary new insight from this study was that the smaller CPA firms and sole practitioners seemed to be "champions of the cause" to modify the auditor's report to a far greater extent than the larger CPA firms; indicating that there may be some significant differences in these two groups' perceptions of the effectiveness and desirability of a new auditor's report.

Pany and Johnson (1985). This study indirectly examined CPAs and bank loan officers' perceptions of the 1980 ASB proposed revised audit report. A set of financial statements for a hypothetical firm seeking a loan were compiled and mailed to 200 randomly selected loan officers and 100 randomly selected members of the AICPA. All information in the financial statements remained the same except for the form of audit report. Half of the bankers received data

Table 3.1. Average Group Responses

	Loan Officers		CPAs
	Proposed Report (n = 20)	Current Report (n = 27)	Current Report (n = 25)
Grant loan	55	38	—
Interest rate premium	2.36	2.29	—
Perception variables:*			
Free of clerical errors	6.60	7.89	8.12
Conforming with GAAP	7.40	8.85	8.40
Free of material fraud	5.60	7.93	6.44

Note: * Scale: 0 = No confidence; 10 = Extreme confidence

accompanied by an unqualified report using the existing wording; the other half received unqualified audit reports using the 1980 ASB exposure draft proposed wording. All CPAs received the standard unqualified report currently in use. Loan officers were asked to either accept or reject the loan applicant, and if the loan was accepted, to specify what interest rate premium would be charged. If the loan officer rejected the loan, they were asked to estimate at what interest rate premium other institutions might approve the same loan application. The bankers were also asked to indicate their level of confidence that the financial statements: (1) were free from material clerical errors, (2) followed generally accepted accounting principles, and (3) were free of material fraud. The CPAs were only asked to rate their confidence levels regarding the three items mentioned above. Response rates of 23.5 and 25.0 percent were obtained from the bankers and CPAs, respectively. The results are summarized in Table 3.1.

Results of a chi-square test indicate that the difference in loan-rating behavior across reports is not significant ($p < .05$). Similarly, the difference in interest rate premium is also not significant. The loan officers receiving the proposed report had significantly lower confidence ratings than did the officers receiving the current report. On the clerical error and conformity with GAAP variables, CPAs responded significantly different than did loan officers receiving the proposed report, but not significantly different than those receiving the current report. However, on the fraud variable, CPAs responded similarly to loan officers receiving the proposed report, but not to those receiving the existing report.

The authors indicate that their mixed results, in part, support the ASB's resolution to withdraw the proposed report. Loan action was not significantly affected by the proposed report and responses on two of the three confidence variables were more closely aligned with the auditors using the existing report. However, major limitations of the study are the low response rate and the small sample sizes of the groups surveyed. The authors note that their results contradict a large part of the extant research on the auditor's report that calls for its revision. Nevertheless, they conclude that "it would seem that the standard report may not be as problematical as had been believed by the Commission on Auditor's Responsibilities" (p. 258).

Summary

The research on the 1980 exposure draft of the proposed report has also culminated in mixed results. The two studies examining the potential impact of the 1980 proposed report reach opposite conclusions. A possible explanation for these results may have been the different methodologies employed. Bailey et al.'s (1983) laboratory experiment results may have been task driven; while Pany and Johnson's (1985) results may have been the result of a survey instrument that did not adequately examine the proposed effects, or did not properly present the case materials and was plagued by a small sample size. These results suggest that there will need to be a considerable amount of research undertaken on the new auditor's report to resolve the many questions associated with a change in audit report wording.

SUMMARY

This chapter has illustrated that a considerable amount of research has been performed on the auditor's report in recent years. The six sections of the chapter have primarily concluded that research results in these areas has been somewhat contradictory. The research has indicated that, overall, more report users identify the existence of the auditor's report than actually read it. Also, the more sophisticated users "understand" the audit report better than less sophisticated users; however, agreement on auditor responsibility is still relatively poor, even between auditors and "knowledgeable" groups. Capital market studies regarding the effects of audit reports, in the aggregate, have been largely inconclusive because of contradictory results. More capital market studies than not have concluded that the "subject to" report qualification contains little or no information (i.e., stock price impact), but more recent research has found significant results. Also, some evidence supports the notion that more "severe" audit report qualifications produce a greater impact on stock prices. Research on the effect of audit reports on behavior have also produced inconsistent results. However, in general, it appears that once information has been included in the footnotes or as supplemental financial information, the form of the audit report takes on much less significance. Several researchers have analyzed the auditor's reporting decision. A large portion of the studies indicate that it is possible to model the auditor's reporting decision with other publicly available information. Additionally, the last section has also indicated mixed results concerning the proposed report in the 1980 ED.

The need for further research in these areas is evident in order to reach a general consensus on these issues. Also, regardless of earlier findings, the modifications made to the standard unqualified report and the report on uncertainties in 1988 have served to intensify the need for further research on the auditor's report. These initial research projects on *SAS 58* are summarized in Chapter 8.

The next chapter will discuss in detail the research methodology adopted for the remainder of this study which examines reaction to the proposal of the 1987 ED to modify the standard audit report wording.

Note

1. The market model is a simple linear regression model, of the form:

$$\tilde{R}_{it} = \alpha_i + \tilde{\beta}_i \tilde{R}_{mt} + \tilde{\epsilon}_{it}$$

Where: $\tilde{R}_{it}$ = return on security i in period t
$\tilde{R}_{mt}$ = return on the market portfolio

The assumption is made that $E(\epsilon_{it}) = 0$ and $\tilde{\epsilon}_{it}$ and $\tilde{R}_{mt}$ are independent. The $\tilde{\beta}_i$, or *beta* term measures the individual security's *systematic* risk and indicates how the securities return behaves in relation to the overall market portfolio return. The ϵ_{it} or *error* term measures the securities *unsystematic* risk and aggregates all the factors that affect only the individual security's return. See Beaver (1981) or Foster (1986) for a more comprehensive discussion of the market model and its respective applications and limitations.

Chapter 4

Research Design and Methods

There have been many definitions of research design presented in the extant literature. Phillips (1971), for example, describes a research design as "a blueprint for collection, measurement and analysis of data. It aids the scientist in the allocation of his limited resources by posing crucial choices" (p. 93). Similarly, Emory (1985) has presented the following definitions of a research design:

> First the design is a plan that specifies the source and types of information relevant to the research question [and] second, it is a strategy or blueprint [that details] the approaches to be used for gathering and analyzing data.

This chapter will explain the research design and methods employed for the present study.

NATURE OF THE STUDY

The research performed in this study is both exploratory and descriptive and has been conducted using two interactive approaches. The research has first attempted to ascertain, summarize, and describe the written reactions of various audit report preparer and user groups to the ASB's 1987 ED on the auditor's report. These reactions are then examined, along with the ASB's process of modifying the 1987 ED, in an effort to determine whether the various groups' reactions affected the board's final decision and decision-making process.

Additionally, in order to discern a causal relationship between these responses and the board's final decision, ASB meetings on the development and resolution of this ED were attended and numerous discussions with ASB and AICPA task force members were conducted. This latter research strategy has enabled the researcher to more adquately describe the other significant influences on the ASB as they attempted to resolve this issue of auditor communication. Each of these interactive research phases will be more fully discussed in this chapter.

95

PHASE I: THE CONTENT ANALYSIS
RESEARCH APPROACH

A direct approach to ascertaining reaction to the proposed audit report changes is to examine the written responses submitted to the ASB on the exposure draft. The response letters represent an archival data source and are likely to be well thought out and reflect truthful reactions to the proposed changes because they are a direct attempt to influence the ASB—the body that will actually make the final decision as to what, if any, changes must be implemented by all public auditors. An appropriate unobtrusive research technique for analyzing these response letters is content analysis, which allows the researcher to utilize original unstructured communications data (Buckley et al. 1976).

Content analysis, like any other research technique, has as its purpose to gain knowledge and new insights, and to provide a representation of the "facts" (Krippendorff 1980). Content analysis is a research technique used to make replicable and valid inferences from archival data. Holsti (1969, 601) has defined content analysis broadly as, "any technique for making inferences by systematically and objectively identifying specified characteristics of messages."

Accordingly, whenever an individual has interpreted *any* communication, they have employed some form of content analysis. However, this is an extremely broad definition of content analysis, and one could argue that, inherent in a systematic and objective identification of message characteristics or content, is the imposition of some form of quantification or weighting, whether or not it is explicitly formalized. Berelson (1952, 18), among others, has focused on this quantitative aspect and has defined content analysis as, "a research technique for the objective, systematic and quantitative description of the manifest content of communication."

The proposed research has adopted this quantitative approach to describing the content of the messages in the responses to the exposure draft. In this study, each written response to the exposure draft has been treated as a single communication.

In order to accurately capture the message content of the response letters, the researcher must establish meaningful categories for the types of respondents, as well as categories that will identify all the relevant attributes of the communications. This categorization process, in essence, must attempt to derive a logical and meaningful structure from the originally unstructured communications. In order to accurately capture the underlying attributes of the response letters, a "detailed" content analysis has been employed that has established categories at a finer level than overall "agreement" or "disagreement" with the entire exposure draft. Broad categorizations, as primarily utilized by Brown (1981) and Dillard and Jensen (1983), may not capture the many distinctions and variations among the specific response letters, and may not capture the different reasons for respondent agreement or disagreement. This research has attempted to analyze the responses in more detail in an effort to ascertain and document differences in communications between respondents and respondent groups.

The data base, once derived, is solely dependent on those attributes or categories that have been utilized. These categories attempt to capture the messages conveyed in the written communications. It is not difficult to see, then, that the results of any content analysis cannot be separated from the categories established to represent the content of the communications. Accordingly, Berelson (1952, 147) notes:

> Content analysis stands or falls by its categories. Particular studies have been productive to the extent that the categories were clearly formulated and well adapted to the problem and to the content.

Category Identification

This study has considered attributes—categories—established prior to the start of analysis of the responses, as well as categories that have been identified as relevant during the course of the analysis itself. This adaptive approach has allowed the researcher to embark on the initial analysis of the content and still retain the ability to capture all the relevant attributes communicated in the letters. An allowance for the introduction of new or modified categories is central to a well-performed content analysis. It is virtually impossible to establish *a priori* categories for *all* the possible fundamental message attributes that could be communicated—even in a simple context. To be insensitive to the richness of the communications' context by not allowing new category identification would prove to be a severe constraint on the analysis and resulting research conclusions.

In order to become familiar with the messages communicated in the response letters, and to properly establish the communication attribute categories, all of the response letters were read twice prior to embarking on the actual coding of content attributes. All of the letters were read initially as they were received by the researcher from the ASB's Auditor Communications Task Force (simultaneously with all other ASB members). Then they were all read a second time and more detailed notes were taken as to what messages the letters contained. These readings established a familiarity with the messages, as well as giving the researcher insight into the myriad of ways the respondents could potentially articulate their respective viewpoints. In addition, the ED itself has also aided in the identification of probable response categories based on areas of documented concern and highlighted changes from the existing report.

An initial list of 140 response categories was derived and given to the Auditor Communications Task Force chairman and technical staff member, David Landsittel and Mimi Blanco-Best, respectively, for their review. Both of these individuals noted the need for some minor editorial modification or regrouping of some of the categories, but both indicated that, overall, the categories established by the researcher were more than adequate in number and that they believed the categories would capture the salient messages contained in the responses to the ED. In fact, a concern was raised that potentially too many categories were being employed in the analysis. David Landsittel noted that most of the respondents would only mention a few of the potential attributes in their response, and that a number of categories that were established were not mentioned at all by the letters. This concern will be shown to be accurate, however, the need to establish a comprehensive list of possible messages is an essential part of the content analysis methodology and has overshadowed the desire to minimize the number of response categories.

Content analysis can only be considered valid if it has reliably captured the content of the messages that it is intended to capture. The review of the categories by AICPA officials was a way for two independent reviewers, who are also intimately familiar with the messages communicated in the response letters, to validate the researcher's categories. These two reviewers reaffirmed that the categories established for analysis are content valid, that is, they represent the actual content of the response letters to the ED.

Additionally, an initial coding of approximately 40 response letters indicated that some additional categories should be modified and several added to more easily and fully capture the messages communicated. Also, a few other categories were added during the course of analysis. In order to accommodate this interactive approach, Krippendorff (1980) recommends that coding sheets be employed for each communication. These coding sheets have facilitated the addition of new categories throughout the analysis, along with providing a record of when a new category was adopted, or an old one modified, so that earlier analyzed responses could be reevaluated.

A final set of 182 response attribute categories have been utilized for this study and are presented in Table 4.1. This set of response attributes is felt to have adequately captured all of the relevant messages contained in the comment letters regarding the 1987 ED on the auditor's report. The set is divided into five sections: (1) general respondent data, (2) topical issues related to the wording of the auditor's report, (3) topical issues related to the examples of audit report modifications, (4) overall positions, and (5) general issues. These sections will be analyzed and further discussed in the data analysis of Chapter 6.

Table 4.1. Response Attribute Categories

I. General Data

1. Number given to response letter by the ASB.
2. Date of response letter.
3. Number of days between exposure draft issuance (February 14, 1987) and date of response letter.
4. Number of pages included in the response letter.
5. Is response handwritten or typed?
6. Type of respondent (per listing of respondent categories).
7. Respondent also responded to the exposure draft on ability of clients to continue in existence.
8. Respondent also responded to the exposure draft on errors and irregularities.
9. Respondent also responded to the exposure draft on illegal acts by clients.
10. Respondent also responded to the exposure draft on assessing control risk.
11. Respondent also responded to the exposure draft on analytical procedures.
12. Respondent also responded to the exposure draft on auditing accounting estimates.
13. Respondent also responded to the exposure draft on communications of control-structure related matters.
14. Respondent also responded to the exposure draft on communications with audit committees.
15. Respondent also responded to the exposure draft on examination of management's discussion and analysis.
16. Respondent also responded to the overall direction of all 10 exposure drafts in a general comment letter.

II. Topical Issues Related to the Length and Wording of the Standard Unqualified Report

17. Reference is made to the change in length of the proposed standard report.
18. Respondent indicates agreement with the addition of the word "independent" to the report title.
19. Respondent indicates disagreement with the addition of the word "independent" to the report title.
20. Respondent indicates agreement with the inclusion of the statement that the financial statements are representations of the company's management.
21. Respondent indicates disagreement with the inclusion of the statement that the financial statements are representations of the company's management.
22. Reference made to revise the report to state that financial statements are management's "responsibility," not management's "representations."
23. Reference is made that the report of management and not of the auditor should state management's responsibility.
24. Reference is made to delete mention of "X Company" by name in the second sentence of the introductory paragraph because it is redundant.
25. Respondent indicates agreement with the change from "examined" to "audited."
26. Respondent indicates disagreement with the change from "examined" to "audited."
27. Respondent indicates agreement with the ED report's retention of the reference to GAAS.
28. Respondent indicates disagreement with the ED report's retention of the reference to GAAS.
29. Respondent makes positive reference to a potential rewording that would state that standards are established by the AICPA.
30. Positive reference is made to reword the report to state "we performed our audit in accordance with GAAS standards established by the AICPA."

(continued)

Table 4.1. (Continued)

31. Respondent indicates that GAAS should be more explicitedly defined in the auditor's report and/or the new SAS.
32. Respondent indicates agreement with the statement "that an audit be designed to evaluate."
33. Respondent indicates disagreement with the statement "that an audit be designed to evaluate."
34. Reference is made to modify "an audit be designed to evaluate" to wording explicitly referring to planning and performance of an audit.
35. Respondent indicates agreement with the phrase "are materially misstated."
36. Respondent indicates disagreement with the phrase "are materially misstated."
37. Respondent disagress with the phrase "materially misstated" because of its lack of congruence with "fairly presented" in the opinion paragraph.
38. Respondent disagrees with the phrase "materially misstated" because of its negative tone, and indicates that more positive wording should be used.
39. Respondent indicates that the phrase "are materially misstated" should be modified to say "are *not* materially misstated" or "are free of material misstatement" in the scope paragraph.
40. Respondent indicates that the phrase "are materially misstated" should be modified to say "are fairly presented" in the scope paragraph.
41. Respondent indicates that reference to GAAP should also be made in the scope paragraph.
42. Respondent indicates that the term "materially" should be defined in the new auditor's report and SAS.
43. Respondent indicates agreement with the report inclusion of "intentionally or unintentionally."
44. Respondent indicates disagreement with the report inclusion of "intentionally or unintentionally."
45. Respondent does not concur with inclusion of "intentionally or unintentionally" because it is irrelevant given the preceding report wording.
46. Respondent does not concur with inclusion of "intentionally or unintentionally" because of its negative connotation toward management.
47. Respondent does not concur with inclusion of "intentionally or unintentionally" because it may give the implicit message that auditors actually must classify errors as "intentional" or "unintentional."
48. Respondent does not concur with inclusion of "intentionally or unintentionally" because it would implicitly increase the auditor's responsibility for detecting fraud.
49. Respondent does not concur with inclusion of "intentionally or unintentionally" because it could create confusion on the part of the reader as to the level of assurance provided by an audit.
50. Respondent indicates preference to retain modifiers of "materially misstated," however, another pair of modifiers like "errors and irregularities" should be used.
51. Respondent indicates agreement with the addition of "reasonable assurance."
52. Respondent indicates disagreement with the addition of "reasonable assurance."
53. Respondent indicates that reasonable assurance should be linked to the audit and not to the auditor's evaluation of the financial statements, per se.
54. Respondent indicates that reasonable assurance should be more directly linked to the financial statements and not to the auditor's evaluation, per se.
55. Respondent agrees with the exclusion of "but not absolute" as possible modifiers of reasonable assurance.
56. Respondent indicates a desire to modify reasonable assurance with a phrase like "but not absolute."

(continued)

Table 4.1. (Continued)

57. Respondent indicates general agreement with the sentence beginning, "Reasonable assurance...."

58. Respondent indicates disagreement with the sentence beginning, "Reasonable assurance..." and would prefer an editorial modification to enhance its readability.

59. Respondent indicates that the sentence beginning "Reasonable assurance..." should be deleted because one cannot "educate" readers about the nature of an audit in one sentence or brief report.

60. Respondent would like the sentence beginning, "Reasonable assurance..." to indicate that the auditing procedures listed are not all inclusive.

61. Respondent indicates agreement with the statement that auditors examine evidence "on a test basis."

62. Respondent indicates disagreement with the statement that auditors examine evidence "on a test basis."

63. Respondent indicates agreement with the term "supports."

64. Respondent indicates disagreement with the term "supports."

65. Respondent indicates agreement with the term "amounts."

66. Respondent indicates disagreement with the term "amounts."

67. Respondent indicates that this sentence should be modified to mention more than just financial statement "amounts" (i.e., disclosures).

68. Respondent indicates agreement with the phrase "assessing the appropriateness of the accounting principles used."

69. Respondent indicates disagreement with the phrase "assessing the appropriateness of the accounting principles used."

70. Respondent would prefer modifying the "appropriateness" reference, when referring to accounting principles selected, to "acceptability" or "reasonableness," so as to clearly indicate that the auditor does not select the principles used.

71. Respondent indicates agreement with the inclusion of "assessing the appropriateness of the...significant estimates made by management."

72. Respondent indicates disagreement with the inclusion of "assessing the appropriateness of the...significant estimates made by management."

73. Respondent would prefer modifying the "appropriateness" reference to "reasonableness" when referring to estimates made by management.

74. Respondent indicates agreement with the reference to assessing "the appropriateness of the overall financial statement presentation."

75. Respondent indicates disagreement with the reference to assessing "the appropriateness of the overall financial statement presentation."

76. Respondent indicates agreement to the inclusion of "assessing the appropriateness of disclosures."

77. Respondent indicates disagreement to the inclusion of "assessing the appropriateness of disclosures."

78. Respondent indicates a desire for the explicit reference to the footnotes to the financial statements by the new report.

79. Respondent indicates agreement with the last sentence of the scope paragraph.

80. Respondent indicates that the last sentence of the scope paragraph should be modified.

81. Respondent indicates that the last sentence of the scope paragraph should be deleted.

82. Respondent indicates a desire to expand the list of audit procedures mentioned in the scope paragraph in order to more fully discuss major auditing procedures or a GAAS audit.

(continued)

Table 4.1. (Continued)

83. Respondent agrees with the lack of mention of analytical procedures in the scope paragraph.
84. Respondent indicates that analytical procedures should be mentioned in the scope paragraph.
85. Respondent agrees with the lack of mention of client's internal control in the revised report.
86. Respondent indicates that the client's internal control should be mentioned in the revised report.
87. Respondent indicates that the client's internal control should be mentioned in a separate paragraph in the revised report.
88. Respondent mentions that the client's internal control should be mentioned in the auditor's report if the company's management mentions it in their report.
89. Respondent mentions that the client's internal control should be mentioned in the auditor's report only if the auditor disagrees with management's assessment of the control environment as depicted in management's report.
90. Respondent agrees with the lack of explicit reference to the use of auditor judgment by the report.
91. Respondent indicates that the report should specifically reference the use of auditor judgment.
92. Respondent indicates agreement with the inclusion of "in all material respects."
93. Respondent indicates disagreement with the inclusion of "in all material respects."
94. Respondent indicates agreement with the phrase "fairly presented."
95. Respondent indicates disagreement with the phrase "fairly presented."
96. Respondent indicates that they would modify the ED report wording to say "present fairly" instead of "fairly presented."
97. Respondent indicates that the term "fairly" is redundant and should be deleted from the report.
98. Respondent indicates that the term "fairly" is ambiguous and should be eliminated in order to clarify the report.
99. Respondent indicates that "fairly" should be eliminated because conformity with GAAP leads to a fair presentation.
100. Respondent indicates agreement with the deletion of the phrase "the financial position of X Company as of December 31, 19XX, and its results of operations and changes in financial position for the year then ended."
101. Respondent indicates disagreement with the deletion of the phrase "the financial position of X Company as of December 31, 19XX, and its results of operations and changes in financial position for the year then ended."
102. Respondent indicates agreement with the retention of "in conformity with GAAP."
103. Respondent indicates disagreement with the retention of "in conformity with GAAP."
104. Respondent indicates agreement with the deletion of "applied on a consistent basis."
105. Respondent indicates disagreement with the deletion of "applied on a consistent basis."
106. Respondent indicates that they would like to see some supporting arguments or rationale provided by the ASB in the ED for the deletion of the reference to consistency.
107. Respondent provided to the ASB their actual preferred modifications or rewordings for part of the standard auditor's report with their response.
108. Respondent provided to the ASB their actual preferred modifications or rewordings for all of the standard auditor's report with their response.

III. Topical Issues Related to the Examples of Report Modifications

109. Respondent includes mention of the ED wording of the report qualified because of a departure from GAAP.

(continued)

Table 4.1. (Continued)

110.	Respondent includes mention of the ED wording of the report qualified because of a scope limitation.
111.	Respondent includes mention of the ED wording of the report "modified" because of an uncertainty.
112.	Respondent indicates agreement with the elimination of the present "subject to" report qualification.
113.	Respondent indicates disagreement with the elimination of the "subject to" report qualification.
114.	Respondent concurs with the ED wording proposed for the auditor's report when material uncertainties exist.
115.	Respondent indicates disagreement with the ED wording proposed for the auditor's report when material uncertainties exist.
116.	Respondent indicates that the wording proposed in the ED does not properly highlight the entity's unresolved uncertainty to report readers.
117.	Respondent indicates that a separate paragraph should be used in the auditor's report to properly highlight the entity's unresolved uncertainty to report readers.
118.	Respondent believes that the "qualification for a material uncertainty" reporting category should be eliminated and such reports should be treated as an "emphasis of a matter" report.
119.	Respondent indicates the need for more guidance on when to use the new report modification for uncertainties.
120.	Respondent mentions the ED on continued existence in their response discussion of the uncertainty modification.
121.	Respondent includes mention of the ED wording of the adverse opinion report.
122.	Respondent indicates that the phrase "in all material respects" should be eliminated from the adverse opinion report wording.
123.	Respondent includes mention of the ED wording of the disclaimer of opinion.
124.	Respondent indicates a desire for more types of modified report examples to be illustrated in the Appendix.

IV. Overall Issues

125.	Respondent indicates that, overall, a new standard report is not needed.
126.	Respondent indicates that, overall, a new standard report is needed.
127.	No general indication as to the desirability of a new auditor's report could be discerned from the response letter.
128.	Respondent indicates that the report in the ED is acceptable without modification.
129.	Respondent indicates that, overall, the report in the ED is acceptable, but offers suggestions for its improvement.
130.	Respondent indicates that the report in the ED is not acceptable unless suggested modifications are made.
131.	Respondent indicates that a new report is *not* needed, however, modifications to the ED report are offered in an attempt to influence any future report adoption.
132.	Respondent indicates that a new report is not needed, because it is intended to be read by a knowledgeable user that does not need to be "educated."
133.	Respondent indicates that the time is right to modify the standard report to better communicate with report readers.
134.	Respondent indicates that the auditor's role does not need to be communicated any better through the auditor's report.

(continued)

Table 4.1. (Continued)

135. Respondent indicates that the purpose of the auditor's report is to present the results of an audit, and not to "educate" report readers about an audit.
136. Respondent indicates that the current report is a symbol.
137. Respondent indicates that any new report will remain a symbol.
138. Respondent indicates that the current report is an adequate communication to report readers.
139. Respondent indicates that the current report is not an adequate communication to report readers.
140. Respondent indicates that the proposed report will be a more adequate communication to report readers.
141. Respondent indicates that the proposed report will not be a more adequate communication to report readers.

V. General Issues

142. Respondent believes that, overall, the proposed report should be modified to take a more active voice.
143. Respondent believes that, overall, the proposed report should be modified to become more positively worded.
144. Respondent indicates that the requirement of a management report stating management's responsibility for the financial statement will aid in communicating responsibility in the financial reporting process.
145. Respondent indicates that the profession should also use other educational efforts in conjunction with the change in auditor's report to enhance the public's level of audit knowledge.
146. Respondent indicates the need for a supplemental report that describes the role of the auditor in regard to the financial statements.
147. Respondent makes reference to the current legal climate of auditors.
148. Respondent indicates that a new auditor's report will have an impact on the legal liability of the auditor, the direction of which can not be determined *a priori*.
149. Respondent indicates that the proposed report will increase the legal liability of the auditor.
150. Respondent indicates that the proposed report will decrease the legal liability of the auditor.
151. Respondent indicates that the proposed report will stabilize the legal liability of the auditor.
152. Respondent believes that the ED report revision will increase auditor responsibility.
153. Respondent believes that the ED report revision will decrease auditor responsibility.
154. Respondent believes that the ED report revision properly depicts the current level of auditor responsibility.
155. Respondent indicates that no matter what new report is adopted, it will be misunderstood by users as an attempt to reduce auditor responsibility.
156. Respondent believes that a new standard report *should* increase auditor responsibility.
157. Respondent believes that a new standard report *should not* increase auditor responsibility.
158. Respondent indicates that auditors should increase their responsibility for fraud detection.
159. Respondent indicates that auditors should not increase their responsibility of fraud detection.
160. Respondent indicates that the auditor should sign his name, and not that of the firm, to the audit report.
161. Respondent mentions the existence of a current "expectations gap" between auditors and users.
162. Respondent indicates that there presently is *no* "expectations gap" between auditors and users.

(continued)

Table 4.1. (Continued)

163.	Respondent mentions another current exposure draft in their response.
164.	Respondent includes comments regarding the rewording of the actual proposed SAS (i.e., footnote references or particular wordings), excluding the auditor's report, per se.
165.	Reference made to the House Subcommittee on Investigations and Oversight—Representatives Dingel and Wyden.
166.	Reference made to the "Wyden Bill."
167.	Reference made to the Treadway Commission.
168.	Reference made to the FASB.
169.	Reference made to the SEC.
170.	Reference made to the AICPA.
171.	Reference made to the ASB.
172.	Reference made to the FEI.
173.	Reference made to the report proposed by the CAP.
174.	Reference made to the report proposed by the Cohen Commission.
175.	Reference made to the report proposed in the 1980 ED.
176.	Reference made to any research regarding the present auditor's report or any earlier proposed modifications of the auditor's report or other research supporting their position.
177.	Respondent mentions existing SASs in their response letter.
178.	Respondent indicates that all SAS sections regarding auditor's reports should be reworded to indicate implementation of the standard report modifications, and that these sections should be issued to practitioners for reporting guidance.
179.	Respondent indicates a desire for more explicit guidance during the transition period (i.e., when comparative statements are issued and the auditor's report was modified in an earlier year).
180.	Respondent believes that the new SAS should also give reporting guidance when financial statements are based on a comprehensive basis of accounting other than GAAP.
181.	Respondent mentions the cost to auditors to implement a new auditor's report.
182.	Respondent mentions the cost to the profession of altering existing literature to incorporate all the proposed report revisions.

Category Definition

Category identification and definition are central to a well-constructed content analysis. These category definitions must fit the investigator's theory; they should be exhaustive, to ensure that every item relevant to the study has been identified; and they should be mutually exclusive, so that no attribute can be scored more than once within a category set (i.e., one response cannot be both "for" and "against" on the *same* attribute). Additionally, well-established and defined categories should also enhance the ease of identification and categorization of an attribute into one of the mutually exclusive categories. Category definitions for this study are relatively straightforward given the categories themselves, and are presented in Table 4.2.

Table 4.2. Category Definitions

Category	Definition
1	Number assigned to the response upon receipt by the ASB; appears in upper right-hand corner on the first page of the response.
2	Date indicated by ASB as the date response was received; if no ASB date, the date of the letter is used; if neither of these two exist, then the date of the mailing of response letters to board members was used.
3	Number of days which have elapsed between date of the ED (February 14, 1987) and date identified in Category 2.
4	Number of pages included in response letter; recorded in one-quarter page increments.
5	Was the response handwritten or typed?
6	Number of the response group of which the respondent is a member. (See Table 6.1 in Chapter 6 for a listing of respondent groups and their respective group number.)
7-15	Per the list of respondents to the various exposure drafts dated February 14, 1987, this respondent also responded to the respective exposure drafts.
16	Per the list of respondents regarding the overall direction of all 10 exposure drafts dated February 14, 1987, this respondent also separately commented on the general direction of all 10 exposure drafts in the aggregate.
17	Respondent made explicit reference to the three-paragraph length of the proposed audit report.
18-108	Respective statement is made somewhere within the response, or approval/disapproval may be inferred from any alternate wordings of the report suggested by the respondent in their response on the individual topical issues related to report wording. For example, if the respondent suggests an alternate report wording that does not include the words "reasonable assurance," Category No. 52 would be met, even though there is no explicit statement that "reasonable assurance" should be deleted from the proposed report.
109-124	Statement is present within the letter specifically including mention of the respective attribute category regarding audit report modifications.
125-127	Respondent indicates their overall reaction to the need for a new standard report. If no overall reaction can be clearly discerned, then category 127 would be coded. These three categories are mutually exclusive and the existence of one must be noted for each response letter.
128-141	Respondent indicates their aggregate overall reaction to these remaining overall issues regarding the existing auditor's report and the proposed modification presented in the ED.
142-182	Statement is present within the response specifically mentioning these respective individual general issues.

Coding Enumeration

The first six attribute categories have been coded according to the definitions set forth in Table 4.2. For the remainder of the attribute categories, numbers 7 through 182, the study has adopted a dichotomous coding scheme. If an attribute, as defined in Table 4.2, was identified as being present in the response letter the corresponding category was coded a "1," and if the communication attribute was not present within the response letter the corresponding category was coded a "0." Holsti (1969, 659) indicates that the dichotomous-decision technique has the advantage of facilitating focus on a single decision at a time "and is particularly useful when many categories are employed."

Additionally, by using dichotomous coding, the mean of the category is also the proportion of responses containing that particular characteristic or statement. Dichotomous codings, then, are both easy to interpret and increase the efficiency of the statistical processing of the information found in the communications.

Coding Reliability

The researcher has served as the principal judge and after reading each letter at least two times, sequentially coded all of the response letters on all attribute categories twice. All response letters were coded the first time in numerical sequence from 1 to 183, then coded a second time in the same sequence without referring to the initial codings. These two codings were then compared and any discrepancies were resolved to arrive at the final coding of all letters. This final coding was used for all analysis discussed in the next chapter.

This double blind coding was performed so the researcher could assure coding reliability as to: (1) capturing all the messages communicated in the response letters and, (2) consistently recording those communication attributes identified in the response letters. Figure 4.1 indicates the cumulative coding adjustments (i.e., changing "0" to "1" or vice versa) for both the first and second coding. These coding adjustments are based on a comparison between the respective first and second codings and the final coding that resolved any comparative discrepancies.

Several aspects of Figure 4.1 should be highlighted. First of all, and as would be expected, the second coding has fewer coding adjustments than the first coding. This should be expected because the researcher has by this time completely read each letter at least four times and has become extremely familiar with the content of the letters. Second, there were relatively few coding adjustments compared to the total number of categories coded for all letters. There were 97 and 52 adjustments made based on the first and second codings, respectively. In comparison, 33,306 categories in total were coded for the 183 response letters for each of the codings. Also, the "cumulative coding adjustments" include adjustments for both items noted above; missing a communication attribute altogether and also changing an original coding, for example, from "agreement" to "disagreement" on a particular topic. A review of the nature of the coding adjustments for the second coding indicate that 77 percent (40) were made due to lack of identification of a communciation attribute contained within the response letter. Only 23 percent (12) were from

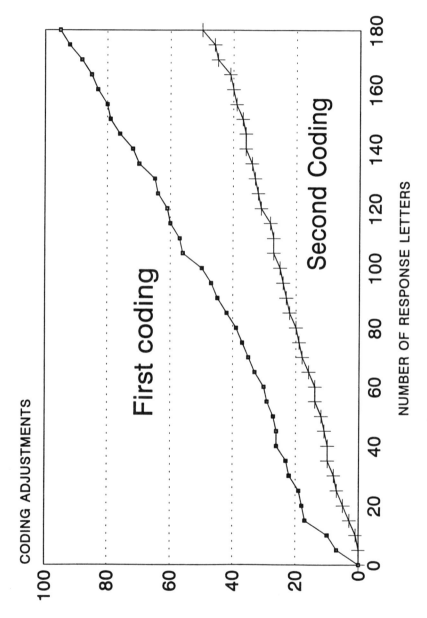

Figure 4.1. Cumulative Coding Adjustments

changing an original agree/disagree position on any topic. This result indicates that, in a majority of cases, the researcher has consistently coded the identified attributes contained in each letter. Consequently, after coding all response letters twice, and deriving the final codings, the researcher is confident that substantially all relevant attributes communicated by the respondents have been identified and properly included in the analysis.

In order to check for any systematic coding bias on the part of the researcher, two panels of judges were selected among Ph.D. candidates in accounting at the Pennsylvania State University and presented with random sets of 20 response letters. Each panel was given the 11 overall response categories 125-131 and 138-141 to code, along with 19 other randomly selected categories for a total of 30 categories. Each panel consisted of six individuals, and every member coded each of the 20 letters for all 30 categories. A comparison of these codings to those of the researcher is presented in Table 4.3.

The results of this reliability check indicate that the overall percentage of agreement between the researcher and the other coders is extremely high at 96.7 percent. This reliability test is a dual test both for items coded by the researcher but not by a panel member and vice versa. A review of the coding differences for all categories, except 125-141, indicates that 75.6 percent are items which the researcher indicated as being present while the individual panel member did not. This is indicative of the researcher "finding" more items as being present in the letters, while the other coders may have overlooked some attributes. This result is to be expected because the researcher read the letters more than the other coders and was, due to familiarity with the letters, able to pick up a greater number of items.

Overall categories 125-131 and 138-141 were coded by all 12 coders for each of their respective 20 letters, for a total of 240 "checks" on each category. On the categories 125-127 for overall indication of desire for a new report, most of the differences in codings arose because of differences in classifying letters as "indeterminate." Panel members classified letters as indeterminate 20 times (category 127), while the researcher coded 14 of them as in favor and 6 as not in favor of a new report. Also the researcher, as compared to the other 240 codings, coded 7 letters "indeterminate" while the panels coded them all as in favor of a new report. More importantly, only once did a panel member indicate that a letter was not in favor of a change when the researcher indicated that it was in favor of a change and vice versa. Thus, the results of the reliability test for these items indicate that the researcher may have had a minimal tendency not to classify a letter as "indeterminate" compared to the panel members. The discussion in Chapter 6 will note that the ASB was extremely reluctant to label any letter as "indeterminate." Thus, the researcher's responses fall somewhere in between these two groups.

Additionally, the extremely high percentage of agreement between the panel of coders and the researcher also indicates that the percentage of agreement

Table 4. Coding Reliability

Panel A		Panel B		Panels A and B	
Category	Percent Agreement (N = 120)	Category	Percent Agreement (N = 120)	Category	Percent Agreement (N = 240)
20	95.0	35	92.5	125	96.7
21	95.8	36	89.2	126	91.7
22	96.7	37	96.7	127	90.4
23	99.2	38	99.2	128	99.2
24	100.0	39	99.2	129	97.5
25	94.2	40	98.3	130	97.5
26	100.0	51	94.2	131	99.6
43	100.0	52	95.8	138	97.1
44	97.5	104	98.3	139	84.2
71	95.8	105	99.2	140	89.6
72	95.8	112	95.0	141	95.0
73	97.5	113	99.2		
85	99.2	143	99.2		
86	98.3	147	96.7		
100	100.0	148	100.0		
101	99.2	149	97.5		
135	100.0	150	99.2		
161	97.5	151	100.0		
162	99.2	177	94.2		

Note: Average percentage of agreements across all categories tested is 96.7 percent.

between panel members is also high. The high percentages of agreement between all coders indicates that the categories established for coding have been derived in such a manner that all coders have usually agreed with the existence or nonexistence of an attribute. Thus, the "codability" of the categories established for analysis also appears to be strong. In summary, there does not appear to be a significant researcher bias present in the final codings used for analysis in the sixth chapter.

The second phase of the research is an attempt to describe some of the more salient influences on the ASB's resolution of this ED, including the response letters. This is discussed in the next section.

PHASE II: DETERMINING CAUSAL RELATIONS

Phase II of this study is necessary to accurately depict the relative influences on the board and is what separates this research from most other research that has analyzed responses to standard-setting bodies and attempted to infer a causal relationship between formal written inputs and final resolution (Brown 1981; Puro 1984).

Content analysis alone will not enable the researcher to appropriately infer a direct cause and effect relationship between the messages communicated in the response letters and the board's final decision regarding the proposed changes in the ED. To more accurately assess whether these and other attempts at influencing the board were fruitful, the researcher attended ASB meetings that included discussions and final decisions concerning the ED. During these meetings, the board deliberated at considerable length over each agenda item with board members, AICPA project staff, and board consultants offering comments for discussion. These discussions have incorporated responses to the ED as well as other potential inside and outside influences. This longitudinal analysis has enabled the researcher to determine if the respondents' views communicated in their letters had an impact on the board's decisions and has also allowed the researcher to more fully comprehend and document the processes involved in the board's standard-setting procedures.

Additionally, numerous interviews with board members and AICPA project staff and consultants have been conducted throughout the process by the researcher at board meetings and over the telephone regarding the development of this ED and the resolution of the proposed report rewordings. The researcher was on the ASB mailing list for all documentation pertaining to this ED and received all documentation regarding this ED and its final resolution at the same time as board members. Also, the researcher received copies of all comment letters to all 10 "expectations gap" exposure drafts.

This study has analyzed the formal written responses to the ASB using an appropriate detailed analytic technique and has additionally attempted to address various other influences on the standard-setting process of the ASB not depicted in response letters alone. The result has been a richer appreciation and understanding of the standard-setting process.

RESEARCH LIMITATIONS

Phase I

Content analysis is a powerful unobtrusive research technique for analyzing archival unstructured communications data. Like all research techniques, however, content analysis does have its limitations. Meaningful and accurate category identification and definition forms the nucleus of content analysis, and is crucial to a proper application of the technique. In order to address this potential limitation, this study has utilized two independent individuals at the AICPA to review the attribute categories for completeness and accuracy. However, there still exists the potential that the established categories did not enable the researcher to fully capture the messages conveyed in the response letters.

Limitations due to lack of coding reliability on the part of the researcher have been addressed earlier in this chapter and do not appear to be a substantial limitation of the study. However, the use of only one primary coder, even though full codings were done twice on each letter and randomly checked by independent panels of coders, may have introduced an undesirable bias into the analysis.

Krippendorff (1980, 22) also notes that messages do not have a single meaning that needs to be "unwrapped"; and that meanings need not be shared. It is for these reasons that multiple detailed categories have been established—to attempt to capture as many meanings behind the communication as possible. However, these categories will, at best, capture the most obvious or "manifest" aspects of the communications. In order to capture any more meaning from some of the communications, the researcher would need to share the same cultural and sociopolitical perspective as each respondent. Because this cannot be achieved, this research phase is limited to summarizing and describing the manifest messages in the response letters.

Another limitation of this phase of the research methodology is that each response letter is assigned the same weight. All response letters have been coded in the same manner and no allowance or adjustment for weighting the responses from various groups, firms, or individuals has been made. Undoubtedly, some respondents have more eloquently articulated the reasoning behind their positions and have had more of an impact on the deliberations of the board and the task force. Additionally, some respondents may have had more impact than others by virtue of their reputations alone. Also, no attempt has been made to capture the intensity with which a respondent agrees or disagrees within any given category. Categories have been coded either a "1" or "0" depending on the presence or absence of an attribute.

A final limitation of the use of content analysis on the actual response letters to the ASB is that of self-selection bias on the part of the respondents. These respondents may differ on some characteristic which has caused them to respond to the exposure draft. The response letters, accordingly, cannot be considered as fully representative of the opinions of the population to which the respondents belong. Any conclusions drawn from the analysis of these responses cannot be generalized to the underlying populations. However, these respondents are considered to be of interest because they have actually attempted to influence the ASB with their response letters.

Phase II

This research phase attempted to describe the salient influences on the ASB and Auditor Communications Task Force regarding this one particular SAS. Even though all relevant documentation was received on a timely basis, numerous conversations and interviews transpired between the researcher and prominent individuals involved, and the relevant ASB meetings were attended, the researcher did not actually become a "board member" and could have misinterpreted or not identified some of the forces impinging on the decision-making process and final outcome. The researcher could not in reality become a board member and experience the process from their precise point of view, however, the tremendous amount of candid interaction enabled the resarcher to, as closely as possible, "see through the eyes of a board member." In an additional attempt to minimize this potential limitation, the influences discussed and interpretations derived have been reviewed by members of the AICPA and have been found to be valid representations of the interplay of forces during this particular standard-setting process.

SUMMARY

This chapter has discussed the cross-sectional and longitudinal nature of the study and has indicated that it is both exploratory and descriptive, and that it has been conducted in two interactive phases. Phase I is an exploration into the documented concerns of the respondents to the ED on the auditor's report. Phase II attempts a depiction of the salient influences on the board as evidenced in the deliberation and resolution of this particular issue. Analyses of these two research endeavors constitute the remainder of the chapters presented in this study. The next chapter will discuss the process of arriving at the audit report version presented in the ED released February 14, 1987 for comment.

Chapter 5

AICPA Deliberations Leading to an Exposure Draft

This chapter will highlight the deliberations on the part of the AICPA that led to the ED issued in early 1987 proposing a modification to the existing standard unqualified audit report. Chapter 3 discussed some of the external forces impinging on the profession during this time period and these will not be specifically addressed further. This chapter will focus on the internal standard-setting process of the AICPA as it relates to this particular ED, and will focus primarily on the actual report wordings proposed, as opposed to the ED document itself.

ESTABLISHMENT OF THE TASK FORCE

A summary of the ASB's standard-setting procedures, may be found in an AICPA in-house document, *Auditing Standards Division Summary of Operating Policies* (AICPA 1987b, 108-110), which sets forth a general 14-point procedure for establishing a Statement of Auditing Standards (SAS). This sequence of steps, documented in Chapter 1, starts with topic identification and ends with the distribution of a final adopted SAS. The procedural list indicates that once the topic is added to the ASB's agenda by the ASB Planning Subcommittee, it is assigned to an existing or new AICPA "component." The component created in late 1985 to handle the issue of the auditor's report was the Auditor Communications Task Force (TF). David Landsittel, who recently served as ASB chairman, was asked to chair the TF at its inception in late 1985 and remained the chairman through the resolution of the final SAS in early 1988. The general charge for the TF was to address issues of auditor communication, including the auditor's report, and to make recommendations for improvement. The TF eventually served to also facilitate the ASB in its consideration of a report modification by offering suggestions for change, implementing changes directed by the board on any documents being proposed, and after the ED was issued, coordinating and disseminating responses to the ED to ASB members and other involved parties. Along with identifying the need for a more effective auditor's report, the TF also identified two other topics ultimately leading to EDs in 1987—auditor's communications with audit committees and possible auditor's association with management's discussion and analysis in financial reports.

The 1986 TF consisted of a chairman, a full-time AICPA Auditing Standards Division technical staff member, Eileen Demichelis, and the following ASB members: John Ellingsen, Deloitte Haskins & Sells; Samuel Gunther, sole practitioner; Howard McMurrian, Cole, Evans & Peterson; and Robert Temkin, Arthur Young & Co. Additionally, the AICPA also asked Henry Jaenicke of Drexel University to serve on the TF.

In discussions with Eileen Demichelis, she indicated that the 1986 TF, as with most issues addressed by the ASB, did not perform any "original" empirical research. That is, no alternate versions of potential wordings were given to any outside groups or individuals to determine how potential changes were viewed by individual users or outside groups. The TF did, however, consider some of the extant literature on modifying the auditor's report such as CAR's report and the various background research papers developed for the commission by the AICPA. This approach is typical for issues addressed by the AICPA because most of the issues have a practical orientation and often do not benefit directly from *a priori* rigorous scrutiny by auditing researchers. Changes contemplated by the AICPA are usually the result of professional deliberation as opposed to answering a research question, per se.

The TF deliberated and studied the issue of the auditor's report in early 1986 and eventually presented the following three-paragraph report for the board's consideration at their August 1986 meeting:

(Title to include the word *independent*)

We have audited the accompanying balance sheet of X Company as of (at) December 31, 19XX, and the related statement of income, retained earnings and changes in financial position for the year then ended. These financial statements, including the accompanying notes, are the representations of X Company's management.

Our audit work was performed in accordance with standards established by our profession. These standards require extensive tests including, to the extent considered necessary, confirmation of certain matters with outside parties, physical observation of some assets, inspection of the documentation for selected transactions and balances, and inquiries of company personnel and of persons outside the company. The standards also require an assessment of the accounting principles used and the significant estimates made by management in preparing the financial statements. An audit is designed to provide reasonable assurance that the financial statements do not contain material misstatements resulting from mistakes or fraud. We believe that our auditing procedures were adequate in the circumstances to express our opinion presented below.

In our opinion, the financial statements referred to above, present fairly, in all material respects, the financial position of X Company as of (at) December 31, 19XX, and the results of its operations and the changes in its financial position for the year then ended in conformity with generally accepted accounting principles.

This proposed three-paragraph report more closely resembles the multiple-paragraph report proposed by CAR than does the earlier 1980 ASB proposed report. The proposed report included "independent" in the title, replaced "examined" with "audited," stated that the financial statements and notes are management's representations, greatly expanded the scope paragraph to discuss attributes of an audit, including the concept of "reasonable assurance," eliminated the reference to GAAS, added "in all material respects" and deleted the reference to consistency in the opinion paragraph. The expanded discussion in the report, and particularly in the scope paragraph, was an attempt by the TF to address various concerns within the profession that users did not fully understand the nature of an audit. Therefore, an effort was made to more directly communicate to report readers some of what an audit entails. The discussion of an audit prepared by the TF was one of the most comprehensive of the recent proposals to modify the report. The next section will discuss the ASB meetings that modified this proposal before arriving at the ED.

AUDITING STANDARDS BOARD MEETINGS LEADING TO THE EXPOSURE DRAFT

August 1986

At the August meeting, the ASB, led in discussion by David Landsittel, concluded that a new three-paragraph audit report would improve communication to users, but decided to substantially revise the TF's proposed report. The introductory paragraph was modified to say "All information included in" these financial statements are management's representations, along with some other minor editorial modifications. The most extensive modifications made to the proposed report were in the scope paragraph. The reference to auditing standards established by "our profession" was changed to "the American Institute of Certified Public Accountants." The next two sentences in the scope paragraph were essentially switched and substantially modified to read:

Those standards require that an audit be designed to evaluate whether the financial statements are materially misstated. Reasonable assurance regarding that evaluation is achieved by examining support, on a test basis, for the amounts included in the financial statements, by assessing the appropriateness of the accounting principles used and the significant estimates made by management, and by assessing the appropriateness of the overall financial statement presentation and disclosures.

This rewording eliminated direct reference to confirmations with outside parties, physical inspection of assets, and inquiries of company personnel in support of the amounts included in the financial statements. After considerable discussion, the ASB eliminated direct reference to causes of materially misstated financial statements—"mistakes and fraud." The TF indicated that it included this phrase in response to the Treadway Commission's concern that fraud be more explicitedly included under the perview of the auditor. However, the board felt that an explicit reference to "fraud" in the audit report was not necessary. Overall, the implemented modifications to the wording shortened the report and eliminated some direct references to types of audit evidence evaluated in an audit, and the explicit reference to the auditor's responsibility for detection of material fraud.

The opinion paragraph was also modified to reposition "in all material respects," switch "present fairly" to "fairly presented" and eliminate the reference to "the financial position of X Company...." This last modification was considered to be an editorial shortening of the report, but was later shown to have been a substantive change and was reinstated in the audit report. The opinion paragraph, as modified by the board in August, read:

> In our opinion, the financial statements referred to above are, in all material respects, fairly presented in conformity with generally accepted accounting principles.

The board also discussed in August deletion of the reference to consistent application of GAAP in the opinion paragraph. As discussed in the previous chapter, APB No. 20 requires consistent application of accounting principles between periods, or appropriate disclosures if a change is made. Thus, the TF and the ASB considered consistency a part of GAAP which need not be mentioned separately if the auditor states that the financial statements are in conformity with GAAP. Accordingly, it was concluded by the board that no reference to consistency needed to be made in the standard unqualified report, or even in the auditor's report when a change in principle is made, if proper disclosures are included by management in the notes to the financial statements.

The TF also presented the ASB with an appendix that illustrated auditor's reports other than the standard unqualified report based on the proposed new wording. At this point, the proposed wording of the TF for the auditor's report when a material uncertainty existed still was considered a qualified opinion and retained the "subject to" language. The ASB would later amend this preliminary position with regard to the "subject to" audit opinion.

After the TF suggested its report version to the board, the TF's role changed to primarily implementing the decisions of the board regarding the proposed report. However, throughout the process, board members still listened to and considered suggestions regarding wording of the report made by the TF, and especially those of the TF chairman. Thus, the potential influence of the TF, as a separate body, was considerably limited because of the ASB's final authority over any decisions regarding the issues addressed. At this point, the TF became more of a facilitator for the ASB rather than a decision maker.

October 1986

The next time the ASB met to discuss the auditor's report was in October 1986. At this meeting the TF presented a revised audit report wording that implemented the modifications agreed upon by the board in August. At this meeting, the TF chairman reaffirmed that the intent of a changed audit report was to provide a positive statement regarding the auditor's responsibility and to more clearly communicate what an audit entails to all report readers. Again, the concept of the report being a positive statement surfaced and was discussed when a suggestion was made to begin the report with the sentence stating that the financial statements were representations of management. The resounding consensus was that such a starting sentence would sound much too negative. Also, the board noted that the 1980 ED started with a similar sentence and was viewed by the respondents to the 1980 ED as being too negative and self-serving on the part of the auditing profession.

At this October 1986 meeting, only the scope paragraph of the proposed report was modified. Through recent discussions with the SEC, Jerry Sullivan, the chairman of the ASB, found that the SEC was not in favor of the elimination of the reference to GAAS and its replacement with "standards established by the AICPA." However, the board voted in October to retain their new wording and to make further inquiries of the SEC on this issue before the next discussion. Two overriding concerns were presented by the board regarding the second sentence of the scope paragraph: (1) it was too negative and implied that financial statements were likely to be misstated, and (2) it did not address fraud and irregularities, which some members believed the Treadway Commission wanted in a modified audit report.

After considerable debate, no change was made with regard to (1) above; however, the the board voted 10-to-3 in favor of mentioning reasons for material misstatement in the report. The discussion centered around the issue of a perceived "expectations gap," and it was felt that explicit reference to the responsibility of the auditor in the audit report would directly address this disparity. Another vote indicated that seven members were in favor of using "intentionally and unintentionally," while only five members were in favor of using "fraud and error" in order to modify the report to attempt to lessen the "expectations gap." When the TF returned to the board in December, this modification would be included in parentheses to emphasize the split decision on the appropriate wording on the part of the ASB. The remainder of the unqualified report wording remained essentially the same as after the August meeting.

In regard to reports qualified because of uncertainty, the TF proposal in October still maintained the existing "subject to" qualified-opinion wording. Per discussions with the TF chairman, it was his impression that the TF, in general, was not entirely satisfied with the "subject to" report language, and that it did fall under the perview of the TF as an auditor communication problem. However, the TF first attempted to establish a need for a new standard audit report and the actual wording it should take, and then address issues such as reporting on uncertainties or the wording of other audit reports. However, the TF was not far enough along on the wording issues involved in the standard unqualified report in October to propose changing any other report wordings.

The task force assessing the auditor's responsibility in questions of the client's ability to continue in existence (i.e., the Continued Existence TF) was relatively further along in its discussions and had addressed auditor reporting requirements in this area. In fact, the Continued Existence TF proposed the elimination of the "subject to" wording at the October ASB meeting. This TF proposed to replace the "subject to" qualified audit opinion with an unqualified audit opinion that also referred the report reader to the footnote disclosures elaborating on whether the client had the ability to continue in existence. The continued existence TF proposed the following opinion paragraph instead of the standard unqualified audit opinion:

> In our opinion, the financial statements referred to above are, in all material respects, fairly presented in conformity with generally accepted accounting principles. The financial statements do not include adjustments for the uncertainty of future effects of the possible discontinuance of X Company discussed in Note A, including the effect on the recoverability and classification of assets and the amounts and classification of liabilities described therein.

This report wording was proposed prior to the ASB's discussion of the standard unqualified report in October. The board upheld the position of the Continued Existence TF that the existing "subject to" report language was confusing to report readers and that it should be replaced with an expanded *unqualified* opinion paragraph instead of the current explanatory middle paragraph.

When the Auditor Communications TF later addressed the board in the October meeting, in general, only issues concerning the wording of the standard unqualified report were discussed. However, the board agreed that the Auditor's Communication TF should adopt the substance of the Continued Existence TF's proposal to eliminate the "subject to" wording. The Auditor Communications TF, however, was charged with assessing all auditor reporting requirements, and it was believed that the proposals of the two TFs should be congruent and that all audit reports concerning uncertainties should be modified to eliminate the existing "subject to" wording.

Hence, the ASB in 1986 again proposed the elimination of the "subject to" report for uncertainties. The actual impetus for this change was the Continued Existence TF and not the Auditor Communications TF. The proposal to replace the qualified report with an expanded unqualified opinion paragraph was similar to the ASB's 1985 ED which proposed to eliminate the "subject to" audit report wording. This ED, however, was tabled by the board in 1985 because the respondents to the ED were not generally enthusiastic about the proposal. Discussion of the 1985 ED was taken up by the board later in 1987 when attempting to finalize the 1987 ED. In late 1986, the ASB felt that, because appropriate disclosures of all significant uncertainties are required by GAAP (*SFAS 5*), failure to provide appropriate disclosure is a GAAP exception that would result in an "except for" opinion qualification (similar to the logic behind deletion of the consistency reference). Once proper disclosure is made under GAAP, no further reference needs to be made in the auditor's report. However, as discussed in ASB meetings, it was believed that a reference to the discussion of the uncertainty in the footnotes, although not technically required, would serve to help alert users of financial statements to the existence of such uncertainties. Thus, the elimination of the "subject to" wording was proposed, and in its place was proposed an unqualified report that would still serve to provide report readers with a useful "warning signal."

December 1986

As noted above, the Auditor Communications TF was charged with implementing in its proposed ED the decisions of the ASB at the October 1986 meeting. When the TF returned to the board in December 1986 to finalize the ED on the auditor's report, they presented an example of a report "modified" because of an uncertainty that had the same first two paragraphs as the standard unqualified report and the following opinion paragraph:

> In our opinion, the financial statements referred to above are, in all material respects, fairly presented in conformity with generally accepted accounting principles. As discussed in Note X to the financial statements, the company is a defendant in a lawsuit alleging infringement of certain patent rights and claiming royalties and punitive damages. The company has filed a counter action, and preliminary hearings and discovery proceedings on both actions are in progress. The ultimate outcome of the lawsuit cannot presently be determined. Accordingly, no provision for any liability that may result upon adjudication has been made in the accompanying financial statements.

This opinion paragraph incorporated the substance of the conclusions made by the ASB in October regarding reporting on uncertainties. No modification to this proposed wording was made in December and the report "modified" for uncertainties was issued for comment as presented by the TF in December.

In December the TF also presented a proposed unqualified report wording that incorporated the resolutions made by the board in October. The topic of the auditor's report, however, was specifically not addressed by the board until after they further discussed and resolved the issues mentioned in the ED on continued existence and its reporting requirements. At this December meeting, their earlier stance on the "subject to" elimination was upheld.

A few final modifications to report wording were made on the report presented by the Auditor Communications TF in December. The second sentence of the introductory paragraph was modified to eliminate the references to "all information included in" and "including the accompanying notes."

The issue of deleting the reference to GAAS was once again addressed by the board. The switch from GAAS to "standards established by the AICPA" was reviewed by the legal counsel of the AICPA and it was believed that the two phrases legally said essentially the same thing. However, the ASB chairman, through further discussions with Clarence Sampson, chief accountant for the SEC, found that the SEC did not favor the switch from GAAS because Sampson believed GAAS was a well-understood phrase and that a change would convey an unintended different message to report readers. Sampson believed that there might be a mistaken perception of a narrowing of audit responsibility by changing from GAAS to stating that auditing standards were established by only one organization—the AICPA. It was also noted in the board's discussion that the phrase GAAS is used in reports on government municipalities and other areas not directly under the perview of the AICPA.

The ASB finally decided, with a 9-to-5 vote, to reinstate GAAS into the auditor's report. There was a general consensus on the board that sentiment did not run deep enough for the proposed change to warrant challenging and debating the SEC. So, if the SEC felt strongly about it, the ASB did not feel that changing the reference from GAAS was worth further deliberation.

In an attempt to give the report a more active voice, the phrase "our audit was performed" was changed to "we performed our audit" in the first sentence of the scope paragraph. Also, as discussed earlier, in order for ED readers to understand that the ASB was contemplating including "intentionally or unintentionally" as modifiers of "materially misstated," they decided that, along with including the phrase in parentheses in the ED, it should also be footnoted. It was concluded that the footnote should specifically indicate that the addition of these words was being contemplated and that ED commentators should state their positions on this item.

The TF also had the AICPA's in-house public relations division review the proposed new audit report wording and presented those results to the board in December. The public relations division indicated that a new report would be beneficial for the profession, and that the revision of the ASB in this regard was a considerable improvement in attempting to communicate with report readers. Their only substantial criticism of the proposed audit report was that the sentence beginning with "reasonable assurance" in the scope paragraph was too long and complex. They suggested that the sentence be broken down and that the audit attributes mentioned in the sentence be presented in the form of a list instead of in one long sentence in order to be more effectively communicated and better understood by the report readers. This suggestion was discussed by the board which decided to expose the proposed report as it was, without modifying this sentence, and see what the reaction to the report would be.

After continued discussion, the balance of the proposed report remained unchanged and was unanimously approved by the board for exposure at the conclusion of a meeting in December 1986. This report wording was then reviewed and approved by the AICPA's legal counsel prior to its release as an ED. Thus, the final proposed auditor's report exposed for comment on February 14, 1987, read as follows:

Independent Auditor's Report

We have audited the accompanying balance sheet of X Company as of December 31, 19XX, and the related statements of income, retained earnings, and changes in financial position for the year then ended. These financial statements are the representations of X Company's management.

We performed our audit in accordance with generally accepted auditing standards. Those standards require that an audit be designed to evaluate whether the financial statements are materially misstated (intentionally or unintentionally). Reasonable assurance regarding that evaluation is achieved by examining evidence, on a test basis, that supports the amounts included in the financial statements, by assessing the appropriateness of the accounting principles used and the significant estimates made by management, and by assessing the appropriateness of the overall financial statement presentation and disclosures. We believe that our auditing procedures were appropriate in the circumstances to express our opinion presented below.

In our opinion, the financial statements referred to above are, in all material respects, fairly presented in conformity with generally accepted accounting principles.

SUMMARY

This chapter has highlighted the significant steps in the process that the 1987 ED passed through in order to finally be approved for exposure by the ASB in December 1986. This particular ED took approximately one year to get from the establishment of a TF that intensely studied and addressed the issue, to the final approval of the ED by the ASB. The discussion has indicated that, throughout the process, the board was intent on attempting to make the revised report sound more positive than earlier revision attempts, as well as making the proposed report more easily comprehensible by directly stating some of the messages only implied in the old report. Discussions at the board meetings and the respective changes implemented on the proposed report have illustrated that the establishment of an ED is a difficult, time-consuming, and sometimes circular task.

This chapter has attempted to portray some of the salient features of the wording proposals of the TF and the discussions held at the board meetings, and how this process shaped the wording of the auditor's report proposed in the ED released in 1987. It was also noted that, with the exception of the SEC's disapproval of changing the GAAS reference to "standards established by the AICPA," the report wording proposed in the 1987 ED was largely shaped and developed by professional deliberations within the AICPA. The procedural steps in establishing SAS, as outlined in Chapter 1, indicate that the initial stages are, appropriately, more internally oriented prior to issuing an ED for public comment.

The chapter has noted that the only significant outside influence on the process of establishing the ED was the SEC. The SEC has the legislative authority to accept or reject a new audit report wording issued to corporations that are SEC registrants. Therefore, the SEC has the potential to exert significant influence on the final audit report wording, unless the ASB was willing to establish dual reporting—one report required for SEC registrants and another report for all other entities. This possible resolution was briefly discussed by the board in 1986 and generally dismissed as an undesirable reporting alternative. The continuing influence of the SEC will also be seen in the analysis of SAS finalization presented in Chapter 7.

The next chapter will presefnt the analysis of the response letters commenting on this ED.

Chapter 6

Analysis of Response Letters

The Auditing Standards Board received a total of 1,105 response letters in 1987 on all 10 "expectations gap" exposure drafts released for comment on February 14, 1987. An additional 154 letters were also received offering general comments on the combined package of the 10 exposure drafts. The exposure draft receiving the most letters was the proposed audit report modification which received 183 letters.

James Loebbecke, ASB member, in an address to the Pennsylvania State University Graduate Accounting Conference on September 11, 1987, noted that the board views the response letters "not as a vote, but as a way of getting insights into the potential standards." However, he also stated that, on the issue of identifying whether the EDs were favorably received, "it is hard not to count them up," and indicated that the ED on the auditor's report received support from the majority of respondents. This chapter will analyze the content of those letters addressing the ED on the auditor's report by using the attribute categories established in the preceding chapter. Overall response patterns found in 1987 will also be compared to those identified in the letters of comment on the 1980 ED that proposed a change in audit report wording.

In discussing the procedural steps in performing a content analysis study, Kidder (1981, 288) describes the final analysis stage as follows:

> with content analysis the most straightforward analysis is the straightforward presentation of the data in summary form, such as numbers represented and percentage representation.

This chapter has adopted the summary form approach suggested by Kidder (1981), and will straightforwardly present the results of the coding process, as well as provide appropriate discussion of the results.

WHO RESPONDED

The number and types of respondents commenting on the 1987 ED are presented in Table 6.1. The 16 categories of respondents were established at the conclusion of the letter coding and are believed to adequately represent the major respondent groups. A list of all respondents to this ED, along with their group classification, is included in Appendix I.

As would be expected, a majority of the respondents were from within the public accounting profession. Other closely associated groups like governmental auditors, academics, and corporations also contributed considerable percentages of the comment letters.

Comparison with 1980

In 1987, the ASB received 183 response letters to the ED on the auditor's report, compared to an unprecedented 443 letters received on the 1980 ED. Mitchell (1983) noted that 272 letters were received from the public accounting profession alone in 1980. Several factors in the process of eliciting comments might have caused the number of responses in 1987 to be lower than in 1980. First, the exposure draft was mailed to every member of the AICPA in 1980, which was not the case in 1987. Most individuals and organizations typically had to request copies of the 1987 ED from the AICPA, thus limiting its dissemination. Second, there was no public hearing to discuss the potential modification of the auditor's report in 1987 as there was in 1980. The ASB is not required to hold a public hearing during its standard-setting process, but in 1980 a public hearing was held prior to issuance of the 1980 ED. This lack of a public hearing in 1987 could have also led to a lower level of public interest compared to 1980. Third, the 1987 ED on the auditor's report was part of the "package" of 10 "expectations gap" EDs all issued for comment on February 14, 1987. This "package" approach may have resulted in fewer response letters being received than if each ED (including the one on the auditor's report) had been issued separately or at different times. In fact, most of the general comment letters on all 10 exposure drafts resembled a form letter, which, in part, asked the ASB to extend the comment period in order to permit a proper review of all 10 EDs.

In an attempt to minimize these deterrants to potential respondents, the board established a five-month comment period for these 10 exposure drafts instead of the usual three-month comment period. In fact, all letters received by the ASB, whether or not received before the comment deadline of July 15, 1987, were read and considered by the Auditor Communications Task Force (TF), and copies of all letters were given to ASB members. Still, the 183 response letters received on this ED were the most for any of the 10 EDs and were in excess of the average 80 to 120 comment letters received on a typical

Table 6.1. Types of Respondents

Respondent Group	Number	Percent of Total
I. *Public Auditors*		
Big Eight CPA firms	7	4
Next 15 largest CPA firms*	5	3
Smaller CPA firms	49	26
Individual CPAs	36	20
State and local CPA societies	18	10
AICPA officials and committees	8	4
	123	67
II. *Governmental Audit Agencies*		
State and local municipal auditors	12	6
Federal governmental audit agencies	3	2
	15	8
III. *Issuers of Financial Statements*		
SEC-filing corporations	9	5
Non-SEC-filing corporations	2	1
Governmental and not-for-profit agencies	3	2
Organizations representing issuers	4	2
	18	10
IV. Academics	19	10
V. Lawyers and Legal Groups	3	2
VI. Report Users and User Groups	0	0
VII. Miscellaneous Respondents	5	3
Total	183	100

Note: * Per the list of the 23 largest CPA firms obtained from the AICPA on November 17, 1987.

AICPA ED, evidencing an above average interest in the proposal to change the auditor's report.

Table 6.2 shows a comparison of 1987 respondents and Mitchell's (1983) categorization of the 1980 respondents. A completely accurate comparison cannot be made between the two lists due to establishment of slightly different respondent groups, however, a gross comparison can still provide useful insights.

The most striking differences are that, in 1987 fewer issuers of financial statements responded than in 1980, and, regretably, *no* users of financial statements (i.e., bankers, security analysis, investment firms, investors, etc.) responded in 1987. However, the Financial Executives Institute (FEI) did respond in writing to the ASB in 1987. The FEI represents the view of

Table 6.2. Comparison of Respondents in 1987 and 1980

Respondent Group	1987		1980	
Public accounting profession	67%	(123)	61%	(272)
Issuers of financial statements	10	(18)	23	(104)
Governmental agencies	8	(15)	2	(7)
Users of financial statements	0	(0)	5	(21)
Academics	10	(19)	6	(24)
Lawyers and legal groups	2	(3)	NA	
Miscellaneous	3	(5)	3	(15)
Total	100%	(183)	100%	(443)

Note: ( ) indicates raw number.

thousands of corporate financial executives and will be shown in the next chapter to have significantly influenced the ASB. Not withstanding this influential letter and strong voice for issuers, more insight might have been gleened from views of other financial statement issuers.

The nonresponse from users of audit reports is disappointing in that these potential respondents could have provided the ASB useful feedback on the ED; even if only to state their overall agreement or disagreement. User groups, by definition, are the prime recipients and beneficiaries of audit reports. Reaction from this group concerning the proposed report could have helped the ASB in assessing whether implemented or contemplated changes to the ED wording or any changes to auditor's report would have potentially elicited the desired results. Because better communication to users of audit reports was a prime goal of this ED (AICPA 1987a), reaction of user groups to the ED would have allowed the ASB to make more informed decisions.

It is evident that in both 1980 and in 1987, the ASB's method of soliciting comments was inadequate in encouraging members of the financial statement preparer and user groups to respond to issues that affected them. The ASB may need to consider other methods to ascertain the reactions of these groups to the issues addressed by the AICPA which would benefit more directly from outside commentary. Typically, issues addressed by the ASB are more internally oriented. However, in cases such as the proposed modification of the auditor's report, an alternate process for soliciting relevant views from outside parties should be contemplated.

1987 Respondents

In 1987, fully two-thirds of the letters were from the public accounting profession, while another eight percent were from governmental audit agencies, making a total of 75 percent of the respondents from auditing professions. The public auditor groups were categorized as the Big Eight, the 15 next largest CPA firms, smaller CPA firms, and individual CPAs in order to capture any differences across firm size of the respondent. Dillard and Jensen (1983) combined all CPAs and CPA firms into one group for analysis. However, Mitchell (1983) noted distinct differences across the larger CPA firms compared to smaller CPA firms and individual CPAs. Mitchell (1983) notes that overall reaction to the proposed report in 1980 was negative, and that the majority (56%) of the larger CPA firms favored the existing report. However, smaller CPA firms and individual CPAs were most inclined to support the thrust of the 1980 proposed report over the existing report (60% and 62%, respectively). A similar type of reaction pattern was anticipated in 1987 and will be discussed in later sections of this chapter.

The only Big Eight firm that did not respond in writing to this ED (and the other nine EDs) was Touche Ross & Co. Tom Bittinger, a partner of Touche Ross & Co. and an ASB member, indicated that it was the position of Touche Ross & Co. that his presence on the board was sufficient to voice their concerns and opinions and that written responses were thus unnecessary. All other Big Eight firms submitted formal written letters of comment to the ASB on each of the 10 exposure drafts.

The federal governmental audit agencies category consists of audit regulators at the federal level and includes letters from the U.S. Comptroller General, the President's Council on Integrity and Efficiency, and the Federal Financial Institutions Examination Council. Organizations representing issuers includes letters from organizations like the Financial Executives Institute and the National Association of Accountants. Both professors and students were included in the academics group. Letters from the American Bar Association and individual lawyers were included in the lawyers and legal groups category. As noted earlier, regretably no letters were received from any individual or organization representing users of financial statements. Finally, the miscellaneous category includes those respondents who did not properly fall into any of the established groups and those respondents for whom no identification could be made.

GENERAL DATA ITEMS

Along with capturing the overall and specific concerns of the respondents, some general data items were collected or calculated for each letter of comment. The inclusion of these items was an attempt to provide more general information on the respondents and how they responded to the ASB on this one ED. Table 6.3 provides the mean for all groups for the average number of days it took to respond, the average number of pages included in the response and the percentage of letters typed.

Table 6.3. General Data Items

Respondent Group	N	Average Number of Days (Cat. 3)	Average Number of Pages (Cat. 4)	Percent of Letters Typed (Cat. 5)
I. Public Auditors				
Big Eight CPA firms	(7)	126	3.00	100
Next 15 largest CPA firms	(5)	102	2.90	100
Smaller CPA firms	(49)	125	1.04	63
Individual CPAs	(36)	112	1.51	56
State and local CPA societies	(18)	153	1.54	100
AICPA officials and committees	(8)	109	1.44	100
II. Governmental Audit Agencies				
State and local municipal auditors	(12)	138	1.08	92
Federal governmental audit agencies	(3)	160	1.67	100
III. Issuers				
SEC-filing Ccrporations	(9)	153	1.75	100
Non-SEC-filing corporations	(2)	104	1.13	100
Governmental and not-for-profit agencies	(3)	150	.92	100
Organizations representing issuers	(4)	145	2.06	100
IV. Academics	(19)	108	1.64	63
V. Lawyers and Legal Groups	(3)	146	5.58	100
VI. Report Users and User Groups	(0)	—	—	—
VII. Miscellaneous Respondents	(5)	119	.85	100
Total	183	126	1.52	77

The averages included in Table 6.3 (and all succeeding tables) should be analyzed in light of the small number of respondents in some of the groups. In general, the results presented in Table 6.3 indicate that there was relatively little variation among the groups on these three general data items. Most of the small variations can be readily understood based on the type of group responding. Larger organizations appear to have taken longer to respond and typically typed their response, while smaller organizations or individuals responded more quickly and were more likely to submit a handwritten response. Additionally, response letters were typically one to two pages in length, and a large majority of respondents took most of the five-month exposure period to respond, with no group mean response time less than 100 days.

It appears that large CPA firms wrote longer responses than the other CPA groups, while individual CPAs were relatively quick to respond and were fairly evenly split between handwriting their response and typing it. State societies and groups outside auditing took a little longer to respond and typically typed their response. One additional noteworthy item is the average length of the lawyers and legal group letters of 5.58 pages. This average is based on only three comment letters, including the one received by the American Bar Association which totaled nine pages. This length of response can also be expected from this group due to their thorough examination of the issues and alternatives regarding wording of the auditor's report.

In an attempt to ascertain the respondents' level of interest on the other nine exposure drafts, the lists of commentators to the other EDs were examined to see if the individual respondent to the ED on the auditor's report also responded to any of the other "expectations gap" EDs. The results presented in Table 6.4 indicate that the respondents were not only interested in the auditor's report, but they were also generally interested in the other EDs. Roughly 40 to 45 percent of all respondents to this ED also responded to the other EDs. However, there was a larger percentage of auditor's report respondents responding to the ED on continued existence and auditor's responsibility for errors and irregularities, at 50 and 55 percent, respectively.

This general pattern of responses to the other EDs is also fairly consistent with the overall number of responses received on these individual EDs. One noted exception, however, is that of the response level to the 10 EDs as a whole. Only four firms or individuals responding to this ED also responded separately to the "package" of 10 EDs. A large majority of those submitting general comments on all the EDs taken together used a type of form letter. Reviewing all lists of ED respondents, typically these respondents did not submit any comments on any of the other nine EDs. Hence, a majority of these "general" commentators had no specific documented response to any of the EDs taken individually.

WHAT WAS SAID

The analysis in this and subsequent sections of this chapter present percentages of respondent groups identified as reacting to the respective items. However, due to a low number of raw responses for some groups, certain large percentages for some groups may be misleading and represent only one or two respondents. Percentages should be cautiously interpreted in the context of the number of respondents for the respective item. Accordingly, the raw numbers of respondents have also been indicated within the tables.

Overall Responses

Reaction to the Need for a New Report. Each response letter was coded as to an overall disagreement or agreement on the need for a new standard audit report (Cat. 125 and 126, respectively); or, if no general indication could be discerned from the letter, Cat. 127 was coded. The overall positions of

Table 6.4. Percentage of Respondents Responding to Other EDs

Respondent Group	N	Group Percentage Responding									
		CE	EI	IA	CR	AR	EST	CS	AC	MD&A	GEN
I. Public Auditors											
Big Eight CPA firms	(7)	100	100	100	86	100	100	100	100	100	29
Next 15 largest CPA firms	(5)	60	60	80	80	100	100	60	80	80	(0)
Smaller CPA firms	(49)	39	61	35	35	43	29	27	27	20	2
Individual CPAs	(36)	47	50	39	42	36	39	36	36	39	3
State and local CPA societies	(18)	61	72	61	78	56	44	44	61	44	(0)
AICPA officials and committees	(8)	13	25	25	13	50	38	13	38	25	(0)
II. Governmental Audit Agencies											
State and local municipal auditors	(12)	67	42	42	58	50	25	67	67	33	(0)
Federal governmental audit agencies	(3)	100	100	100	100	67	100	100	100	100	(0)
III. Issuers											
SEC-filing corporations	(9)	56	56	78	67	44	56	67	78	89	(0)
Non-SEC-filing corporations	(2)	50	100	50	(0)	50	50	(0)	50	(0)	(0)
Governmental and not-for-profit agencies	(3)	67	67	67	67	(0)	67	33	67	33	(0)
Organizations representing issuers	(4)	100	100	75	100	100	75	100	100	100	(0)
IV. Academics	(19)	42	26	21	32	32	26	37	32	26	(0)
V. Lawyers and Legal Groups	(3)	33	33	33	(0)	(0)	(0)	(0)	(0)	33	(0)
VI. Report Users and User Groups	—	—	—	—	—	—	—	—	—	—	—
VII. Miscellaneous Respondents	(5)	20	20	20	20	20	20	20	20	20	(0)
Total	(183)	50	55	45	47	46	40	41	45	39	2
Total Responses received on ED		110	150	106	107	98	82	85	100	84	154

Notes: ( ) indicates raw number
CE—Continued Existence
EI—Errors and Irregularities
IA—Illegal Acts

CR—Control Risk
AP—Analytical Procedures
EST—Accounting Estimates
CS—Communication of Control Structure

AC—Audit Committee
MD&A—Management's Discussion and Analysis
Gen—Comments on all Ten EDs Combined

132

respondents are summarized in Table 6.5. Exactly two-thirds of all respondents were considered by the researcher to indicate a need for a new audit report, while only 21 percent of all respondents indicated a belief that a new audit report was not needed, and 12 percent did not provide sufficient commentary to make an overall determination.

These overall positions can be compared to the only summary of respondent positions produced by the AICPA's Auditor Communications Task Force. Along with each batch of response letters forwarded to board members, the task force included a cover letter indicating the cumulative number of comments in favor or not in favor of a change in the standard audit report. The last mailing from the AICPA technical manager on the Auditor Communications Task Force, on September 16, 1987, included the following statement with regard to the proposed SAS on the auditor's report:

> Of the 184 comments received to date, 147 appear to favor issuance of the proposed SAS while 34 do not support its release. Three respondents offered no opinion (AICPA File Ref. No. 2347).[1]

The AICPA considered 80 percent of all response letters to be in favor of a new report ("issuance of the proposed SAS"), 18 percent to be not in favor of a new report, and the remaining 2 percent to be noncommittal in their comments. This 4-to-1 margin of favor-to-not-favor was presented by David Landsittel, chairman of the Auditor Communications TF, to the ASB during the subsequent board deliberations concerning this ED. The indication of a more favorable response by the AICPA TF than that presented in Table 6.5 may be a reflection of the author's attempt to be as stringent as possible in classifications of overall agreement or disagreement on the need for a new report. The present study classifies more response letters as "undecided" and less as "favorable" than did the AICPA TF. If no clear indication of overall reaction could be discerned, then the researcher did not hesitate to indicate the response letters as "undecided." In discussing respondents' reactions to specific proposals of the 1980 ED, Dillard and Jensen (1983, 791) note that although there is a "temptation to interpret the absence of a reaction by a respondent as a tacit approval of a specific proposal, it may be misleading to do so." The researcher has tried to minimize such a temptation, while the TF may have been inclined to count more respondents as being in favor of the proposal unless explicit mention was made otherwise. The present analysis, compared to the AICPA TF classifications, may have produced slightly more conservative results in support of a new audit report. The present study indicates that the majority favoring a change in the standard auditor's report is a little more than 3-to-1 instead of the 4-to-1 margin indicated by the TF.

Unfortunately, the task force aggregated all respondents together when assessing reaction to the ED, hence, no detailed comparison can be made by

Table 6.5. Overall Reaction to the Need for a New Report

Respondent Group	N	New Report is Not Needed (Cat. 125)		New Report is Needed (Cat. 126)		No Overall Reaction Indicated (Cat. 127)	
I. Public Auditors							
Big Eight CPA firms	(7)	29%	(2)	71%	(5)	0%	(0)
Next 15 largest CPA firms	(5)	20	(1)	80	(4)	0	(0)
Smaller CPA firms	(49)	16	(8)	70	(34)	14	(7)
Individual CPAs	(36)	42	(15)	50	(18)	8	(3)
State and local CPA societies	(18)	11	(2)	83	(15)	6	(1)
AICPA officials and committees	(8)	0	(0)	63	(5)	37	(3)
II. Governmental Audit Agencies							
State and local municipal auditors	(12)	17	(2)	50	(6)	33	(4)
Federal governmental audit agencies	(3)	0	(0)	67	(2)	33	(1)
III. Issuers							
SEC-filing corporations	(9)	56	(5)	44	(4)	0	(0)
Non-SEC-filing corporations	(2)	0	(0)	50	(1)	50	(1)
Governmental and not-for-profit agencies	(3)	0	(0)	100	(3)	0	(0)
Organizations representing issuers	(4)	25	(1)	75	(3)	0	(0)
IV. Academics	(19)	5	(1)	84	(16)	11	(2)
V. Lawyers and Legal Groups	(3)	0	(0)	100	(3)	0	(0)
VI. Report Users and User Groups	—	—	—	—	—	—	—
VII. Miscellaneous Respondents	(4)	20	(1)	60	(3)	20	(1)
Total	183	21%	(38)	67%	(122)	12%	(23)

Note: ( ) indicates raw number.

respondent group. The reaction by respondent group is presented in Table 6.5. An analysis of Table 6.5 reveals that a majority of all groups indicated agreement with the ASB's position that the current audit report needs to be modified, except for the responding SEC registrants. This result is consistent with the responses to the 1980 ED, in that 51 percent of the comment letters received from SEC registrants in 1980 indicated that a new audit report was not needed. It appears, then, that large public corporations have consistently indicated their belief that the existing audit report wording is adequate and need not be modified. The following quote from the Kimberly-Clark Corporation (Letter No. 82) is representative of the sentiment of this group:

> We do not believe that the present auditor's standard report is in need of change. In our view, it has worked reasonably well for many years, is understood by auditors, preparers, and users of financial statements, is not fraught with overly technical language and its proposed replacement does not represent a clear improvement.

An unexpected result of the 1987 response letters is the reaction from the 36 individual CPAs responding to the ED. The letters of the individual CPAs appeared to be more emotional and, unlike the largely favorable reaction in 1980, the reaction of individual CPAs to the 1987 ED is largely split between agreement and disagreement with the ASB on its premise that the audit report needs modification. Overall positions of individuals in this group ranged from total agreement to total disagreement with the attempted report revision. The following quotes indicate both the emotion displayed by some of these individual CPAs, as well as their overall perceived need for a new audit report:

> Howard M. Siegman, CPA (Letter No. 122)
> I agree with this SAS . . . I am for anything that states things simpler and clearer for the user. I loved you for this SAS.

> George Botschin, CPA (Letter No. 5)
> The AICPA considering the changes [to the auditor's report] should have its management resign for a waste of time and our dues.

This group of 36 respondents presented comments to the ASB that were largely split on the desirability of a new report. This split between desire for a new report and condemnation for the attempted revision will be noted in the subsequent analyses. This result, however, is surprising for several reasons. First, the documented reaction in 1980 would have predicted that a large majority of individual practitioners would have been in favor of a report revision such as the one presented in the 1987 ED. Second, a considerable amount of research, and debate, has largely concluded that those least educated as to the role of an auditor in an audit might benefit from clearer and more accurate communication from the auditor in their report. Because individual practitioners may have a higher probability of interacting with this segment of users, a more positive response to the ED would have been expected. Finally, an analysis of the responses of the state and local CPA societies indicates overwhelming support for the impetus of the ASB's 1987 ED and its proposed report. These societies, for the most part, are representatives of smaller CPA firms and sole practitioners. The strongly positive response of these comment letters does not reflect the split between overall support and disapproval on the part of individual CPAs.

As noted in Chapter 3, the results obtained from this study cannot be validly generalized to any individual or group not responding to this ED due to a self-selection bias on the part of the respondents. Such a limitation is portrayed in the analysis of this group. Respondents may differ compared to nonrespondents on some aspect that has caused them to respond. This may have particularly been the case with the group of CPAs indicating vivid disagreement with this ED, especially if reaction of state and local CPA societies, smaller CPA firms, and the 1980 respondents is any indication of the overall reaction of local practicing CPAs to the need for a modified report.

Thus, with the exceptions noted above, the 1987 respondents indicated a general desire for a report revision in 1987. This generally positive reaction for a new report will be supported in subsequent detailed analyses.

Reaction to the ED Report.   Once a letter was identified as indicating that a new audit report was needed (Category 126), reaction to the specific report wording was assessed, including the potential phrase "intentionally or unintentionally," proposed in the ED. One of three overall reactions was identified for each of these respondents: (1) agreement with the report in the ED without any modification-Category 128; (2) agreement with the report in the ED, but offers suggestions for its improvement—Category 129; and (3) disagree with the report in the ED unless suggested modifications are made—Category 130. These three categories are presented in Table 6.6 and provide more detail for the overall agreement that the existing report needs to be modified. These categories draw attention to reactions concerning the specific report proposed in the ED.

Also, if a firm or individual indicated that, overall, a new report was not needed (Category 125), but then went on in their response to indicate agreement with a proposed change, or made suggested modifications of their own, then Category 131 was coded. These commentors, in effect, have indicated their overall desire for no report change, but have attempted to influence the ASB in the event of a new auditor's report wording. These overall reactions to the proposed report in the ED are summarized in Table 6.6.

The analysis presented in Table 6.6 has categorized a respondent in Category 129, even if the only aspect of the report that was indicated as undesirable was the potential inclusion of the phrase "intentionally or unintentionally" in the scope paragraph. As will be discussed in the next chapter, the potential inclusion of this phrase was quickly withdrawn by the ASB in its first meeting concerning this ED. This classification process, then, has included a considerable number of respondents who desired a modification (specifically "intentionally and unintentionally") which was subsequently addressed and very likely resolved to the respondent's satisfaction.

The ED report version was considered in its entirety as issued on February 14, 1987, without consideration of subsequent modifications. This process, viewed in retrospect, is conservative in its assessment of the general positive response to the ED and particularly to the final report version. However, it is an appropriate measure of reaction to the ED report as actually proposed, and also helps to give an indication of the impact the comment letters actually had on the ASB in finalizing *SAS 58*.

Table 6.6 highlights differences among groups regarding overall reaction to the report in the ED. David Landsittel indicated early on to the researcher

Table 6.6. Overall Reaction to the ED Report

Respondent Group	N	ED Report Is Acceptable Without Modification (Cat. 128)		ED Report Is Acceptable and Offers Modifications (Cat. 129)		ED Report Is Acceptable Only With Modifications (Cat. 130)		ED Report Is Not Acceptable, but .... (Cat. 131)	
I. *Public Auditors*									
Big Eight CPA firms	(7)	14%	(1)	29%	(2)	29%	(2)	14%	(1)
Next 15 largest CPA firms	(5)	0	(0)	80	(4)	0	(0)	20	(1)
Smaller CPA firms	(49)	12	(6)	52	(25)	6	(3)	6	(3)
Individual CPAs	(36)	19	(7)	25	(9)	6	(2)	22	(8)
State and local CPA societies	(18)	6	(1)	71	(13)	6	(1)	0	(0)
AICPA officials and committees	(8)	0	(0)	63	(5)	0	(0)	0	(0)
II. *Governmental Audit Agencies*									
State and local municipal auditors	(12)	0	(0)	50	(6)	0	(0)	17	(2)
Federal governmental audit agencies	(3)	33	(1)	0	(0)	33	(1)	0	(0)
III. *Issuers*									
SEC-filing corporations	(9)	0	(0)	44	(4)	0	(0)	44	(4)
Non-SEC-filing corporations	(2)	0	(0)	50	(1)	0	(0)	0	(0)
Governmental and not-for-profit agencies	(3)	0	(0)	100	(3)	0	(0)	0	(0)
Organizations representing issuers	(4)	0	(0)	75	(3)	0	(0)	25	(1)
IV. *Academics*	(19)	11	(2)	57	(11)	16	(3)	5	(1)
V. *Lawyers and Legal Groups*	(3)	0	(0)	100	(3)	0	(0)	0	(0)
VI. *Report Users and User Groups*	—	—		—		—		—	
VII. *Miscellaneous Respondents*	(5)	40	(2)	20	(1)	0	(0)	0	(0)
Total	(183)	11%	(20)	49%	(90)	7%	(12)	11%	(21)

Note: ( ) indicates raw number.

137

that he felt there was an overall agreement within the profession that a new report was needed, but that agreement on just how a new report should be worded "would not come easily." The general consensus of auditor groups depicted in Table 6.5 indicating agreement with changing the report is not as readily apparent in Table 6.6 when addressing a specific report rewording proposed in the ED.

Big Eight accounting firms indicated a strong support for a new report, yet Table 6.6 indicates relative disagreement as to the desirability of the ED wording. One firm appeared to agree with the ED report without modification, while two firms indicated that modifications would enhance the proposed report, and still two more indicated that they would only support the proposed report if it was appropriately modified to address their concerns. Of the two Big Eight firms indicating that a new audit report was not needed, one went on to suggest modifications to the ED report in order to indicate their position on the specific report wording in the ED in the event of a new audit report adoption.

This lack of consensus regarding the ED report was not noted, however, with the respondents from the next 15 largest CPA firms. These responding firms indicated that the ED report was potentially acceptable, but that specific modifications would enhance its desirability. The sole firm indicating that no new report was needed nevertheless offered comments on the ED report wording.

A majority (52%) of the smaller CPA firms indicated that some improvements could be made on the ED report, while a relatively large percentage (12%) felt that the proposed report was acceptable as exposed. Six percent of this group felt that the ED report would only be acceptable if changes were made, while another 6 percent, although not believing a new report was needed, offered specific comments on the report in the ED.

Table 6.6 also serves to highlight the wide disparity of opinion about the proposed report from the individual CPA group. Of the 50 percent wanting a new report, almost half believed the proposed report was acceptable without modification, while the other half believed modification would improve the proposed report. Only 6 percent felt so strongly as to agree with the proposed report only if their suggestions were implemented. Of the 42 percent not wanting a new report, over half still offered comments concerning the proposed report. Thus, the aggregate positions for this group were as follows: No new report needed, no comments on the ED report (20%); no new report needed, but comments offered (22%); ED acceptable as is (19%); ED basically acceptable, but enhancements could be made (25%); and ED only acceptable if concerns are addressed (6%). This wide dispersion in opinion concerning the ED is similar to the opinion presented by the responding Big Eight firms. Again, this pattern for the individual CPAs was not as positive as expected given the comments received by the 1980 respondents, and those of smaller

CPA firms and the state and local CPA societies. It should be noted, however, that this group did have the highest percentage among the public audit groups for the approval of the ED report as presented. The results on Tables 6.5 and 6.6 indicate that this respondent group had no clear overall desire for a new report or for the proposed report.

Of the remaining groups responding, the majority of respondents favoring issuance of a new audit report believed that the report presented in the ED could be made more desirable with some modification (typically the elimination of "intentionally or unintentionally"). It is also interesting to note that, in all these groups, a majority of respondents indicating that no new audit report was needed still presented comments and their respective positions regarding some aspect of the exposed report wording.

In the aggregate, 10 percent of the letters indicated that a new report was not needed and offered no comment on the ED report; 11 percent of the letters indicated that no new report was needed, but still offered comments on the proposed report; 11 percent approved of the ED report without modification; 49 percent approved of the need for a new report but believed that the report presented in the ED could be enhanced; 7 percent of the respondents indicated the need for a new report, but believed the ED report to be deficient unless their concerns were addressed and appropriate modifications implemented; and 12 percent of the letters did not offer sufficient commentary to properly classify them other than as "indeterminant."

Perceptions of Communicative Characteristics

The comment letters were also read to determine references to the communicative value of both the existing audit report and the report proposed in the ED as compared to the existing audit report. Only those letters commenting on these items were coded, thus the mutually exclusive pairs of categories depicted in Table 6.7 do not necessarily sum to 100 percent.

The first two categories in Table 6.7—current report is an adequate communication to report readers (Category 138) and current report is not an adequate communication to report readers (Category 139)—indicate the same general pattern as depicted in Table 6.5 for the overall reaction to the need for a new audit report. Such results are not surprising and lend some credibility to the consistency of both sets of codings.

The second pair of categories captures the respondent's assessment of the communicative value of the proposed report in the ED in comparison to the existing report wording. Again, explicit references had to be identified for Category 140 (the report in the ED will be a more adequate communication to report readers) and Category 141 (the report in the ED will not be a more adequate communication to report readers). As would be expected, a pattern similar to Tables 6.3 and 6.4 emerges. Big Eight firms, individual CPAs, and

Table 6.7. Perceptions of Communicative Value

Respondent Group	N	Current Report Is An Adequate Communication (Cat. 138)		Current Report Is Not an Adequate Communication (Cat. 139)		Current Report Is a More Adequate Communication (Cat. 140)		Current Report Is Not a More Adequate Communication (Cat. 141)	
I. Public Auditors									
Big Eight CPA firms	(7)	29%	(2)	71%	(5)	43%	(3)	57%	(4)
Next 15 largest CPA firms	(5)	20	(1)	60	(3)	60	(3)	20	(1)
Smaller CPA firms	(49)	10	(5)	35	(17)	43	(21)	16	(8)
Individual CPAs	(36)	17	(6)	28	(10)	25	(9)	28	(10)
State and local CPA societies	(18)	6	(1)	44	(8)	61	(11)	11	(2)
AICPA officials and committees	(8)	0	(0)	25	(2)	25	(2)	0	(0)
II. Governmental Audit Agencies									
State and local municipal auditors	(12)	8	(1)	33	(4)	33	(4)	8	(1)
Federal governmental audit agencies	(3)	0	(0)	67	(2)	33	(1)	33	(1)
III. Issuers									
SEC-filing corporations	(9)	44	(4)	33	(3)	33	(3)	56	(5)
Non-SEC-filing corporations	(2)	0	(0)	0	(0)	0	(0)	0	(0)
Governmental and not-for-profit agencies	(3)	0	(0)	67	(2)	67	(2)	0	(0)
Organizations representing issuers	(4)	25	(1)	25	(1)	50	(2)	25	(1)
IV. Academics	(19)	6	(1)	37	(7)	42	(8)	6	(1)
V. Lawyers and Legal Groups	(3)	0	(0)	67	(2)	67	(2)	0	(0)
VI. Report Users and User Groups	—	—		—		—		—	
VII. Miscellaneous Respondents	(5)	20	(1)	40	(2)	40	(2)	20	(1)
Total	(183)	13%	(23)	37%	(68)	40%	(73)	19%	(35)

Note: ( ) indicates raw number.

SEC registrants, if they indicated a comparison of the report as presented in the ED to the existing report, believed that the ED report was not an improved communication to report readers. This is a result of the Big Eight and individual CPA's desire to modify the ED report prior to a final adoption, and the SEC registrant group's premise that the existing report did not need revision in the first place.

Again, this analysis is based on the proposed report in the ED without taking into consideration any subsequent modifications of the proposed report. Based on the written responses, a subsequent comparison of the finally adopted standard audit report to the existing audit report would have certainly produced different results, and in the researcher's estimation, considerably more respondents (especially the Big Eight and individual CPAs) would have viewed the final report wording more favorably and would have believed it to be a better communication than the existing audit report. Unfortunately, this direct comparison cannot be performed and this observation is only an informed speculation.

The remaining "overall" response categories, with the exception of Categories 136 and 137, are presented in Table 6.8. Category 136 (explicit indication that the current report is a symbol) and Category 137 (explicit indication that any new report will remain a symbol) were both mentioned in only two response letters and have been excluded from further analysis. Although there has been discussion in the academic and practitioner literature of the current report being a mere symbol of the auditor's work and not a substantive communication to readers, not many respondents explicitly referred to audit reports as symbols. Some other comments may have been interpreted as such, however, very few direct references were made to this "symbolic" aspect of the standard auditor's report.

Table 6.8 presents a pattern similar to Table 6.5; more respondent groups mention that the present time was right for an audit report revision than indicate that the auditor's role did not need to be communicated better in the report, or that the purpose of the auditor's report was to present audit results and not to "educate" report readers. A few comment letters specifically stated that they believed that only relatively knowledgeable users read the audit report and that is why no real "educational" purpose needs to be pursued in the report. Again, all groups, except individual CPAs and SEC filers, more often referred to the time as being right (Category 133) than to the lack of need for better communication between auditors and users through the audit report.

In general, the audit report itself was portrayed by those indicating a need for change, as not *the* way of communicating to user groups and educating them as to the role of the auditor and the process of an audit, but as an

Table 6.8. Remaining "Overall" Categories

Respondent Group	N	Time is Right to Modify Report (Cat. 133)		Auditor's Role Does Not Need to Be Communicated Better in the Report (Cat. 134)		The Purpose of Report is to Present Results, Not Educate (Cat. 135)		Only Knowledgeable Useres Read the Audit Report (Cat. 132)	
I. *Public Auditors*									
Big Eight CPA firms	(7)	71%	(5)	29%	(2)	29%	(2)	0%	(0)
Next 15 largest CPA firms	(5)	40	(2)	20	(1)	20	(1)	0	(0)
Smaller CPA firms	(49)	31	(15)	14	(7)	12	(6)	2	(1)
Individual CPAs	(36)	14	(5)	28	(10)	17	(6)	6	(2)
State and local CPA societies	(18)	33	(6)	6	(1)	0	(0)	0	(0)
AICPA officials and committees	(8)	25	(2)	0	(0)	0	(0)	0	(0)
II. *Governmental Audit Agencies*									
State and local municipal auditors	(12)	33	(4)	8	(1)	0	(0)	0	(0)
Federal governmental audit agencies	(3)	33	(1)	0	(0)	33	(1)	0	(0)
III. *Issuers*									
SEC-filing corporations	(9)	11	(1)	56	(5)	0	(0)	0	(0)
Non-SEC-filing corporations	(2)	0	(0)	0	(0)	0	(0)	0	(0)
Governmental and not-for-profit agencies	(3)	33	(1)	0	(0)	0	(0)	0	(0)
Organizations representing issuers	(4)	25	(1)	25	(1)	25	(1)	0	(0)
IV. *Academics*	(19)	53	(10)	5	(1)	0	(0)	0	(0)
V. *Lawyers and Legal Groups*	(3)	67	(2)	0	(0)	0	(0)	0	(0)
VI. *Report Users and User Groups*	—	—		—		—		—	
VII. *Miscellaneous Respondents*	(5)	40	(2)	0	(0)	0	(0)	0	(0)
Total	(183)	31%	(57)	16%	(29)	9%	(19)	2%	(3)

Note: ( ) indicates raw number.

important component in the communication process. A representative comment from Deloitte, Haskins & Sells (Letter No. 2) reads as follows:

> We support the issuance of the proposed statement because we believe that the revised form of report does a substantially better job of communicating the nature of the auditor's work, the level of assurance provided by an audit and the auditor's conclusions about the financial statements. We believe that the current report is generally misunderstood and is, as a result, treated as a symbol that is often not read...we believe it is time that a change is made. We realize that the revised report will not solve the communication problem by itself, but it will represent an essential part of the solution to this problem.

Likewise, a few comment letters were adamant in their belief that the purpose of the auditor's report, was in no way to "educate" report readers. For instance:

> William V. Allen, Jr., CPA (Letter No. 133)
> Let's do a better job responding to the public's needs instead of trying to protect ourselves ... Let's educate CPAs, not the public. Educating the public is "Not Our Business."

> R. L. Daniels, Jr., CPA (Letter No. 3)
> Auditing is a *technical* occupation and technical language is required ... Non-CPA's should not ever be expected to understand verbiage of a CPA, i.e., you don't understand medical terms, but you do what the doctor advises anyway (emphasis in original).

> J. R. Deputy of Deputy, Montgomery, Inc., CPAs (Letter No. 14)
> Since we are not trying to address the average high school dropout, I cannot see the reason for any changes.

This section has depicted the response letters as to their overall agreement with the need for a new auditor's report, or their belief that currently no report modification is needed. The overwhelming majority (67%) of the response letters were in favor of a new audit report, while only 21 percent were opposed to a modified audit report. The one group not in favor of a new report were the SEC registrants, while only half of individual CPAs were in favor of changing the report wording. Assessments as to the desirability of the audit report proposed in the ED were also made. A large majority of those supporting the effort for a new audit report felt that the wording of the ED report could be enhanced by some modification.

The analysis was based on the exact report wording proposed in the ED. With an overriding desire for a report modification on the part of the respondents, the ASB set out in 1987 to modify and finalize the exact audit report wording. The next sections will discuss the responses to specific issues regarding the wording of the audit report presented in the ED.

Actual Wording of the Proposed Report

This section will discuss the respondents' comments on Categories 17 through 108. These categories were established to capture the respondents' agreement or disagreement with specific wording issues regarding the audit report proposed in the ED, as well as alternate wordings suggested by the respondents that were not initially included in the ED.

Many response letters explicitly indicated their agreement or disagreement with the wording of parts or all of the proposed audit report by directly stating their position. Others, however, stated a particular position and then suggested an alternative wording in their letter to illustrate their preferred verbiage. Still others did not specifically state their position on an issue, but offered suggested rewordings without direct comment on any specific issue. Categories 107 and 108 captured the occurrences of letters that included suggested rewordings of part or all of the proposed report, respectively. In all, the ASB received 50 letters that offered alternative wordings for part of the proposed report and another 17 letters that offered illustrations of respondents' preferred wording for the entire report. Thus, 67 comment letters (37% of all letters) offered actual alternative rewordings to the ASB for consideration. Some rewordings included relatively small changes while others offered considerable departures from the proposed audit report. All of these positions, whether explicitly stated or directly implied from any alternate wording presented, were included in the remaining Categories 17 to 106. However, only the prominent and more interesting results will be discussed in this section. A final summary of the content analysis coding results for all categories is presented in Appendix II, which presents the mean of each category in total and by respondent group.

Historical Issues.   Several historical issues concerning the possible revision of the auditor's report were identified and summarized at the end of Chapter 2. In several instances it is difficult to make a direct comparison between the changes proposed in 1987 and those proposed in earlier revision attempts. The exact placement, particular wording, and the overall responses elicited by each proposed report have differed. Nevertheless, it is important to determine how the respondents perceived the ASB's attempt to resolve these issues in 1987. First, the more comparable modification proposals will be addressed, followed by the remaining proposals.

Identical Changes.   Table 6.9 presents the results for three changes in 1987 that are identical to earlier modification attempts. This table also indicates the overall agreement or disagreement with these proposed changes in 1980 as reported by Mitchell (1983).

Independent—The proposed requirement to include the word independent in the report title is not new and received relatively little comment in 1987.

Table 6.9. Proposed Modifications Identical to Earlier Revision Attempts

Respondent Group	N	Add "Independent" Agree (Cat.18)	Add "Independent" Disagree (Cat. 19)	"Audited" Agree (Cat. 25)	"Audited" Disagree (Cat. 26)	Delete "Consistency" Agree (Cat. 104)	Delete "Consistency" Disagree (Cat. 105)
I. *Public Auditors*							
Big Eight CPA firms	(7)	14% (1)	0% (0)	43% (3)	14% (1)	57% (4)	43% (3)
Next 15 largest CPA firms	(5)	20 (1)	20 (1)	40 (2)	0 (0)	40 (2)	0 (0)
Smaller CPA firms	(49)	16 (8)	2 (1)	20 (10)	2 (1)	16 (8)	8 (4)
Individual CPAs	(36)	19 (7)	3 (1)	22 (8)	3 (1)	22 (8)	14 (5)
State and local CPA societies	(18)	6 (1)	6 (1)	22 (4)	6 (1)	17 (3)	0 (0)
AICPA officials and committees	(8)	0 (0)	0 (0)	0 (0)	0 (0)	13 (1)	13 (1)
II. *Governmental Audit Agencies*							
State and local municipal	(12)	8 (1)	0 (0)	25 (3)	0 (0)	25 (3)	8 (1)
Federal governmental audit agencies	(3)	0 (0)	0 (0)	0 (0)	0 (0)	0 (0)	33 (0)
III. *Issuers*							
SEC-filing corporations	(9)	33 (3)	0 (0)	33 (3)	22 (2)	0 (0)	67 (6)
Non-SEC-filing corporations	(2)	0 (0)	0 (0)	50 (1)	0 (0)	50 (1)	0 (0)
Governmental and not-for-profit agencies	(3)	0 (0)	0 (0)	33 (1)	0 (0)	0 (0)	33 (1)
Organizations representing issuers	(4)	25 (1)	0 (0)	25 (1)	0 (0)	0 (0)	0 (0)
IV. Academics	(19)	26 (5)	0 (0)	21 (4)	0 (0)	26 (5)	11 (2)
V. Lawyers and Legal Groups	(3)	67 (2)	0 (0)	33 (1)	0 (0)	33 (1)	33 (1)
VI. Report Users and User Groups	—	—	—	—	—	—	—
VII. Miscellaneous Respondents	(5)	0 (0)	0 (0)	0 (0)	0 (0)	0 (0)	0 (0)
Total	(183)	16% (30)	2% (4)	22% (41)	3% (6)	20% (36)	14% (25)
Totals from 1980 Responses		55%	11%	61%	20%	47%	30%

Note: ( ) indicates raw number.

145

Only 34 out of the 183 letters, commented on this item, with 30 in favor of the addition and 4 not in favor of the addition (Categories 18 and 19, respectively). This "modification" to the report appears to have elicited very little interest on the part of the 1987 respondents, but in general, appears to be a favorable change.

Audited—As in earlier modification attempts, the 1987 ED also proposed to change the reference from "examined" to "audited." Twenty-two percent (41) of all respondents indicated agreement with the modification, while only 3 percent (6) of respondents did not favor the change (Categories 25 and 26, respectively). Again, respondents appeared to generally agree with this modification in 1987 and 1980 that attempted to more accurately state that an "audit" was performed in regard to the financial statements.

Consistency—Presently, consistent application of GAAP is required under Accounting Principles Board (APB) Opinion No. 20. The ASB, in 1980 and 1987, proposed to delete all reference to consistency in the standard auditor's report. The reasoning behind such a deletion, as outlined in the ED, was that to properly conform to GAAP (including APB No. 20), financial statements must either consistently apply their adopted generally accepted accounting principles, or state in the financial statements that a change has been made. This requirement of APB No. 20, in essence, requires disclosure of changes in adopted GAAP within the financial statements. If no mention of a change is made, then a departure from GAAP results, which would require an "except for" qualified report on the part of the auditor. Hence, the reference to consistency is technically not necessary in the standard unqualified auditor's report after reference to the adherence to GAAP has been made. This deletion was also proposed in CAR's audit report in 1978.

Categories 104 and 105 indicate the positions of the respondents to the 1987 ED on the deletion of the reference to consistency in the opinion paragraph. The reaction to this proposal was largely mixed. Of the 61 respondents commenting on this change, 36 (20% of all letters) were in favor of the change, while 25 (14% of all letters) indicated disagreement with this deletion.

This divided respondent opinion will be shown to have eventually filtered into the ASB discussions regarding this issue. In general, all respondent groups mentioning this item, except SEC filers and federal audit agencies, were in favor of this modification. The same general pattern of response was noted in 1980. All groups except for the users and issuers of financial statements were in agreement with the deletion of the reference to consistency, while the large CPA firms and state societies were evenly split on the issue in 1980 (Mitchel 1983). Hence, the "proper" handling of the reference to consistency in the auditor's report was neither decisively resolved by respondents in 1980, nor in 1987. However, more respondents approved of the deletion than disapproved.

Similar Changes. In addition to suggesting changes that were "identical" to earlier modification attempts, the ASB in 1987 also suggested changes that were "similar," but not identical to earlier proposed reports. These themes were identified in Chapter 2 as recurring themes with respect to the auditor's report, however, the approach to resolving these issues is different in 1987 compared to earlier modification attempts. These "similar" modifications and the reaction to them are summarized in Table 6.10.

Management's representation—The 1980 proposed report began with a statement that the accompanying financial statements "are management's representations." This initial statement was viewed in 1980 as overly negative and was perceived by some as an attempt to artificially reduce auditor responsibility (Mitchell 1983). Inclusion of a statement regarding management's role in the financial reporting process was an attempt to address problems borne out by earlier research (surveyed in Chapter 3) and a belief within the profession that a considerable number of audit report users attribute financial statement responsibility to the auditor and not to management. Because of this apparent misperception, an explicit statement regarding management's role was deemed a necessary addition to the auditor's report.

In 1987, the ASB attempted to include the same explicit message in the ED, but with a less negative tone. Hence, this statement was not the first sentence of the proposed report, but was made as the second sentence in the introductory paragraph, following an explanation that the financial statements have been audited. Thus, the same message was communicated—"the financial statements are representations of X Company's management"—but its placement in the second sentence diminished the impression that the audit report was a self-serving attempt at limiting auditor responsibility.

In 1987, respondents were generally in favor of this modification, except for the SEC-filing corporations. Sixty-seven percent of the SEC filers did not favor the inclusion of the statement that financial statements were representations of the company's management, nor did the FEI favor this statement in its response to the ASB. However, if the wording of the phrase was modified to say management's "responsibility" instead of management's "representation" (Category 22), 15 of the 27 respondents disagreeing with the specific proposed ED wording would have favored inclusion of the statement. Of those 15 who preferred "responsibility" over "representations," four were among the six SEC-filing corporations indicating disagreement with the ED proposed wording, and another was the FEI. Use of the term "responsibility" was later adopted by the ASB and will be discussed in the next chapter. In sum, most 1987 respondents favored the inclusion of a statement explicitly stating management's role, especially if the term "responsibility" instead of "representation" was adopted.

Reasonable assurance—A sentence including the words "reasonable assurance" was included in the 1987 ED, as was a similar sentence in 1980.

Table 6.10. Proposed Modifications Similar to Earlier Revision Attempts

Respondent Group	N	Statement About Management Representation		Add "Reasonable Assurance"		Add "In All Material Respects"	
		Agree (Cat. 20)	Disagree (Cat. 21)	Agree (Cat. 51)	Disagree (Cat. 52)	Agree (Cat. 92)	Disagree (Cat. 93)
I. *Public Auditors*							
Big Eight CPA firms	(7)	29% (2)	29% (2)	43 (3)	29% (2)	43% (3)	0% (0)
Next 15 largest CPA firms	(5)	20 (1)	40 (2)	40 (2)	0 (0)	60 (3)	0 (0)
Smaller CPA firms	(49)	27 (13)	10 (5)	25 (12)	16 (8)	10 (5)	8 (4)
Individual CPAs	(36)	28 (10)	11 (4)	14 (5)	17 (6)	19 (7)	8 (3)
State and local CPA societies	(18)	17 (3)	11 (2)	39 (7)	6 (1)	17 (3)	0 (0)
AICPA officials and committees	(8)	0 (0)	0 (0)	50 (4)	0 (0)	0 (0)	0 (0)
II. *Governmental Audit Agencies*							
State and local municipal	(12)	25 (3)	33 (4)	8 (1)	8 (1)	25 (3)	8 (1)
Federal governmental audit agencies	(3)	0 (0)	0 (0)	0 (0)	0 (0)	0 (0)	0 (0)
III. *Issuers*							
SEC-filing corporations	(9)	11 (1)	67 (6)	11 (1)	56 (5)	33 (3)	22 (2)
Non-SEC-filing corporations	(2)	50 (1)	0 (0)	50 (1)	0 (0)	50 (1)	0 (0)
Governmental and not-for-profit agencies	(3)	33 (1)	33 (1)	0 (0)	0 (0)	0 (0)	0 (0)
Organizations representing issuers	(4)	25 (1)	25 (1)	0 (0)	25 (1)	25 (1)	0 (0)
IV. *Academics*	(19)	32 (6)	0 (0)	21 (4)	0 (0)	11 (2)	5 (1)
V. *Lawyers and Legal Groups*	(3)	33 (1)	0 (0)	33 (1)	0 (0)	33 (1)	0 (0)
VI. *Report Users and User Groups*	—	—	—	—	—	—	—
VII. *Miscellaneous Respondents*	(5)	0 (0)	0 (0)	20 (1)	0 (0)	0 (0)	0 (0)
Total	(183)	24% (43)	15% (27)	23% (42)	13% (24)	18% (32)	6% (11)
Totals from 1980 Responses		47%	27%	40%	30%	NA	NA

Note: ( ) indicates raw number.

148

However, the 1980 reference to reasonable assurance was qualified with the words "but not absolute," to read "reasonable, but not absolute, assurance." The addition of this concept of *reasonable* assurance is similar in the two drafts, however, the wording surrounding the phrase implies a slightly different meaning. Overall, the inclusion of "reasonable assurance" was favorably received in 1987 by all groups except SEC filers and organizations representing issuers. These two groups were also not in favor of the 1980 proposed wording regarding this potential addition (Mitchell 1983). The analysis in 1987 has also attempted to identify whether the respondents preferred the qualifier "but not absolute" when referring to reasonable assurance, as was proposed in 1980. Of those for which a determination could be made, 14 percent did not favor including "but not absolute," while 8 percent did prefer inclusion of such a phrase. The majority of those in favor of adding "but not absolute" came from smaller CPA firms and state and local CPA societies. These two groups were also noted by Mitchell (1983) to have had the highest rate of approval for the 1980 ED report wording of this item.

Some of the noted dissatisfaction with this wording in 1980 was, again, that it sounded too negative and self-serving and should be properly modified or eliminated from further consideration. The majority of those disagreeing with the inclusion of "reasonable assurance" in 1987 were not disagreeing specifically with this item, but were in general disagreement that the auditor's report should attempt to more explicitly discuss the nature of an audit in the auditor's report.

In all material respects—In 1987, the ASB proposed inclusion of the phrase "in all material respects" in the opinion paragraph. This addition was not proposed in 1980, but was proposed by CAP and CAR in their suggested report modifications. This suggested modification was the latest attempt to address the continuing variation in interpreting "presents fairly in conformity with GAAP" in the opinion paragraph. The CAP and CAR reports suggested that the term "fairly" be dropped from the report and that the phrase "in all material respects" be inserted in its place. In 1980, the ASB decided that the term "fairly" should be dropped, but did not propose that the phrase "in all material respects" take its place. Earlier discussion of this 1980 ED focused on the problem created by this proposed modification and the eventual reinstatement of the term "fairly" by the ASB in later deliberations. Once the board reinstated "fairly," there was felt to be a lack of any substantive improvement over the existing report and the ED was rescinded in March 1981.

To combat this potential problem in 1987, the ASB addressed the issue of "fair presentation" in the scope paragraph and modified the opinion paragraph. The scope paragraph stated that auditors are to make an assessment of the overall financial statement presentation and disclosures; while the opinion paragraph stated that the financial statements are, "in all material respects, fairly presented in conformity with GAAP." Hence, the reference to "fairly" and inclusion of the phrase "in all material respects" was maintained in the ED.

Categories 92 and 93 (Table 6.10) indicate agreement and disagreement, respectively, with the inclusion of "in all material respects." Few respondents noted a preference either way on this item, indicating that it may have been perceived as a minor change proposed in the ED. All groups responding to this item generally favored inclusion and, in total, agreement to disagreement was about 3-to-1.

Categories 94 to 99 attempt to analyze respondents' positions with respect to the term "fairly," which was retained in the 1987 ED in the phrase "fairly presented." Respondents were coded as agreeing with the phrase "fairly presented" (Category 94) or disagreeing (Category 95). If disagreement was noted, several reasons may have been given: (1) the respondent preferred current wording, "present fairly" (Category 96); or (2) the respondent preferred deleting "fairly" because it is redundant (Category 97), or ambiguous (Category 98), or because conformity with GAAP leads to a fair presentation of financial statements (Category 99). Multiple reasons for the deletion of "fairly" were allowed for each respondent, so the total of Categories 97 through 99 is more than the actual number of response letters indicating that "fairly" should be deleted from the report. Table 6.11 presents the responses to this issue as indicated in the comment letters.

Table 6.11 indicates that of those responding to the issue of "fairly," 19 explicitly approved of the ASB's ED wording, and 22 disapproved. Of those 22 disapproving of "fairly presented," seven would prefer a reversal of the phrase to "present fairly," while the other 15 respondents (8% of all letters) would prefer to delete the term "fairly." The most often cited reason for deletion was that the term "fairly" is ambiguous and is not precisely defined by the auditing literature or the auditor's report. However, there appears to be very little support in 1987 for deleting the term "fairly." Tables 6.10 and 6.11 taken together indicate that, in general, the 1987 respondents were in agreement with the way the ASB approached and resolved the issue of "presents fairly in confirmity with GAAP" in the ED—by adding "in all material respects" and retaining "fairly."

No Changes Proposed. Along with proposing "identical" and "similar" changes to those proposed in earlier report modification attempts, the 1987 ED did not propose a possible modification to the report that was previously discussed and contemplated by the profession.

Internal control—An issue of continuing debate has been whether or not to mention auditor involvement, if any, with the client's system of internal control. Chapter 2 noted that audit reports preceding the existing report typically mentioned auditor involvement with the client's internal control system. The Treadway Commission in 1987 also concluded that the auditor's report should indicate the degree of auditor evaluation and reliance on internal control. The ASB, however, did not suggest such a report modification in the

Table 6.11. "Fairly Presented"

Respondent Group	N	"Fairly Presented"		Prefer "Present" Fairly (Cat. 96)	Disagree with "Fairly Presented"	Delete "Fairly"	
		Agree (Cat. 94)	Disagree (Cat. 95)		Redundant (Cat. 977)	Ambiguous (Cat. 98)	GAAP Leads to Fair... (Cat. 99)
I. Public Auditors							
Big Eight CPA firms	(7)	43% (3)	14% (1)	0% (0)	0% (0)	14% (1)	0% (0)
Next 15 largest CPA firms	(5)	60 (3)	0 (0)	0 (0)	0 (0)	0 (0)	0 (0)
Smaller CPA firms	(49)	12 (6)	4 (2)	6 (2)	4 (2)	2 (1)	2 (1)
Individual CPAs	(36)	8 (3)	19 (7)	6 (2)	6 (2)	6 (2)	6 (2)
State and local CPA societies	(18)	0 (0)	17 (3)	0 (0)	11 (2)	11 (2)	0 (0)
AICPA officials and committees	(8)	0 (0)	0 (0)	0 (0)	0 (0)	0 (0)	0 (0)
II. Governmental Audit Agencies							
State and local municipal	(12)	17 (2)	0 (0)	0 (0)	0 (0)	0 (0)	0 (0)
Federal governmental audit agencies	(3)	0 (0)	0 (0)	0 (0)	0 (0)	0 (0)	0 (0)
III. Issuers							
SEC-filing corporations	(9)	0 (0)	22 (2)	22 (2)	0 (0)	0 (0)	0 (0)
Non-SEC-filing corporations	(2)	50 (1)	50 (1)	0 (0)	0 (0)	50 (1)	50 (1)
Governmental and not-for-profit agencies	(3)	0 (0)	0 (0)	0 (0)	0 (0)	0 (0)	0 (0)
Organizations representing issuers	(4)	0 (0)	50 (2)	25 (1)	0 (0)	0 (0)	0 (0)
IV. Academics	(19)	5 (1)	16 (3)	11 (2)	0 (0)	0 (0)	5 (1)
V. Lawyers and Legal Groups	(3)	0 (0)	33 (1)	0 (0)	0 (0)	33 (1)	0 (0)
VI. Report Users and User Groups	—	—	—	—	—	—	—
VII. Miscellaneous Respondents	(5)	0 (0)	0 (0)	0 (0)	0 (0)	0 (0)	0 (0)
Total	(183)	10% (19)	12% (22)	4% (7)	3% (6)	4% (8)	3% (6)

Note: ( ) indicates raw number.

1987 ED. This research has additionally looked for respondents' agreement or disagreement with the continued lack of mention of internal control in the proposed report. Few respondents addressed this issue directly; however, their positions could often be determined through their suggested report wordings. Agreement and disagreement with the lack of mention of internal control in the auditor's report was measured by Categories 85 and 86, respectively. Additionally, Categories 87 through 89 indicate the occurrence of respondents' preferences to mention internal control in the report by means other than a standard sentence in the scope paragraph. The possible alternatives to a standard sentence mentioned by the respondents were: (1) mention in a separate new paragraph (Category 87); (2) mention in the report only if management refers to internal control in the management report (Category 88); and (3) mention in the report only if the auditor disagrees with management's assessment of internal control as depicted in the management report (Category 89). Table 6.12 presents the respondents' expressed views on mentioning internal control in the audit report.

Twenty-six percent of all respondents commented on this issue. Twenty-two percent indicated that they favored not mentioning the system of internal control in the auditor's report, while only 4 percent (7 respondents) indicated a preference for including the mention of internal control within the perview of the auditor's report. One comment letter indicated that internal control should be mentioned in a separate paragraph in the new report, one letter indicated a preference to mention internal control only if mentioned by management, and by deduction, the remaining five preferred that internal control be included as a standard part of the three-paragraph format—typically in the scope paragraph (one letter preferred mention in the introductory paragraph).

In order to address this issue, the AICPA prepared an "Issues Paper" in 1987 setting forth various alternatives for mentioning internal control in the auditor's report. This document anticipated the Treadway Commission's conclusions and will be discussed further in the next chapter. The 1987 respondents, however, resoundingly indicated agreeement not to mention internal control in the proposed revised auditor's report.

"New" Proposed Modifications. Several of the modifications proposed in the 1987 ED are relatively new to the debate surrounding the wording of the audit report. The largest proposed change was the substantial expansion of the scope paragraph to describe the nature of an audit. Although attempted in the 1980 and earlier proposed reports, the discussion in 1987 represented a considerable departure from most earlier modification attempts. The 1987 ED included several new additions in the reworded scope paragraph: (1) a statement that an audit is designed to evaluate whether the financial statements are materially misstated; (2) the possible addition of "intentionally or

Table 6.12. Internal Control

| Respondent Group | N | No Mention of Internal Control | | Ways to Include Other Than by Standard Sentence in Scope Paragraph | | |
		Agree (Cat. 85)	Disagree (Cat. 86)	Always in a Separate Paragraph (Cat. 87)	In a Paragraph if Management Mentions (Cat. 88)	In a Paragraph if Disagree with Management (Cat. 89)
I. *Public Auditors*						
Big Eight CPA firms	(7)	43% (3)	29% (2)	0% (0)	14% (1)	0%
Next 15 largest CPA firms	(5)	40 (2)	20 (1)	0 (0)	0 (0)	0
Smaller CPA firms	(49)	20 (10)	0 (0)	0 (0)	0 (0)	0
Individual CPAs	(36)	19 (7)	3 (1)	0 (0)	0 (0)	0
State and local CPA societies	(18)	28 (5)	6 (1)	0 (0)	0 (0)	0
AICPA officials and committees	(8)	0 (0)	0 (0)	0 (0)	0 (0)	0
II. *Governmental Audit Agencies*						
State and local municipal	(12)	17 (2)	0 (0)	0 (0)	0 (0)	0
Federal governmental audit agencies	(3)	0 (0)	3 (1)	0 (0)	0 (0)	0
III. *Issuers*						
SEC-filing corporations	(9)	56 (5)	0 (0)	0 (0)	0 (0)	0
Non-SEC-filing corporations	(2)	50 (1)	0 (0)	0 (0)	0 (0)	0
Governmental and not-for-profit agencies	(3)	0 (0)	0 (0)	0 (0)	0 (0)	0
Organizations representing issuers	(4)	25 (1)	0 (0)	0 (0)	0 (0)	0
IV. Academics	(19)	11 (2)	5 (1)	5 (1)	0 (0)	0
V. *Lawyers and Legal Groups*	(3)	33 (1)	0 (0)	0 (0)	0 (0)	0
VI. *Report Users and User Groups*	—	—	—	—	—	—
VII. *Miscellaneous Respondents*	(5)	20 (1)	0 (0)	0 (0)	0 (0)	0
Total	(183)	22% (40)	4% (7)	1% (1)	1% (1)	0%

Note: ( ) indicates raw number.

153

unintentionally" to modify materially misstated; (3) examining evidence on a test basis that supports amounts in the financial statements; (4) assessing the appropriateness of accounting principles used and estimates made by management; (5) assessing the appropriateness of the overall financial statement presentation and disclosures and (6) an explicit statement that the procedures performed were appropriate in the circumstances to express the opinion presented.

Category 57 indicates that only 8 percent of all respondents agreed with the exact wording of the sentence beginning with "Reasonable assurance," while 19 percent explicitly indicated that they would have preferred some type of editorial modification to make this long complex sentence easier to read and understand, and 10 percent of the respondents (mainly those who did not favor a new report) believed that this sentence should be eliminated entirely because no effort should be made to educate report readers as to the nature of an audit in the auditor's report.

Categories 60 through 78 capture the many issues included in the "Reasonable assurance" sentence. Several of the topics listed above have been broken down for the content analysis of the response letters. All of these categories will not be discussed in detail; however, overall reactions will be noted.

Seven percent of the respondents would have modified the report to more clearly indicate that the auditing procedures listed in the report are not all-inclusive. Twenty-one and 13 percent indicated agreement and disagreement, respectively, to inclusion of examining evidence "on a test basis" in the report. Fifteen percent of the respondents agreed and 19 percent disagreed with the use of the term "supports." Most of those disagreeing with "supports" believed that the verbiage in the report appeared to say that only collaborative, or "supporting" evidence is examined in an audit, but that potentially nonsupportive evidence is not examined. On the use of "amounts," 15 percent agreed while 16 percent disagreed with its inclusion. Four percent of the respondents felt that the report should be modified to include more than just financial statement "amounts." Fourteen percent agreed with the phrase "assessing the appropriateness of the accounting principles used," while 21 percent disagreed with this phrase. Nine percent (almost half) of these dissenters would modify the phrase to say "acceptability" or "reasonableness" of accounting principles instead of "appropriateness." Fourteen percent indicated agreement with "assessing the appropriateness" of the significant estimates made by management, while 18 percent disagreed. Four percent specifically indicated that "appropriateness" in this phrase should be modified to say "reasonableness" when referring to estimates made by management. Regarding "assessing the appropriateness of the overall financial statement presentation," 18 percent agreed and 14 percent disagreed with its inclusion. On the issue of assessing the appropriateness of "overall disclosures," 16 percent agreed and 14 percent disagreed with its inclusion.

These overall results indicate that, in general, few respondents reacted to these detailed items, but slightly rewording the report would appear to satisfy a significant number of those originally disagreeing with the wording proposed in the ED. The next chapter will discuss how the ASB eventually incorporated a number of the suggestions made in the comment letters regarding the scope paragraph, and this long sentence in particular.

With regard to the last sentence in the scope paragraph, 7 percent indicated that it was satisfactory as proposed, 10 percent indicated that it should be modified, and 14 percent believed it should be eliminated altogether. Those respondents indicating a need for modification or deletion of this sentence included not only those opposed to a new report, but all types of respondents. Typical modification suggestions either eliminated "in the circumstances" or "presented below" from the proposed wording of this sentence. In general, the comments indicated a pervasive desire to alter or eliminate the proposed last sentence of the scope paragraph.

In 1980, the proposed report stated that the purpose of an audit was to provide "reasonable, but not absolute, assurance as to whether financial statements taken as a whole are free of material misstatements." In 1987, the proposed report stated that the purpose of an audit is to "evaluate whether the financial statements are materially misstated." The 1987 reaction to this statement is included in Table 6.13. Respondents indicated a definite dislike of the phrase "materially misstated." Forty-two percent of the respondents indicated their position on this issue, with more than twice as many (29%) opposing it as favoring it (13%). Thirty-six out of 53 respondents in disagreement with "materially misstated" indicated their reason for dissatisfaction. Twenty-five (14%) felt the phrase was too negative in tone. The implication of the proposed report, as articulated by some respondents, was that financial statements are naturally in a state of material misstatement— which is certainly not the case. The wording was viewed as implying that management was attempting to misstate financial statements. Another 11 respondents (6%) indicated that the phrase should be more congruent with the opinion paragraph that states an opinion of "fair presentation." Multiple responses were allowed for these two categories of disapproval.

Of respondents offering suggested rewordings, 5 percent (9 letters) indicated that they preferred "not materially misstated," while 14 percent (25 letters) preferred "are fairly presented." Additionally, 8 percent (15 letters) explicitly indicated a preference to include mention of GAAP in the scope paragraph as well as in the opinion paragraph.

The overwhelming response from the 1987 letters was that the phrase "materially misstated" was too negative and generally not acceptable. The

Table 6.13. Materially Misstated

Respondent Group	N	Phrase "Materially Misstated" Agree (Cat. 35)	Disagree (Cat. 36)	Reasons for Disagreement — Lacks Congruence Without Opinion (Cat. 37)	Too Negative (Cat. 38)	Modify to Say "Not Materially Misstated" (Cat. 39)	Modify to Say "Are Fairly Presented" (Cat. 40)	Refer to GAAP in Scope Paragraph (Cat. 41)
I. Public Auditors								
Big Eight CPA firms	(7)	43% (3)	29% (2)	14% (1)	14% (1)	0% (0)	29% (2)	29% (2)
Next 15 largest CPA firms	(5)	0 (0)	40 (2)	20 (1)	20 (1)	20 (1)	20 (1)	20 (1)
Smaller CPA firms	(49)	8 (4)	31 (15)	8 (4)	12 (6)	4 (2)	12 (6)	4 (2)
Individual CPAs	(36)	6 (2)	28 (10)	6 (2)	8 (3)	3 (1)	8 (3)	8 (3)
State and local CPA societies	(18)	17 (3)	50 (9)	6 (1)	17 (3)	11 (2)	22 (4)	17 (3)
AICPA officials and committees	(8)	25 (2)	25 (2)	13 (1)	13 (1)	0 (0)	13 (1)	13 (1)
II. Governmental Audit Agencies								
State and local municipal	(12)	17 (2)	8 (1)	8 (1)	8 (1)	0 (0)	8 (1)	0 (0)
Federal governmental audit agencies	(3)	0 (0)	0 (0)	0 (0)	0 (0)	0 (0)	0 (0)	0 (0)
III. Issuers								
SEC-filing corporations	(9)	0 (0)	56 (5)	0 (0)	44 (4)	0 (0)	11 (1)	11 (1)
Non-SEC-filing corporations	(2)	0 (0)	50 (1)	0 (0)	50 (1)	50 (1)	0 (0)	0 (0)
Governmental and not-for-profit agencies	(3)	0 (0)	0 (0)	0 (0)	0 (0)	0 (0)	0 (0)	0 (0)
Organizations representing issuers	(4)	0 (0)	75 (3)	0 (0)	75 (3)	25 (1)	50 (2)	25 (1)
IV. Academics	(19)	27 (5)	11 (2)	0 (0)	6 (1)	6 (1)	6 (1)	0 (0)
V. Lawyers and Legal Groups	(3)	0 (0)	33 (1)	0 (0)	0 (0)	0 (0)	0 (0)	33 (1)
VI. Report Users and User Groups	—	—	—	—	—	—	—	—
VII. Miscellaneous Respondents	(5)	40 (2)	0 (0)	0 (0)	0 (0)	0 (0)	0 (0)	0 (0)
Total	(183)	13% (23)	29% (53)	6% (11)	14% (25)	5% (9)	12% (22)	8% (15)

Note: ( ) indicates raw number.

issuers of financial statements in particular took exception to the proposed wording, with no respondents in favor of this wording as proposed.

The final specific wording issue to be addressed regarding the scope paragraph is the EDs inclusion of the possible modifiers "intentionally or unintentionally" to "material misstatement." As noted in Chapter 4, the board oscillated on whether or not to include in the report any reference to the auditor's responsibility for fraud, and if so, how to word that reference. The board did not resolve this issue and decided to solicit comments in the ED on the possible modifiers "intentionally and unintentionally," representing, in essence, "fraud and error."

This specific proposal was suggested by the ASB in order to receive feedback from respondents, and was enclosed in parentheses to emphasize that the addition was still being contemplated by the board at the time of exposure. More respondents commented on this proposal than any other item. In fact, this was the only issue that received comment by more than half of all the 1987 response letters. Table 6.14 presents the positions of the respondents.

The respondents indicated an overwhelming dissatisfaction with the possibility of "intentionally or unintentionally" being included in the auditor's report. Fully 55 percent of all respondents indicated disagreement with this item. Categories 45 through 49 capture some of the expressed disagreeement with the potential phrase (multiple responses permitted). Of those indicating the reasoning behind their disagreement, most felt that the inclusion of "intentionally or unintentionally" was irrelevant given the preceding wording of the report. A considerable number of respondents (30 letters) also felt the potential phrase projected a negative connotation toward management, or created more confusion than clarification in describing the auditor's role (28 letters). Also, 23 respondents felt that inclusion would extend auditor responsibility for detecting fraud. Additionally, Category 50 (not shown in the table) indicated that dissatisfaction was more with the idea of including modifiers to materially misstated, than with the actual two modifiers selected, because only two respondents indicated that an alternate set of modifiers would be preferable to the ones proposed. This resounding response in the comment letters will be shown to have caused the board to drop from further consideration the potential phrase "intentionally or unintentionally."

The final actual wording issue to be addressed is the proposed deletion from the opinion paragraph of "the financial position of X Company as of December 31, 19xx, and the results of its operations and changes in financial position for the year then ended." This deletion was not highlighted or identified in the cover letter to the ED that discussed the changes proposed. Subsequent discussion by the board in 1987 indicates explicitly that this modification was originally intended to be editorial, but was later considered to be a substantial change from the former report. Table 6.15 indicates that only a few of the respondents to this ED indicated a specific position on this proposed modification.

Table 6.14. "Intentionally or Unintentionally"

Respondent Group	N	"Intentionally or Unintentionally"		Reasons for Disagreement				
		Agree (Cat. 43)	Disagree (Cat. 44)	Irrelevant (Cat. 45)	Negative (Cat. 46)	Classify (Cat. 47)	Extended Responsibility Cat. 48	Confusing (Cat. 49)
I. *Public Auditors*								
Big Eight CPA firms	(7)	0% (0)	100% (7)	71% (5)	43% (3)	29% (2)	14% (1)	29% (2)
Next 15 largest CPA firms	(5)	40 (2)	60 (3)	20 (1)	20 (1)	0 (0)	40 (2)	0 (0)
Smaller CPA firms	(49)	4 (2)	49 (24)	12 (6)	14 (7)	6 (3)	14 (7)	12 (6)
Individual CPAs	(36)	11 (4)	28 (10)	3 (1)	8 (3)	3 (1)	6 (2)	6 (2)
State and local CPA societies	(18)	0 (0)	94 (17)	56 (10)	28 (5)	6 (1)	17 (3)	28 (5)
AICPA officials and committees	(8)	0 (0)	75 (6)	63 (5)	38 (3)	0 (0)	0 (0)	13 (1)
II. *Governmental Audit Agencies*								
State and local municipal	(12)	0 (0)	83 (10)	50 (6)	8 (1)	0 (0)	25 (3)	42 (5)
Federal governmental audit agencies	(3)	0 (0)	33 (1)	33 (1)	0 (0)	0 (0)	0 (0)	0 (0)
III. *Issuers*								
SEC-filing corporations	(9)	0 (0)	56 (5)	0 (0)	22 (2)	22 (2)	0 (0)	11 (1)
Non-SEC-filing corporations	(2)	0 (0)	50 (1)	0 (0)	50 (1)	0 (0)	50 (1)	50 (1)
Governmental and not-for-profit agencies	(3)	0 (0)	67 (2)	67 (2)	0 (0)	0 (0)	33 (1)	33 (1)
Organizations representing issuers	(4)	0 (0)	75 (3)	25 (1)	50 (2)	25 (1)	0 (0)	0 (0)
IV. Academics	(19)	21 (4)	47 (9)	11 (2)	11 (2)	16 (3)	16 (3)	16 (3)
V. *Lawyers and Legal Groups*	(3)	0 (0)	33 (1)	33 (1)	0 (0)	0 (0)	0 (0)	0 (0)
VI. *Report Users and User Groups*	—	—	—	—	—	—	—	—
VII. Miscellaneous Respondents	(5)	20 (1)	20 (1)	0 (0)	0 (0)	0 (0)	0 (0)	20 (1)
Total	(183)	7% (13)	55% (100)	22% (41)	16% (30)	7% (13)	13% (23)	15% (28)

Note: ( ) indicates raw number.

Table 6.15. "Delete Financial Position and Results of Operations . . ."

Respondent Group	N	Agree with deletion (Cat. 100)		Disagree with deletion (Cat. 101)	
I. *Public Auditors*					
Big Eight CPA firms	(7)	29%	(2)	14%	(1)
Next 15 largest CPA firms	(5)	40	(2)	0	(0)
Smaller CPA firms	(49)	14	(7)	0	(0)
Individual CPAs	(36)	11	(4)	8	(3)
State and local CPA societies	(18)	6	(1)	0	(0)
AICPA officials and committees	(8)	0	(0)	0	(0)
II. *Governmental Audit Agencies*					
State and local municipal auditors	(12)	17	(2)	0	(0)
Federal governmental audit agencies	(3)	0	(0)	0	(0)
III. *Issuers*					
SEC-filing corporations	(9)	0	(0)	33	(3)
Non-SEC-filing corporations	(2)	50	(1)	0	(0)
Governmental and not-for-profit agencies	(3)	0	(0)	0	(0)
Organizations representing issuers	(4)	0	(0)	50	(2)
IV. *Academics*	(19)	11	(2)	11	(2)
V. *Lawyers and Legal Groups*	(3)	33	(1)	0	(0)
VI. *Report Users and User Groups*	—	—	—	—	—
VII. *Miscellaneous Respondents*	(5)	0	(0)	0	(0)
Total	(183)	12%	(22)	6%	(11)

Note: ( ) indicates raw number.

This item was not typically discussed by the respondents, and those that did indicate a position most often preferred to delete the phrase. This low response rate may have been a function of not mentioning this change in the cover letter to the ED, and could also be because respondents may have also viewed the change as editorial and thus not worth particular attention. The discussion in the next chapter will indicate that even though there were few respondents to this issue, their comment letters had a significant impact on *SAS 58* and caused the ASB to readdress their original position in the ED.

This section has indicated that there was a considerable amount of diversity in the response patterns of groups to some issues, while other issues elicited similar responses from all groups. The most notable similarities in the letters were: (1) the overwhelming desire of all groups to drop "intentionally or unintentionally" from further consideration; (2) the dissatisfaction with "materially misstated"; (3) the general desire to modify the scope paragraph to make it more readable and to clearly and more accurately describe the nature of an audit, including the discussion of some of the factors involved in an audit; (4) the general agreement on the modification of fairly presents in conformity with GAAP to include "in all material respects"; (5) to retain the term "fairly," and (6) the general agreement that the auditor's report should not refer to the client's system of internal control.

Modifications to the Standard Unqualified Audit Report

The 1987 ED included in an appendix examples of five auditor report modifications to illustrate how the proposed new wording would be implemented for reports other than the standard unqualified audit report. Examples of report modifications were presented for: (1) qualifications of opinion due to a departure from GAAP; (2) qualifications of opinion because of a scope limitation; (3) modifications of the report due to an uncertainty; (4) adverse opinions; and (5) disclaimers of opinion due to a scope limitation. Categories 109, 110, 111, 121, 123 measure the number of response letters commenting on the report modifications presented in the ED. All of these report illustrations, except the modification for uncertainty, received comments from 6 percent or less of all respondents. Most of the respondents appeared more interested in commenting on the standard report or the modification for uncertainty than on the other illustrations of new report language, probably because these other illustrations are basically driven by the wording of the standard unqualified report. These other report wordings will not be discussed further. Twenty-five percent of the respondents, however, did include comments on the report modified for an uncertainty. *Statement of Financial Accounting Standards (SFAS) 5, Accounting for Contingencies*, requires financial statement disclosure of material unresolved uncertainties. The lack of appropriate disclosure would be considered an exception to GAAP. Thus, because disclosure is required by GAAP, all the relevant information should, theoretically, be included in the financial statements and no reference to uncertainties, if properly disclosed, would be necessary in the auditor's report. However, if material uncertainties exist at the balance sheet date, under *SAS 2*, the auditor is generally required to qualify the audit opinion "subject to" the effect on the financial statements, if any, of the resolution of the uncertainty, and refer the reader to the appropriate footnote disclosures in the financial statements.

In 1987, the ASB proposed to eliminate the former "subject to" qualified report and replace it with an unqualified report that refers to the footnote disclosures discussing the existing uncertainty. Table 6.16 presents the numbers and percentages of respondents in favor and not in favor of the elimination of the "subject to" report and the related issues regarding the proposed new language for "uncertainty" reports.

In general, the reaction to the elimination of the "subject to" report category received a mixed blessing. The Big Eight CPA firms typically agreed with the proposed elimination, along with all of the AICPA officials, academics, and

Table 6.16. Reports on Uncertainty

Respondent Group	N	Referred to Report on Uncertainty (Cat. 111)	Eliminate "Subject to" Agree (Cat. 112)	Eliminate "Subject to" Disagree (Cat. 113)	Actual Wording Proposed in ED Agree (Cat. 114)	Actual Wording Proposed in ED Disagree (Cat. 115)	Does Not Properly Highlight Uncertainty (Cat. 116)	Separate Paragraph is Needed (Cat. 117)
I. Public Auditors								
Big Eight CPA firms	(7)	100% (7)	71% (5)	29% (2)	57% (4)	29% (2)	29% (2)	29% (2)
Next 15 largest CPA firms	(5)	80 (4)	40 (2)	40 (2)	20 (1)	20 (1)	20 (1)	0 (0)
Smaller CPA firms	(49)	10 (5)	6 (3)	4 (2)	2 (1)	6 (3)	4 (2)	2 (1)
Individual CPAs	(36)	14 (5)	8 (3)	6 (2)	3 (1)	11 (4)	8 (3)	6 (2)
State and local CPA societies	(18)	39 (7)	17 (3)	6 (1)	6 (1)	28 (5)	17 (3)	22 (4)
AICPA officials and committees	(8)	38 (3)	38 (3)	0 (0)	0 (0)	25 (2)	13 (1)	13 (1)
II. Governmental Audit Agencies								
State and local municipal	(12)	8 (1)	0 (0)	8 (1)	0 (0)	8 (1)	8 (1)	0 (0)
Federal governmental audit agencies	(3)	33 (1)	0 (0)	33 (1)	0 (0)	33 (1)	33 (1)	0 (0)
III. Issuers								
SEC-filing corporations	(9)	44 (4)	11 (1)	33 (3)	0 (0)	33 (1)	11 (1)	0 (0)
Non-SEC-filing corporations	(2)	50 (1)	0 (0)	0 (0)	0 (0)	0 (0)	0 (0)	0 (0)
Governmental and not-for-profit agencies	(3)	33 (1)	33 (1)	0 (0)	33 (1)	0 (0)	0 (0)	0 (0)
Organizations representing issuers	(4)	50 (2)	0 (0)	50 (2)	0 (0)	50 (2)	50 (2)	0 (0)
IV. Academics	(19)	16 (3)	11 (2)	0 (0)	5 (1)	5 (1)	5 (1)	0 (0)
V. Lawyers and Legal Groups	(3)	67 (2)	33 (1)	0 (0)	0 (0)	33 (1)	33 (1)	5 (1)
VI. Report Users and User Groups	—	—	—	—	—	—	—	—
VII. Miscellaneous Respondents	(5)	0 (0)	0 (0)	0 (0)	0 (0)	0 (0)	0 (0)	0 (0)
Total	(183)	25% (46)	13% (24)	9% (16)	6% (10)	14% (26)	10% (29)	6% (11)

Note: ( ) indicates raw number.

161

lawyers/legal groups responding to this issue. However, the remainder of the public auditing respondents were largely split over the issue, while the preparers of financial statements were generally opposed to the "subject to" elimination. In regard to the actual wording of the report modified for uncertainty, more than twice as many respondents disagreed (14%) than agreed (6%) with its wording. This is in contrast to the slightly favorable reaction to the elimination of the "subject to" report language. Respondents showed an overall pattern of agreement with the "subject to" elimination, but disagreed with the wording proposed in the ED.

Category 116 indicates that 10 percent believed that the proposed wording did not properly highlight to the report reader the uncertainty within the audit report. A majority of these respondents indicating a need to better highlight the existing uncertainty explicitly commented that a separate paragraph discussing the uncertainty would be more appropriate. These respondents, however, indicated that the "subject to" language should not be used in the separate additional paragraph. In general, the respondents commenting on this issue indicated a moderate desire to eliminate the former qualifed "subject to" language, but preferred to retain reference to the uncertainty in the auditor's report, particularly in a separate paragraph.

Other Issues

This section will examine the most prominent occurrences of attribute categories 142 to 182 which attempted to capture a myriad of possible other issues that could be addressed by the respondents. As described in the preceding chapter, an attempt was made to be as comprehensive as possible in defining these categories and to include all potential response attributes that might be included in comment letters. Many of these attributes, however, were not found, or were contained in only a few letters and will not be discussed further. For purposes of analysis, the remainder of this section will use a minimum cut-off of 10 percent of all response letters mentioning the attribute to merit any further discussion. Table 6.17 summarizes the seven categories included in comment letters by more than 10 percent of all respondents.

One of the issues identified in the content analysis was the need for the report to adopt a more generally positive tone. Typically, respondents indicating this explicit overall desire also disagreed with the phrase "materially misstated" and/or with the possible inclusion of "intentionally or unintentionally" in the scope paragraph. These two issues have been addressed previously and it was noted that the ASB did proceed to modify the ED on these two issues.

Twenty-nine respondents (16%) commented on the legal liability of the auditing profession in 1987 (Category 147). Categories 148 through 150 in Appendix II present the positions of those respondents indicating whether a new auditor's report would have any impact on the legal liability of auditors.

Table 6.17. Other Issues

Respondent Group	N	Report Should Be More Positively Worded (Cat. 143)	Reference Made to Current Legal Climate (Cat. 147)	Existence of "Expectations Gap" (Cat. 161)	Refer to Other EDs (Cat. 163)	Refer to AICPA (Cat. 170)	Refer to ASB Cat. 171	Refer to Existing SAS's (Cat. 177)
I. Public Auditors								
Big Eight CPA firms	(7)	43% (3)	0% (0)	29% (2)	43% (3)	0% (0)	57% (4)	86% (6)
Next 15 largest CPA firms	(5)	20 (1)	40 (2)	20 (1)	20 (1)	20 (1)	20 (1)	40 (2)
Smaller CPA firms	(49)	6 (3)	14 (7)	4 (2)	8 (4)	6 (3)	10 (5)	4 (2)
Individual CPAs	(36)	8 (3)	22 (8)	11 (4)	8 (3)	11 (4)	17 (6)	11 (4)
State and local CPA societies	(18)	17 (3)	17 (3)	28 (5)	22 (4)	11 (2)	33 (6)	17 (3)
AICPA officials and committees	(8)	13 (1)	25 (2)	0 (0)	25 (2)	13 (1)	38 (3)	75 (6)
II. Governmental Audit Agencies								
State and local municipal	(12)	0 (0)	0 (0)	8 (1)	0 (0)	17 (2)	8 (1)	0 (0)
Federal governmental audit agencies	(3)	33 (1)	0 (0)	0 (0)	0 (0)	67 (2)	67 (2)	33 (1)
III. Issuers								
SEC-filing corporations	(9)	33 (3)	11 (1)	33 (3)	0 (0)	11 (1)	33 (3)	11 (1)
Non-SEC-filing corporations	(2)	0 (0)	50 (1)	0 (0)	50 (1)	0 (0)	0 (0)	0 (0)
Governmental and not-for-profit agencies	(3)	0 (0)	0 (0)	0 (0)	0 (0)	0 (0)	0 (0)	0 (0)
Organizations representing issuers	(4)	50 (2)	0 (0)	25 (1)	0 (0)	50 (2)	50 (2)	25 (1)
IV. Academics	(19)	5 (1)	26 (5)	26 (5)	11 (2)	21 (4)	32 (6)	0 (0)
V. Lawyers and Legal Groups	(3)	0 (0)	0 (0)	0 (0)	0 (0)	67 (2)	33 (1)	33 (1)
VI. Report Users and User Groups	—	—	—	—	—	—	—	—
VII. Miscellaneous Respondents	(5)	0 (0)	0 (0)	40 (2)	0 (0)	0 (0)	0 (0)	0 (0)
Total	(183)	12% (21)	16% (29)	14% (26)	11% (20)	13% (24)	22% (40)	15% (27)

Note: ( ) indicates raw number.

163

No respondent indicated that a new report would reduce legal liability; 4 respondents (2%) believed that any future impact on the legal climate could not be presently determined; while 14 respondents (8%) believed that a new audit report would serve to increase the legal liability of the auditor.

This response pattern indicates that, in 1987, respondents were not overwhelmingly concerned that a new report would increase auditor liability. Additionally, as would be expected, most of the respondents to this issue were auditors. This further solidifies the idea that the legal liability of auditors was generally not felt to be threatened by the proposed new audit report. Even a cursory review of the response letters would indicate that the major concern was over the communicative value of the report and not over implications for legal liability, as may have been expected *a priori*.

The need to improve the communicative value of the report—on which the ED was essentially founded—is further supported by the respondents noting the actual existence of an "expectations gap" in their letters (Category 161). The indication of the perceived existence of an expectations gap helps to lend credibility to the audit report revision attempt in an effort to help address the differences in beliefs between auditors and users of financial statements.

Categories 163, 170, 171, and 177 had a more than 10 percent response rate and were essentially technical items—referring in their letters to: (1) other current EDs; (2) the AICPA; (3) the ASB; and (4) existing Statements of Auditing Standards (SASs), respectively. As would be expected, more auditors referred to these items or authoritative bodies in their responses than did nonauditor groups. An exception is the 67 percent of federal audit agencies mentioning the AICPA and the ASB in their letters, and also the 67 percent of the lawyer/legal group referring to the AICPA in their letters. These percentages are relatively high for indicated occurrences, but the number of letters in these cases is low.

Also, as would be expected, letters from the larger CPA firms and from AICPA officials and committees were more likely to refer to existing SASs than other groups. These individuals and organizations are more likely to be familiar with the standard-setting process and more apt to evaluate the impact of each ED on existing standards. Additionally, the larger CPA firms have more resources to devote to responding to the ASB's EDs and may be more likely to comprehensively review the issues in the context of the existing SASs.

Assessment of Differences Across Groups

In an effort to determine if any group significantly differed on any category, a response rate of 60 percent or more for one group and 40 percent or less for another on the same item was considered to be indicative of controversy. The 60/40 heuristic was established in order to determine if one group strongly sides one way on an issue, while another group is less enthusiastic or mentions the topic significantly less frequently. A review of Appendix II indicates that the following 22 categories meet the 60/40 response criterion: 18, 21, 27, 36, 38, 44, 45, 69, 105, 111, 112, 126, 129, 133, 139, 140, 167, 170, 171, and 177. Of these categories, only five have not been addressed in the previous analyses. The response patterns of these five categories are presented in Table 6.18 and will be discussed in this section.

Category 27, agreement with the retention of the reference to GAAS in the scope paragraph, was more often noted by the two groups of large CPA firms than by the other groups. This is primarily because large firms also offered the highest percentages of suggested report wordings, which included their desire to retain the reference to GAAS. This issue is not necessarily considered "controversial" because only 2 percent of all respondents indicated that they would delete or modify the phrase "generally accepted auditing standards" in the report.

Disagreement with the phrase "assessing the appropriateness of the accounting principles used" (Category 69) was most apparent among the Big Eight accounting firms. The overall reaction to this issue was discussed in an early part of this chapter, however; Table 6.18 indicates that there are differences across groups. All Big Eight CPA firms responding disagreed with use of this phrase, and most (57%) indicated a desire to replace "appropriateness" with "reasonableness" when mentioning accounting principles. In total, 9 percent of the respondents disagreed with this phrase and would prefer the word "reasonableness" to "appropriateness." This indicates that the disagreement is not with the mention of "accounting principles" in the report, per se, but with the exact wording proposed by the ASB in the ED. An additional 14 percent of all respondents indicated a desire to adopt the phrase as proposed, further supporting the reference to accounting principles in the auditor's report.

Three of the five "next 15 largest CPA firms" indicated that the AICPA should also use additional educational efforts, other than just the audit report, to try to educate financial statement users as to the role and responsibility of the auditor in the financial reporting process (Category 145). Only two other smaller CPA firms and one individual CPA also specifically included mention of any such additional educational efforts on the part of the profession. The following quote from Laventhol and Horwath (Letter No. 21) is indicative of the other respondents' comments that additional efforts at education, in addition to changes in the audit report, would be beneficial:

> The report is only one tool to help users understand what auditors do. This should be only the first step in the AICPA's efforts. Additional steps should include strong education and communication efforts, using public relations and other specialists as appropriate. But even the most ambitious of such efforts will reach only a fraction of users. The report, however, will at least be seen by substantially all users.

Table 6.18. Remaining Significant Differences Across Groups

Respondent Group	N	Disagreement Agreement w/ Retention of Reference to GAAS (Cat. 27)		w/Assessing Appropriateness of Accounting Principles" (Cat. 69)		Use Additional Educational Efforts (Cat. 145)		Comment on Final SAS Wording (Cat. 164)		Reference to Treadway (Cat. 167)	
I. *Public Auditors*											
Big Eight CPA firms	(7)	71%	(5)	71%	(5)	0%	(0)	14%	(1)	29%	(2)
Next 15 largest CPA firms	(5)	60	(3)	20	(1)	60	(3)	60	(3)	0	(0)
Smaller CPA firms	(49)	25	(12)	20	(10)	4	(2)	2	(1)	0	(0)
Individual CPAs	(36)	17	(6)	20	(7)	3	(1)	3	(1)	3	(1)
State and local CPA societies	(18)	28	(5)	17	(3)	0	(0)	22	(4)	0	(0)
AICPA officials and committees	(8)	0	(0)	25	(2)	0	(0)	25	(2)	0	(0)
II. *Governmental Audit Agencies*											
State and local municipal	(12)	17	(2)	0	(0)	0	(0)	8	(1)	0	(0)
Federal governmental audit agencies	(3)	33	(1)	0	(0)	0	(0)	33	(1)	0	(0)
III. *Issuers*											
SEC-filing corporations	(9)	33	(3)	44	(4)	0	(0)	0	(0)	22	(2)
Non-SEC-filing corporations	(2)	50	(1)	50	(1)	0	(0)	0	(0)	0	(0)
Governmental and not-for-profit agencies	(3)	0	(0)	0	(0)	0	(0)	0	(0)	0	(0)
Organizations representing issuers	(4)	25	(1)	50	(2)	0	(0)	25	(1)	0	(0)
IV. *Academics*	(19)	16	(3)	11	(2)	0	(0)	5	(1)	11	(2)
V. *Lawyers and Legal Groups*	(3)	33	(1)	33	(1)	0	(0)	33	(1)	67	(2)
VI. *Report Users and User Groups*	—	—		—		—		—		—	
VII. *Miscellaneous Respondents*	(5)	20	(1)	0	(0)	0	(0)	0	(0)	0	(0)
Total	(183)	24%	(44)	21%	(38)	3%	(6)	9%	(17)	5%	(9)

Note: ( ) indicates raw number.

Also, three of the five "next 15 largest CPA firms" commented on the actual wording of the SAS if adopted, excluding the wording of the audit reports (Category 164). This concern for the actual wording of the SAS (i.e., footnotes, references, and wording of sentences, etc.) would be expected from larger CPA firms which have potentially more time and resources devoted to the development of SASs. What is interesting is that not *more* of the Big Eight CPA firms commented on the wording issues involved in deriving a final SAS. One potential explanation is that these firms all had members on the ASB and may have deferred comments on SAS wording issues until it was more certain that a new SAS would be adopted, and their representatives on the board could properly voice their preferences and concerns. Except for the 60 percent of the "next 15 largest CPA firms," almost all respondents specifically limited their comments to the wording of the proposed audit report and did not comment on any other wording issues related to a potential new SAS on audit reports.

The last issue identified using the 60/40 heuristic is Category 167—references to the Treadway Commission. In general, very few respondents (5%) mentioned the Treadway Commission in their letters. However, two out of the three letters from the lawyer/legal groups did make reference to the Treadway Commission, indicating thier overall concern for the conclusions of this influential body. Nevertheless, this high response rate of 67 percent is based on only a few letters and does not merit further discussion due to the nature of the category and the low number of total responses.

This section has attempted to address any issues for which one group indicated a high response percentage ($\geq 60\%$) while any other group indicated a substantially lower response rate ($\leq 40\%$). This heuristic identified 22 categories, the majority of which were discussed in detail in earlier sections of this chapter. The remaining five categories not previously discussed were not considered to be truly "controversial" issues, and have been appropriately discussed. The next section presents a summary and conclusion based on the analysis presented in this chapter.

SUMMARY

This chapter has discussed the results from Phase I of the study—the content analysis of the response letters. It was noted that the ED on the auditor's report received more comment letters than any of the nine other "expectations gap" EDs issued by the ASB in 1987.

In general, there was agreement among the respondents that a new audit report was needed in 1987. All groups except SEC-registered corporations favored a new report. One unexpected finding was that the individual CPAs responding to this ED were less enthusiastic about a report modification than expected and were largely split (50% for, 42% against) on the need for a new report based on their comment letters. In regard to the proposed report wording in the ED, 74 percent of the respondents agreeing with the need for a new report felt that the ASB's proposed wording could be improved to better clarify the messages communicated in the report. Sixteen percent agreeing with the need for a new report felt that the ED was acceptable as proposed, while the remaining 10 percent would only accept a new report if their suggested changes were adopted.

Some of the strong overall preferences indicated by respondents were: (1) eliminate from further consideration "intentionally or unintentionally," (2) retain a statement regarding management's role in financial reporting; (3) modify "materially misstated" in the scope paragraph; (4) continue not to mention client's system of internal control in the report; (5) retain additions of "independent" to the title, "reasonable assurance" to the scope paragraph, and "in all material respects" to the opinion paragraph; (6) retain "fairly" in the opinion paragraph; (7) retain change from "examined" to "audited," and (8) restructure the scope paragraph to make it easier to read and understand. Additionally, reaction was largely mixed on the deletion of the reference to consistency in the opinion paragraph. The respondents also noted a marginal agreement with the elimination of the "subject to" qualified report, but indicated that a new report on uncertainties should better emphasize the uncertainty and appropriate footnote disclosures contained in the financial statements.

The next chapter will indicate that a majority of the concerns presented in the comment letters were addressed and resolved in subsequent deliberations by TF and the board leading to the adoption of *SAS 58* in early 1988.

The respondents to the 1987 ED on the auditor's report suggested a myriad of new report wordings and suggestions for improving the former report, and primarily, the proposed report. Armed with these new insights, the TF and ASB set out to finalize the new report wording. The next chapter will discuss how these comment letters, along with other factors, influenced the board's standard-setting process and final adoption of *SAS 58*.

Note

1. The task force erroneously included a comment letter both as No. 120 and as No. 180, to arrive at a total of 184 comment letters. The analysis presented in this study excluded the second counting of this letter and appropriately renumbered all subsequent response letters.

Chapter 7

Finalizing the Statement of Auditing Standards

This chapter will discuss the process that the 1987 ED went through in order to become a final adopted SAS. The discussion will focus on the influences that affected the process and final document. Chapter 5 elaborated on the early stages of the ASB's standard-setting process, up to the establishment of the ED proposing a revised auditor's report. This chapter will discuss the salient influences that affected this one "expectations gap" ED and the resulting process of establishing a new standard auditor's report. Although nine other "expectations gap" EDs were under concurrent consideration by the ASB during this period, they will not be specifically discussed in this chapter.

This chapter will discuss each meeting of the ASB in chronological order, starting with the work performed by the Auditor Communications Task Force (TF) prior to the first official board meeting that addressed this ED. Additionally, a section indicating the board's final votes on this proposed SAS will be presented, followed by a summary section.

WORK OF THE TF PRIOR TO THE FIRST 1987 BOARD MEETING ON THE AUDITOR'S REPORT

In 1987, the composition of the TF was changed due to the new and enlarged board membership for the year (increased to 21 members), and some reassignment of existing members. Accordingly, previous TF member Howard P. McMurrian left the board and Robert Temkin was assigned to serve on a different TF. New board members James Brown (Crowe, Chizek & Co.) and Ernest TenEyck (Laventhol & Horwath) were added to the TF. Also, Mimi Blanco-Best took over as Auditing Standards Division technical manager assigned to the Auditor Communications TF.

The new ASB did not meet to formally discuss this, or any of the other EDs, until July 1987. In the interim, however, the TF met regularly in an attempt to improve the ED. One of the major issues that the TF analyzed during this period was whether the auditor should mention the client's system of internal control in the audit report. This effort was a result of the decision by the ASB Planning Subcommittee in February 1987 that the TF should specifically address possible communications regarding internal control in the auditor's report.

In a letter outlining the directive to the TF, Jerry Sullivan, the ASB chairman also indicated that this issue had surfaced in numerous interactions with officials from the General Accounting Office (GAO) and the Treadway Commission. It was believed that auditors should associate themselves with a client's system of internal control and report on this association in the auditor's report. Along with the letter, Jerry Sullivan sent the TF suggestions on several ways such an association with internal control could be achieved in the auditor's report and in the financial statements. He indicated in closing the letter that (Sullivan February 17, 1987, 2):

> ... if we can make progress in this area we will diffuse one common thread of confusion and criticism that we have heard from corporate directors, Treadway Commissioners, Congressional staff, and GAO.

The Treadway Commission concluded shortly thereafter in its April 1987 preliminary statement, that the auditing profession should modify the existing audit report to describe the extent to which the independent public accountant has reviewed and evaluated the system of internal control. Hence, both internal and external forces had focused attention on the possibility of mentioning internal control in the auditor's report.

With this charge from the ASB and the recommendation from the Treadway Commission, the Auditor Communications TF developed an Issues Paper titled *The Communication of the Auditor's Responsibilities for Systems of Internal Control When Conducting an Examination in Accordance with Generally Accepted Auditing Standards*. This 19-page document discussed various issues related to auditor association with systems of internal control, and the potential ways in which reference to internal control could be made within the audit report. Primarily three questions were raised by the TF: (1) Should the standard auditor's report be revised to describe the auditor's responsibility for the system of internal control when conducting a GAAS audit; (2) When a "Report by Management" discusses internal control, should the auditor's report be modified to describe the auditor's responsibility or otherwise respond to the representations contained in the management report; and (3) are the auditor's responsibilities for assertions concerning internal control made by management adequately covered under SAS No. 8, "Other Information Contained in Documents Containing Audited Financial Statements," or the related interpretation in AU Sec.9550? Background information and various arguments regarding each issue were presented in the paper, along with several proposals for possible implementation. The three tentative conclusions reached by the TF, respectively, were as follows (AICPA 1987c):

(1) Because the "minimum study and evaluation of the system" required under existing standards is very limited in examinations in which the auditor does not rely on internal controls, the Task Force believes that any reference to such a study in the standard report would convey greater assurance than is warranted and would serve only to further mislead users. In addition, because the extent of work performed on controls varies significantly from audit to audit, the Task Force believes it would be difficult to convey the degree to which the auditor has reviewed the system in any meaningful manner.

   For these reasons, the Task Force has tentatively concluded that the auditor's standard report should not be revised to include a discussion of the auditor's responsibility for systems of internal control when conducting an examination of the financial statements in accordance with generally accepted auditing standards (p. 7).

(2) The Task Force views the proposed interaction between the "Report by Management" and the auditor's standard report as implying too much assurance with too little work. Its main concern is that the added verbiage will be misunderstood by users to mean an increase in the level of assurance given on the control system while the auditor's responsibility has not increased (nor have his procedures).

   For this reason, the Task Force has tentatively concluded that the auditor's standard report should not be revised to include a statement of assurance on management's representations on internal controls included in a "Report by Management" (p. 17), and

(3) The Task Force agrees that the auditor's statement of assurance in regard to an assertion by management is covered under the provisions of SAS No. 8 and the related interpretation. However, the Task Force also believes that the guidance should be more specific for the auditor who believes the "Report by Management" contains a material misstatement. In addition, it has concluded that any revision of the existing literature for the items discussed above do not deal with auditor communication, per se, and accordingly, should be the responsibility of another task force (p. 17).

Thus, after considerable debate the TF concluded, contrary to the Treadway Commission, that any reference to the client's system of internal control would only serve to further confuse report readers as to the actual level of responsibility assumed by the auditor. However, they did note that *SAS 8* should be expanded to include more guidance when the auditor disagrees with management's evaluation of internal control as presented in the management report. This issues paper was distributed to ASB members and discussed at the July 1987 meeting. At this July meeting the board concurred with the TF's recommendation, and no further consideration was given to the possibility of including a reference to systems of internal control in the auditor's report.

   Along with tackling the issue of internal control during this time period, the TF had the difficult task of determining how the respondents viewed the new audit report, including the actual wording modifications proposed in the

ED. In order to facilitate completion of this task, the TF technical manager prepared a composite of the comment letters arranged by topical issues. All of the segments of the comment letters referring to a specific topic (either positively or negatively) were copied and displayed together within the composite. In this way the TF and ASB members interested in any one topic concerning the modified report could read all of the positive and negative comments from every letter addressing that specific topic without necessarily having to read all the letters individually. However, no count or tabulation of positive versus negative responses was made by the TF for these individual items. The TF focused more on finding ways to improve the existing wording and the expression of new ideas than on conducting a "popularity" vote. A copy of the index to the composite is included in Appendix III. This arduous task eventually produced two composites: one for the first 104 comment letters received through July 10, 1987, and a later one for Letters 105 through 174. The last few letters received by the AICPA (175 to 183), although passed to board members, were received too late to be included in the formal composites.

The TF, in considering modifications to the report included in the ED, relied largely on the first composite. This first composite was distributed to the board members in mid-July, along with the TF's suggested modified auditor's report based on the comments received to date and also on further deliberation by the TF in 1987. This indicates that the earlier comment letters may have had a greater impact on the establishment of the final SAS than later letters. These later letters, as discussed below in this chapter, did not appear to result in any additional proposals for change from the TF. Once the TF presented its revised audit report to the ASB in July 1987, it again assumed the primary role of implementing the board's decisions, as opposed to more directly influencing the outcome of the actual report wording. However, the modifications suggested by the TF in July 1987 were substantially upheld by the board throughout the remainder of the SAS finalization process.

In mid-July, the TF proposed and distributed a modification to the wording of the report contained in the ED that addressed what they believed to be the concerns of the ED respondents. The cover letter to the proposed modified report noted seven changes that were made to the ED: (1) editing the last sentence of the introductory paragraph to eliminate the redundant reference to the company; (2) eliminating "intentionally or unintentionally" from the scope paragraph; (3) restructuring the scope paragraph to improve its readability, relating reasonable assurance to auditing standards, dealing more broadly with performance of audit procedures, and eliminating any inadvertent indication that the description of auditing procedures was all-inclusive; (4) eliminating the "appropriateness" reference in the scope paragraph when discussing accounting principles; (5) modifying the scope paragraph to reflect a more positive, versus a negative, responsibility with respect to material misstatements; (6) editing the last sentence of the scope paragraph; and (7) reinstating in the opinion paragraph an indication of what GAAP financial statements are intended to present—financial position, results of operations and changes in financial position. All of these modifications to the ED, with the exception of numbers 1 and 7, were discussed in detail in the previous chapter.

Only a few letters indicated that the second reference to the audited company's name in the introductory paragraph was redundant. However, the TF considered these comments to be valid and proposed a change to the ED. Additionally, Table 6.15 indicates that only a few letters commented on the deletion of the reference to "financial position, results of operations and changes in financial position" in the opinion paragraph. Two of these letters, however, had a tremendous impact on the TF. Both the TF chairman and technical manager indicated on separate occasions that the letters from Douglas Carmichael (Letter No. 54) and Stephen Zeff (Letter No. 67) were very articulate and pointed out that the proposed deletion was not simply editorial, as was believed in 1986, but was a substantive change. Both of these letters pointed out that the deleted words explained to the report reader what the financial statements mentioned in the introductory paragraph purport to present, and that these explanations were essential in providing information to the report reader. The TF discussed this issue, agreed with these two respondents, and proposed in July that the deleted words be reinstated. The ASB would later debate this issue and would consult with outside legal sources as to the ramifications of the wording proposed in the ED. Overall, however, this indicates how a few well-articulated positions substanially affected the process and the final report wording adopted by the ASB.

The TF's other proposed revisions to the ED report version do appear to address the major concerns of the majority of ED respondents, as discerned by this researcher and discussed in the previous chapter. In its proposal to the board, the TF appeared to take into consideration the respondents' views, and not just their own, when making recommendations to the board in July. Hence, the views expressed by the ED respondents had a measured and direct impact on establishing *SAS 58.*

The report version derived by the TF, and discussed at the July 1987 ASB meeting, that incorporated the seven modifications noted above, was worded as follows:

Independent Auditor's Report
We have audited the accompanying balance sheet of X Company as of December 31, 19XX, and the related statements of income, retained earnings and changes in financial position for the year then ended. These financial statements are the representations of the Company's management.

We performed our audit in accordance with generally accepted auditing standards. Those standards require performance of auditing procedures to obtain reasonable assurance as to whether the financial statements are free of material misstatement. Auditing procedures consist primarily of examining, on a test basis, evidence supporting the amounts and disclosures included in the financial statements. Those procedures also include an assessment of the accounting principles used and significant estimates made by management and an evaluation of the overall financial statement presentation. We believe that the results of our procedures provide a reasonable basis for our opinion presented below.

In our opinion, the financial statements referred to above present fairly, in all material respects, the financial position of X Company as of December 31, 19X1, and its results of operations and changes in financial position for the year then ended in conformity with generally accepted accounting principles.

AUDITING STANDARDS BOARD MEETINGS REGARDING THE AUDITOR'S REPORT

This section will discuss chronologically the ASB meetings and other events pertaining to this new report version proposed by the TF. This meeting-to-meeting analysis will provide a clearer and more thorough understanding of the various influences that acted on the ASB in finalizing the standard auditor's report.

July 1987

The Auditor Communications TF's discussion at the ASB meeting in July focused primarily on the standard audit report wording. In fact, only the report version illustrated above, and not an entire modified ED, was presented to board members so they could more clearly focus on the issues regarding wording of the standard report, and not the wording of a final SAS document. In leading the discussion of the topics under the purview of the Auditor Communications TF, the TF chairman indicated at the outset that reaction to the auditor's report ED was largely favorable, and that the TF wanted to direct most of their attention to this ED and not the other two EDs under their purview. He also indicated that the discussion should focus on issues of report wording, and that topics such as the "subject to" deletion, transitional issues, and the format of the SAS itself should be deferred until the next meeting. This request set the stage for a paragraph-by-paragraph discussion of the report proposed by the TF.

First of all, the ASB agreed that the guidance on the title of the auditor's report presented in the ED was adequate. Thus, the word "independent" was felt to be a meaningful reporting requirement, and was upheld. The change from "examined" to "audited" in the report was also still felt to be appropriate and was agreed to by the 1987 ASB.

The discussion then turned to the sentence stating that the financial statements are the "representations" of the company's management. The TF chairman presented the position of the Financial Executives Institute (FEI), as discussed in the previous chapter, that the term "responsibility" should be used in place of "representations" to more accurately describe management's role. This position had also been articulated to the TF chairman during subsequent discussions with the FEI. The board was also informed that the TF had considered this change, but eventually rejected it, and similar other alternatives, in favor of the ED wording. The board also discussed the possibility of deleting the sentence entirely. After further discussion, a vote indicated that only one member wanted to delete the sentence entirely, four members wanted to modify it to say "responsibility," and the other members were satisfied with the sentence as proposed in the ED. Thus, the reference to management's "representations" in the auditor's report remained unchanged through the July meeting.

The scope paragraph was then discussed, with some initial comments regarding the contemplated phrase "intentionally or unintentionally." It was noted that a resounding cry from the comment letters was to eliminate the phrase from further consideration, which was what the TF had proposed. The board agreed that the phrase did not enhance the communicative value of the auditor's report and agreed to delete it from further consideration.

Overall, the ASB agreed with the TF's restructuring of this paragraph to break up the long sentence in the original ED and to more directly link "reasonable assurance" to the audited financial statements and not to the auditor's "evaluation" of the financial statements as presented in the ED wording. However, considerable debate ensued as to the actual wording of the scope paragraph proposed by the TF.

The issue of modifying the phrase "reasonable assurance" with "but not absolute" was discussed first. Several board members believed that such an attempted caveat made the profession sound overly defensive. A vote indicated that only three members preferred the phrase "reasonable, but not absolute, assurance." The remaining members believed that the reference to "reasonable assurance" was appropriate and that it conveyed the proper level of assurance to report readers without sounding overly negative.

Discussion then turned to the general issue of whether the auditor's report should attempt to include any description of an audit in the scope paragraph. The board's consensus was that a description was necessary and that it was a prime reason for the proposed report modification. However, the ASB chairman indicated that the wording of the two sentences describing an audit proposed by the TF implied a certain order due to the use of the word "primarily" in the first sentence and "also" in the second sentence. To correct this apparent ordering problem, the first sentence was modified to say "auditing procedures include," which parallels the second sentence which begins, "Those procedures also include." The chairman then suggested that the report should refer to planning as well as performance of auditing procedures, and after further discussion the board agreed to modify the second sentence of the scope paragraph to say, "Those standards require planning and performing the audit."

Next, the issue of referring to "materially misstated" in the scope paragaph was discussed at length. It was noted that the TF had discussed a potential rewording of this sentence to read "fairly presented" for consistency with the opinion paragraph. However, the TF believed that the phrase "materially misstated" was sufficiently consistent with the opinion paragraph and suggested that "free of" be added to the phrase to more positively describe the auditor's role. It was explicitly noted that the phrase "free of material misstatement" was adopted by the TF in response to several of the respondents' letters indicating that the tone of the ED was too negative in this regard. This proposal was discussed and upheld by the board.

The last sentence in the scope paragraph was then discussed. The TF chairman indicated to the ASB that the TF wanted to keep some version of this sentence as a bridge and caveat to the auditor's opinion. A vote indicated that only three members wanted to delete this sentence entirely. However, general concern was expressed over the TF's proposed wording. There was general disagreement with the term "results" proposed by the TF. It was felt that a different modification of the ED would have been more desirable. A 10-to-5 vote by the board resolved that "the results of" be eliminated from the proposed report and after subsequent discussion, it was further agreed to delete "presented below" from this sentence.

Discussion then returned to the sentence referring to "free of material misstatement." The board member from Price Waterhouse reiterated his firm's position (Letter No. 171) that determining if financial statements are "free of material misstatement" is not the purpose of an audit. He contended that determining whether the financial statements are "presented fairly" was the focus of an audit and that the auditor's report should be worded to state this positive affirmation in regard to the financial statements. In conjunction with this issue, the board debated whether the phrase "free of material misstatements" should also include "and omissions." After some discussion, a vote indicated that only three board members preferred the inclusion of "and omissions," and only four members preferred to modify the audit report to say "presents fairly in conformity with GAAP" in the scope paragraph. Hence, the ASB voted to retain the wording proposed by the TF on this issue. It should also be noted that the wording proposed by the TF is similar to the recommendation included in the Treadway Commission's April 1987 report to state that an audit provides assurance that the "financial statements are free from material misstatements" (*Report* 1987, p. 51). Thus, it appears that the wording proposed by the TF, and upheld by the ASB, was responsive both to the ED respondents and to the recommendation of the Treadway Commission.

The subject of referencing "disclosures" was then addressed. The TF suggested that it be referred to in conjunction with "amounts" and not added to "overall financial statement presentation." The general consensus of the board was that "overall financial statement presentation" incorporates "disclosures," and that it is more appropriately mentioned in regard to audit procedures as proposed by the TF. Discussion then turned to the issue of evaluating the "overall financial statement presentation." One board member indicated that *SAS 47*, Para. 29 already requires the auditor to assess the overall presentation of financial statements and not just each account or amount individually. This SAS requires auditors to aggregate all representations in the financial statements to assess whether an overall bias exists when the financial statements are presented in their entirety. The board was then reminded by a member that the courts have held auditors responsible for the overall presentation of the financial statements, and cited the case involving Penn Central Railroad as a prime example. The decision in the case of Penn Central Railroad found the auditors liable because the overall presentation of the financial statements was misleading, even though the individual accounts and amounts appeared to have been prepared using individually acceptable GAAP.

Another board member expressed concern regarding the inclusion of this phrase and indicated that he believed it might be misunderstood by report readers to convey more assurance regarding the financial statements than was intended. However, after further deliberation, a vote was taken and no one voted to delete the phrase "evaluation of the overall financial statement presentation" from the report.

The discussion then turned to the wording of the opinion paragraph. At the outset, the TF chairman reiterated four issues identified by respondents' letters that were explicitly considered and rejected by the TF: (1) delete "presents fairly;" (2) delete "in all material respects;" (3) require auditors to sign their name to the report—as opposed to the firm's name; and (4) retain the reference to consistency. The first three issues referred to above were not further discussed in detail by the board.

The TF chairman indicated that the SEC staff position was that the reference to consistency in the auditor's report was a meaningful assertion and that it helped to serve as a "red flag" to report readers when a change in principle was adopted. The SEC staff also believed that it would be difficult to amend Regulation S-X to delete the requirement for auditors to report on the consistent application of GAAP for SEC registrants.

The ASB then debated at length whether the reference to consistency should be included in the auditor's report, even if consistent application of principles is subsumed under GAAP by APB Opinion No. 20, as discussed earlier. One member suggested that the consistency reference be used only when there is a change and not for all audit reports. In that way, the "red flag" would exist for corporations making a change, while it would not require a separate reference in the auditor's report for all other engagements. It was decided at this meeting, however, that the consistency reference was not an important "red flag," and should not be separately mentioned in the audit report when proper disclosures have been made in the financial statements.

The TF chairman then pointed out that the reference to "financial position, results of operations and changes in financial position" was reinstated to the opinion paragraph as a meaningful inclusion. He noted that this was in response to the positions articulated in the letters of Carmichael and Zeff which caused the TF to reconsider the original deletion. Several board members contended that the deletion was only "editorial" and served to unclutter the opinion to more directly relate the concept of fair presentation with GAAP. Other members believed the report essentially had the same meaning either way. After some discussion, a vote indicated that 11 members agreed with inclusion of the phrase while seven members objected to including the phrase. Thus, the proposed reinstatement of "financial position, results of operations and changes in financial position" was upheld by the board in July.

At the conclusion of the discussion of the wording of the standard audit report, the ASB chairman suggested that the TF get an opinion from the AICPA's legal counsel regarding the substantive changes made to the ED. Accordingly, the view of legal counsel was obtained and presented to the board at the next meeting regarding the auditor's report.

At the close of the discussion in July, the proposed standard unqualified audit report read as follows:

Independent Auditor's Report

We have audited the accompanying balance sheet of X Company as of December 31, 19XX, and the related statements of income, retained earnings, and changes in financial position for the year then ended. These financial statements are the representations of the Company's management.

We performed our audit in accordance with generally accepted auditing standards. Those standards require planning and performing the audit to provide reasonable assurance as to whether the financial statements are free of material misstatement. Auditing procedures include examining, on a test basis, evidence supporting the amounts and disclosures included in the financial statements. Those procedures also include an assessment of the accounting principles used and significant estimates made by management and an evaluation of the overall financial statement presentation. We believe that our audit provides a reasonable basis for our opinion.

In our opinion, the financial statements referred to above present fairly, in all material respects, the financial position of X Company as of December 31, 19XX, and its results of operations and changes in financial position for the year then ended in conformity with generally accepted accounting principles.

The July 1987 meeting essentially produced the standard audit report wording that was incorporated in the final SAS. Only a few, but meaningful, changes to report wording were adopted later by the board. After this important meeting regarding the fundamental issues of report wording, the TF again resumed the primary role of facilitating the board regarding the report wording issues. However, the TF will be shown to have had an important role in implementing the proposed wording in the final SAS document itself.

The July 1987 ASB meeting illustrated that the respondents' letters discussed in the previous chapter significantly affected the wording of the auditor's report. In fact, these letters appeared to have had considerably more influence on the board than any other outside sources up to this point. However, other outside influences will be shown to have had a greater impact on the board in subsequent meetings. Thus, the major concerns of the ED respondents regarding audit report wording noted in the previous chapter were also identified by the TF and incorporated into their proposed report wording that was substantially upheld by the ASB in the July 1987 meeting.

September 1987

The next ASB meeting that included the auditor's report on the agenda was held in September 1987. In part of his opening remarks, the chairman indicated that the ASB Planning Subcommittee had decided to assign the issue of reporting on internal control, particularly when management references internal control in their annual report, to the Control Risk Assessment Task Force for further consideration. This recommended analysis by a TF other than the Auditor Communications TF was a result of the issues paper presented at the previous meeting and reflected the board's desire to further analyze this issue. However, the Control Risk Assessment TF was directed to finish work on their current ED ("The Auditor's Responsibility for Assessing Control Risk") before beginning work on this new assignment.

Also, the chairman indicated in his opening comments that the only formal liaison meeting held since the last board meeting was with the FEI. At this meeting, the FEI was informed of the current status of all 10 current EDs. Out of the 10, they had significant concern with the progress of only one ED— the standard auditor's report. The FEI expressed their continuing displeasure with the use of the term "representations" in the introductory paragraph when referring to management's role in the financial reporting process. The FEI believed that the term "representations" was overly negative in its tone toward management, and that a more positive and accurate term would be "responsibilities." The FEI's position was presented and briefly discussed during the chair's opening comments and discussed further when the board formally addressed the issue of the auditor's report later in the meeting.

When the board began discussion of the auditor's report, the TF chairman was once again the discussion leader. He indicated that he would like to see the auditor's report wording, and the related issues, begin to solidify through the discussions of the meeting, and reminded the board that there was "an approximate 4-to-1" ratio of respondents' letters in support of revising the standard auditor's report. He also indicated that the members should have received their copies of the second composite (Letters 105 to 177) prior to the meeting. It was also indicated that the TF was reasonably satisfied with the wording of the scope paragraph because the last meeting and that discussion should start with the first paragraph, move to the opinion paragraph, and then to the scope paragraph.

In discussing the introductory paragraph, the consensus of the board was that if the FEI had a strong distaste for the term "representations," they would consider a change to "responsibilities." However, it was felt that using the term "responsibilities" may appear to be an attempt by the audit profession to shift all responsibility to management. The TF chairman then introduced a recommendation made by the ASB Planning Subcommittee to restructure the sentence to read, "These financial statements are the responsibility of the company's management; we are responsible for expressing an opinion on them based on our audit." The board agreed that this new sentence made a positive statement of the responsibility of both management and the auditor. It was the general consensus that the added portion of the sentence referring to auditors' responsibility for an opinion based on the audit also created a smooth transition to the scope paragraph. The sentence was then revised in further discussion to delete the reference to "them" and say "these financial statements" to better indicate what was being opined on. This sentence, as amended, was felt to adequately address the strong concerns of the FEI, as well as more clearly and positively spell out the responsibility of management and the auditor in the new auditor's report. No other changes were believed to be needed in the introductory paragraph.

Next, the opinion paragraph was addressed. The TF chairman noted that this paragraph still contained two potentially unresolved issues. The first of these discussed was the deletion of the reference to consistency. In July, the board voted to uphold the ED's proposal to delete any reference to consistent application of GAAP in the audit report. It was noted then that the SEC, and Clarence Sampson in particular, may object to this position. The SEC, however, had not responded to the ASB further on this issue since the last meeting. It was felt that Mr. Sampson was turning slightly in favor of the board's position, but it was noted that he wanted to see some cost/benefit analysis in support of the proposed deletion. The board took another vote as to the desirability of deleting the reference to consistency. A unanimous vote was cast (of those members voting) to uphold the proposed consistency deletion in September.

The second potentially unresolved issue discussed was the reinstatement of the phrase "financial position, results of operations and changes in financial position" to the report in July. As requested by the board, the TF consulted with the AICPA's legal counsel on this potential "substantive" modification. A letter was sent to the ASB regarding their legal interpretation of the proposed ED deletion of this phrase. In essence, their conclusion was that the phrase in question should remain in the report in order to establish defensible parameters around what "fairly presents" is intended to mean in the report, and that without these parameters the ED version could be interpreted so as to increase the auditor's exposure to liability.

The last chapter, and earlier sections of this chapter, indicated that only a few respondents articulated reasons why the phrase should be reinstated to the report. The lawyers, in comparing the two potential wordings, actually referred in their letter to the two authors discussed earlier as having alerted the TF and the ASB to a different interpretation of the ED:

> In fact, the two versions of the sentence do not say quite the same thing; in this respect, we agree with the reasoning set out in the comment letters by Messrs. Carmichael and Zeff (Wilkie, Farr & Gallagher, September 4, 1987, 3).

The influence of these two letters by Carmichael and Zeff in causing the ASB to reevaluate a proposed change is, according to the TF technical manager, an excellent example of how the ED process is supposed to work. The exposure process is not intended to be a "popularity contest," but is meant to solicit new insights and ideas regarding the issues being addressed. In this way, each respondent has the potential to significantly influence the board with a valid and well-articulated position. These two letters caused the TF and ASB to reconsider their original position. Ultimately, the board agreed to uphold the position reached in July 1987 to reinstate the phrase "financial position, results of operations and changes in financial position."

Discussion then turned to documenting in the SASs the reason for eliminating the reference to consistency in the report. After some discussion, it was proposed that the TF would provide a "mock up" of the final version of AU Sec. 509, *Reports on Audited Financial Statements*, that would incorporate the new wording of the standard audit report, as well as give more explanation and guidance than was presented in the ED itself. This expanded discussion would then include reasoning behind the consistency deletion— especially because it was an elimination of one of the 10 generally accepted auditing standards. The second standard of reporting formerly stated that, "The report shall state whether such principles have been consistently observed in the current period in relation to the preceding period" (AICPA 1986, AU Sec. 420). Because the new report would not refer to consistency at all, it was felt that there should be a good trail in the SASs to document the change and the reasoning behind it.

At the suggestion of a "mock up" of AU Sec. 509, the TF and board started to shift from discussing the need for a new auditor's report to the actual implementation of the new report into the existing SASs. In the researcher's view, this shift took place because the TF chairman had substantially reached his goal of seeing the new report wording begin to solidify into an acceptable standard report. Also, a few of the board members, after the suggestion of a "mock up" of Sec. 509 was made, indicated that it would be very beneficial from their standpoint to see how the proposed report fit into the existing SASs. The TF then agreed to present to the board, at the next meeting, their version of how the new wording would be presented in the final codification of SASs.

Discussion then moved to the scope paragraph. The TF indicated that it was fairly comfortable with this revised paragraph and had no suggestions for change. However, several of the board members believed that the reference to "auditing procedures" in the third and fourth sentences was slightly obscure and "came out of the blue" because it was not mentioned earlier in the report. It was agreed to modify references to "audit procedures" to "an audit" to facilitate sentence transition in the paragraph and to more clearly associate the procedures mentioned in the report to an auditor's actual performance.

No further wording changes were proposed by the board; however, a member wanted to discuss what was meant by the phrase "evaluation of the overall financial statement presentation." He again articulated his belief that the phrase might be misinterpreted and that auditors might encounter a problem in documenting their "overall evaluation." However, the consensus of the board was that the auditor should essentially "step back" at the end of the engagement and consider the fairness of the overall financial statement presentation. Again, *SAS 47* was discussed and the Penn Central case was mentioned as an appropriate illustation of the need for an overall evaluation of financial statement presentation. Additionally, one member read portions of *SAS 5, The Meaning of "Present Fairly in Conformity with GAAP"* in the Independent Auditor's Report, indicating that the auditor was presently required to assess the fairness of the overall presentation of the financial statements, and that the new report wording simply stated that existing responsibility. The vast majority of the board agreed with this position and with the proposed reference in the audit report. This discussion, however, served to indicate that a consensus interpretation of *SAS 5* is still not fully attained within the auditing profession, even by members of the ASB.

The next issue addressed was the wording of the report on uncertainties contained in the Appendix to the ED. The TF proposed that the opinion paragraph for uncertainties be split in two. The proposal provided that the three standard report paragraphs would be presented unaltered and a new fourth paragraph, consisting of the sentence describing the uncertainty, would follow the opinion paragraph. This proposal literally split the former proposed opinion paragraph.

During the ensuing discussion, it was indicated that the separate paragraph after the opinion paragraph contained the same concept as proposed in the

ED, but that it better highlighted the existing uncertainty. In this regard, the TF chairman mentioned that: "There were a number of comment letters that suggested this during the comment period and the Task Force when reviewing the comment letters considered them appropriate."

Additionally, one member of the Continued Existence TF indicated that they also noted "a lot of respondents" making the same suggestion. The Continued Existence TF decided that it would be appropriate to create the new paragraph, but this decision really rested with the Auditor Communications TF, and that they would support the report wording either way. The discussion that followed indicated that the board approved of this new report structure. They believed it was an appropriate elimination of the "subject to" language that better retained a signal for report readers in the separate paragraph for the unresolved uncertainty. Once again the comment letters on the EDs were seen to have substantially influenced the TF's and ASB's deliberations and final resolution.

The last issue addressed by the board at this meeting was the adequacy of example reports in the ED Appendix. One member suggested that there should also be an example of a report on comparative financial statements with a disclaimer on the first year and an unqualified opinion on the second year. It was noted that such situations occur relatively frequently with new clients and smaller clients. The TF indicated that they would incorporate such an example, along with possible others, in their next presentation to the board.

November 1987

The next time the ASB addressed the issue of the auditor's report was in November 1987. At this meeting, the Auditor Communications TF presented the board with their version of what the final codification of Sec. 509 would look like with the proposed changes incorporated. The TF chairman indicated that, due to the considerably expanded length, the document looked substantially different than the ED, however, in substance it was believed to be essentially the same. He also reminded the board of the "4-to-1" ratio of respondents supporting the board's preference for a new audit report wording.

Discussion first centered around the actual wording of the proposed report. The major wording issue still unresolved was the deletion of the reference to consistency—even though it was voted on several times in the past. The ASB chairman, in opening the meeting, noted that the SEC had made their position against the deletion more pronounced since the last meeting. If the new report wording did not include a consistency reference, then the board felt that the SEC might require a different audit report for SEC registrants that included such a reference. Accordingly, because of this "important later insight," the TF chairman wanted to discuss the issue further.

One member inquired if the SEC always wanted a consistency reference in the audit report, or whether they wanted disclosure only when there was a change in application of principles. The AICPA vice president-auditing indicated that he believed that the SEC would be satisfied with audit report disclosure only when there was a change in accounting principle. He felt that this approach would be viewed by the SEC as a sufficient "red flag" in the auditor's report. The use of a separate paragraph versus a separate sentence in the scope paragraph was then discussed.

Henry Jaenicke, TF member, voiced his belief that the report wording in the ED was conceptually the correct approach, but that a separate paragraph identifying any change in principle might be needed as a step in the right direction toward the total elimination of the reference to consistency in the audit report. He noted that inclusion of a separate paragraph would be consistent with the "red flag" reports on uncertainty, and that this might represent a reasonable compromise. He also noted that, in the future, a separate paragraph may be easier to eliminate from the report than if it was incorporated in the unqualified opinion paragraph. Thus, this suggested compromise would position the audit report wording for total elimination of the reference to consistency the next time the ASB addressed the wording of the auditor's report.

Some board members agreed with this proposal of a separate paragraph only when a change is made. They believed that there should be a consistent way to point things out to the report reader, and believed the way the board had established was a separate paragraph following the opinion paragrah. However, other members believed that inclusion in the report was not important and that the proper way to make additional reference to inconsistent application of GAAP was with a separate sentence at the end of the opinion paragraph. A vote was taken which indicated that eight members preferred a separate sentence and seven members preferred a separate paragraph that referenced the inconsistency. Because of this split decision on the part of the board, the TF chairman indicated that the TF would draft a version of a separate sentence and a separate paragraph and have the SEC comment on both so that a final determination on this issue could be made at the next meeting in December.

The TF also proposed several smaller editorial changes to the report wording in November. For example, they proposed to eliminate "on these financial statements" from the introductory paragraph, to change "We performed our audit" to "We conducted our audit" and to change "provide reasonable assurance" to "obtain reasonable assurance" in the scope paragraph. The actual report wording presented by the TF to the ASB in November read as follows:

Independent Auditor's Report

We have audited the accompanying balance sheet of X Company as of December 31, 19XX, and the related statements of income, retained earnings, and changes in financial position for the year then ended. These financial statements are the responsibility of the Company's management; our responsibility is to express an opinion based on our audit.

We conducted our audit in accordance with generally accepted auditing standards. Those standards require that we plan and perform the audit to obtain reasonable assurance as to whether the financial statements are free of material misstatement. An audit includes examining, on a test basis, evidence supporting the amounts and disclosures in the financial statements. An audit also includes an assessment of the accounting principles used and significant estimates made by management, as well as an evaluation of the overall financial statement presentation. We believe that our audit provides a reasonable basis for our opinion.

In our opinion, the financial statements referred to above present fairly, in all material respects, the financial position of X Company as of December 31, 19XX, and the results of its operations and the changes in its financial position for the year then ended in conformity with generally accepted accounting principles.

The ASB discussed the changes proposed by the TF and agreed with all of them except for the elimination of "on these financial statements" in the last sentence of the introductory paragraph. The board decided to reinstate this phrase and to make two sentences out of the existing last sentence by replacing the semicolon with a period. Thus, the new sentences read: "These financial statements are the responsibility of the company's management. Our responsibility is to express an opinion on these financial statements based on our audit."

The final editing of the introductory paragraph was aimed at improving the flow and readability of the report by explicitly stating what the audit opinion is on, and by eliminating the seemingly cumbersome structure of the original sentence.

The final issue regarding report wording addressed in November was the implementation of the new FASB requirement for a *Statement of Cash Flows* (*Statement of Financial Accounting Standards* (*SFAS*) *95*) that would replace the Statement of Changes in Financial Position. The ASB Planning Subcommittee had already addressed this issue prior to the November meeting in order to avoid having a large number of companies being issued a consistency exception audit report if they did not retroactively issue a cash flow statement when statements of changes in financial position were formerly presented. The Planning Subcommittee believed that the statement "results of operations" in the opinion paragraph of the report could be interpreted to include the income statement *and* the statement of changes in financial position. Thus, the reference to statement of changes in financial position could be eliminated from the opinion paragraph. This position was drafted and disseminated to AICPA members in a notice included in the November 16, 1987, issue of *The CPA Letter*.

The position of the ASB Planning Subcommittee was not well received by the remaining members of the ASB. The position of the remainder of the board was that "results of operations" and "changes in financial position" were two separate concepts that relate to the income statement and statement of changes in financial position, respectively. They also believed that a similar logic would hold for the statement of cash flows. It was suggested that both the TF and the ASB Planning Subcommittee confer with the FASB for their interpretation of the meaning of "results of operations" and how the new cash flow statement would fit in. The TF was directed to then propose what they believed to be the correct report wording referencing the financial statements to the board in December. Most of the board believed that the results of cash flows should be referenced in the opinion paragraph if the statement of cash flows is mentioned as an audited financial statement in the introductory papagraph.

After the discussion of cash flows, the standard unqualified audit report wording was substantially finalized. Discussion at the board continued on some conceptual and implementation issues (e.g., cash flows), however, only two minor adjustments to the actual report wording were made in December. Thus, as indicated in September, the board continued to shift from focusing on report wording to incorporating the desired report wording into the existing SASs.

This was largely accomplished by the TF presenting the board in November with what amounted to a proposed final version of the Codification of Statements on Auditing Standards AU Sec. 509. This approach did not create a document that resembled the ED or a typical SAS that would eventually have to be incorporated into the existing SASs (i.e., "codified"). Due to the pervasive changes in the codification of the SASs mandated by a new standard audit report wording, the TF and ASB chose to discuss the final version of the codification of a new report wording in what was referred to as a "mini codification SAS." This mini codification attempted to summarize all of the major issues on how to phrase the audit report, and all of the related issues, when conducting an audit of historical cost financial statements. The TF chose to exclude from the proposed SAS such issues as special reports and comfort letters, even though it was acknowledged that these reports would eventually need to be addressed. This document prepared by the TF for the November meeting became the proposed final SAS.

In order to logically present all of the audit reporting issues in one place, AU Sec. 509 was essentially restructured and expanded to incorporate all, or portions, of other existing AU sections. Some of the existing sections that were brought into the proposed document by the TF were: AU Sec. 543—use of other auditors and the sections on procedural guidance, AU Sec. 505—reports on comparative financial statements, AU Sec. 546—reporting on consistency, AU Sec. 420—consistency of application of GAAP, along with the interpretation of AU Sec. 509 in AU Sec. 9509.

The general consensus of the board was that such a summary document was certainly needed to illustrate the implementation of the proposed wording changes, as well as cohesively summarize some of the existing codification sections. Also, one TF member pointed out that this summary document was also partially in response to some of the ED respondents expressing concern for adequate guidance and more audit report illustrations. Similarly, it was noted that the final SAS could be formatted like the ED, but that there really needed to be more total guidance provided in order to be sensitive to the practical issues of how to apply the new reporting requirements.

Interestingly, the TF chairman indicated at the meeting that in drafting the proposed SAS, the TF referred to the rescinded 1985 ED proposing an elimination of the "subject to" report discussed earlier, which had more guidance on when to issue uncertainty reports than was included in the existing SASs. This 1985 ED elaborated on when an auditor would be required to render a modified report due to uncertainties, and also included an elaborate discussion of what constitutes a GAAP departure. The AICPA VP-auditing also commented that several firms had looked individually to the 1985 ED for guidance on reporting on uncertainties subsequent to its withdrawal.

In general, the ASB was in favor of excerpting relevant passages from the 1985 ED to be used in the new SAS. However, it was noted that the 1985 ED, when issued, was considered controversial and could have potentially contaminated the final SAS. To provide more background information on the 1985 ED, the TF indicated that it would give the following items to the ASB members for their review:

1. A copy of the 1985 ED,
2. a copy of the last draft of the proposed SAS before it was dropped from further consideration in 1986,
3. copies of some of the comment letters received on the ED to discern the respondents' concerns, and
4. a copy of a letter from the TF chairman summarizing the discussions for the ASB in 1985.

These items were sent to the ASB members prior to the next meeting. The TF chairman noted that he wanted any additional input (based on these items) from the ASB members as soon as possible. Otherwise, the TF would incorporate the remaining guidance they believed appropriate from these documents.

The remainder of the November ASB meeting was spent addressing the wording of the actual SAS document itself, and implementation issues such as whether the audit report should mention that a former uncertainty has been resolved, the proper guidance on uncertainty reports issued on comparative financial statements and the effective date for implementing the proposed SAS.

December 1987

It was imperative for the board to finalize the wording and content of this and the other proposed SASs in December 1987 because a new ASB would be formed in 1988. Some existing members would be off the board and new members would take their place. This could have created a substantial problem in that the new members would not have been as familiar with the status of the proposed SASs, and they would have needed some start-up learning time in order to be comfortable with the board's existing positions. It would inevitably have required a rehashing of many of the issues that the board had already addressed and resolved.

In order to minimize this potential problem, the ASB chairman obtained special approval for the existing 1987 ASB to have one last meeting in early 1988, if needed, to clean up any remaining issues regarding the 1987 EDs. This meeting would be necessary if the board was unable to finalize the proposed SAS wording in the form of a ballot draft that could be voted on individually by the ASB members. As it turned out, the ASB was able to finalize the wording of the auditor's report and the remainder of the SAS documents in December, and did not need to address the issue of auditor reports as a board in early 1988.

At the outset of the December meeting, the chairman outlined the balloting procedures to be used by the board in finalizing the SASs. He indicated that, after the ballot drafts were completed and sent to each board member, a written vote on each SAS was to be returned to the respective TFs. Board members were to vote either: (1) unqualified approval; (2) qualified approval, or (3) dissent to publication as a SAS. If the ASB member either approved with qualification or dissented, a written statement as to what aspects of the document were objectionable needed to be included with their returned ballot. This specification was necessary because a positive vote from two-thirds of the members was needed on each issue addressed for approval of the potential SAS. That is, if the number of those that dissented plus those that gave qualifications on the same issue exceeded seven, then the entire proposed SAS would not be approved. Thus, it was necessary for those who gave qualified approvals to indicate the issues to which they dissented so that the issue-by-issue accumulation of positive votes could be made. The final ballots of the board members will be discussed in the next section.

The December discussion regarding the auditor's report initially centered around the two unresolved issues of consistency and how to properly reference the newly required cash flow statement. The TF chairman indicated that, even though earlier positions were articulated regarding the consistency reference, the board needed to solidify its position in light of knowing how the SEC viewed the issue.

The ASB chairman told the board that the SEC held that a reference to consistency was a separable issue from fair presentation under GAAP and that it could be separately addressed. The SEC's position was also articulated by an SEC staff member attending the ASB meeting. It was noted that the staff at the SEC believed that reporting on consistency should be further researched to determine if the reference in the auditor's report was perceived as meaningful to report readers. The board was informed that the research contemplated by the SEC could eventually suppport the existing report wording, support elimination of all reference to consistency, or even support expanding the consistency reference to attest on consistent application of accounting estimates along with accounting principles. The SEC staff member further indicated that they believed a research study should be performed regarding consistency regardless of the position adopted by the ASB. However, the SEC did inform the board that they would accept, for the time being, a new report that only mentioned consistency when there was a change in accounting principle. This would allow for research over a reasonable period of time before the SEC would possibly recommend an amendment to Regulation S-X to formally allow the new method of reporting on consistent application of GAAP in the auditor's report. Accordingly, after some discussion, the AICPA VP-auditing and the ASB chairman indicated that the AICPA would be willing to commit to a research project that assessed the perceived usefulness of referencing consistency in the auditor's report.

In general, most of the board believed that the SEC's approach was reasonable. That is, before fully accepting the new "modified" audit report approach and amending Regulation S-X, they would initially accept the new report and concurrently ensure that research was being conducted on the desirability of various alternative ways to reference consistency.

The board, as in November, then discussed the issue of requiring a separate paragraph or a separate sentence to be added to the opinion paragraph that would highlight an inconsistency. However, at this meeting the consensus was that if the reference to an inconsistency was important enough to warrant mention in the audit report, then it should be handled like the uncertainty "red flag" and put in a separate paragraph. A final vote on this issue indicated that a large majority of members (14-to-3) believed that the proper approach was disclosure in a separate paragraph following the opinion paragraph.

Thus, the ASB finalized the decision to reference consistency in the audit report only if there is a change. This was done even though the majority of board members felt that, conceptually, it was not a necessary component of the audit report, but, from a practical standpoint, a middle ground was needed between their position and the SEC's. Additionally, the final decision of the board did not eliminate one of the existing 10 generally accepted auditing standards, but modified it to require reference in the auditor's report only when there is a change in principle.

The next substantive issue addressed was the handling of the new cash flow statement. The TF chairman, as directed by the board at the November meeting, conferred with the staff at the FASB regarding their position on whether "results of operations" in the opinion paragraph of the auditor's report could be interpreted to incorporate both the income statement and the statement of cash flows. It was the FASB staff's position that it could not, and that "cash flows" should be separately mentioned in the auditor's opinion paragraph to indicate what the statement of cash flows purports to present. Additionally, the TF copied and disseminated to the board page 75 from Appendix D of *SFAS 95, Statement on Cash Flows*, that indicated how the FASB believed references to the statement of changes in financial position in earlier pronouncements should be modified. The paragraph discussing this issue was paragraph 152, and read as follows (Financial Accounting Standards Board 1987, 75):

> Many pronouncements issued by the Accounting Principles Board (APB) and the FASB contain references to the phrase: (a) *a complete set of financial statements that present financial position, results of operations, and changes in financial position*; (b) *statement of changes in financial position*, or (3) *changes in financial position*. All such references appearing in paragraphs that establish standards or the scope of a pronouncement are hereby replaced by references to the phrase: (a) *a complete set of financial statements that present financial position, results of operations, and cash flows*; (b) *statement of cash flows*, or (c) *cash flows*, respectively (emphasis in original).

Based on this documented position of the FASB, the board concluded that the intent was for the new cash flow statement to be a substitute for the old statement of changes, and that it should be separately mentioned in the opinion paragraph just like the statement of changes was mentioned. A separate 17-to-2 vote confirmed this position. It was also agreed to issue a "Notice to Practitioners" in the January 15, 1988 issue of *The CPA Letter* that would supersede the earlier November 16, 1987 notice and require a reference to cash flows in the opinion paragraph when a statement of cash flow was included as an audited financial statement in the first paragraph of the audit report.

After these two substantive issues were addressed, the TF opened the discussion up to any other concerns regarding the wording of the report. A specific concern was expressed for the lack of parallelism in the scope paragraph for the three objectives of an audit: "examining," "assessment," and "evaluation." The board agreed to modify "an assessment of" and "an evaluation of" to "assessing" and "evaluating," respectively, to state all three points in parallel form. This editing was the last change made to the actual wording of the auditor's report included in the proposed SAS.

In order to assess whether this final report wording had a significant probability of being adopted, and before discussing the remaining wording of the proposed SAS document, the TF chairman called for an indication of support for the proposal. First, however, he reiterated what he felt to be the major changes from the current report:

1. A new explicit mention of management's responsibility.
2. Explicit reference to materiality in the scope and opinion paragraphs.
3. Explicit reference to reasonable assurance.

4. The incorporation of a more elaborate "thumbnail sketch" of an audit, including the notion of auditor judgment and estimation.
5. Elimination of the "subject to" wording, but not the uncertainty "red flag."
6. Elimination of the reference to consistency, but not the "red flag" when there is a change in accounting principle.

A vote of hands indicated the following:

Unqualified approval	13
Qualified approval	3
Dissent	2
Obstain	1
Absent	2
	21

Again, the document needed 14 positive votes on each issue to pass, and it was believed that the qualified approval votes did not all qualify on the same issue. Thus, the board approved the document for final written ballot before they again discussed the actual wording of the entire proposed SAS, including the illustrations of types of audit reports and some remaining implementation issues.

Interestingly, the TF chairman indicated to the researcher that, subsequent to the vote of hands taken at the meeting, several of the persons indicating qualified approval would, if needed, would change their vote on the final ballot to an unqualified approval if their vote kept the document from passing. Their belief was that the proposed report modification was too important for their dissatisfaction with a particular issue to stop the entire document from becoming a SAS. This sentiment on the part of the board members evidenced a strong desire for the passage of the proposed modification to the auditor's report—even if practical compromises were made along the way. This sentiment also afforded the TF a high probability of the board passing this document.

In discussing the remainder of the document, the board decided, as proposed earlier by the TF, to separately address special reports (i.e., AU SEC. 621) after the finalization of the current document regarding audit reports. It was concluded that the Auditor Communications TF and the new ASB would separately address special reports in 1988 with the intention of releasing a separate ED setting forth their position for comment. Thus, the existence of the Auditor Communications TF was extended well beyond 1987. These deliberations would eventually lead to *SAS 62, Special Reports* in April 1989 (AICPA 1989a).

After wording adjustments were made to the body of the proposed SAS, the TF chairman informed board members that any further comments regarding any aspect of the document needed to be communicated promptly to the TF in order for the final ballot draft to be mailed by January 8, 1988, and written votes returned by the deadline of January 22, 1988. The next section will discuss the results of the final vote.

Final Ballot

There were no comments regarding the revised wording of the auditor's report received after the December 1987 meeting that were incorporated into the final ballot. However, some minor modifications were made to the remaining portions of the body of the document. Thus, the report wording agreed upon in December, and presented below, was included in the final proposed SAS to be voted on in early January 1988:

Independent Auditor's Report

We have audited the accompanying balance sheet of X Company as of December 31, 19XX, and the related statements of income, retained earnings, and cash flows for the year then ended. These financial statements are the responsibility of the Company's management. Our responsibility is to express an opinion on these financial statements based on our audit.

We conducted our audit in accordance with generally accepted auditing standards. Those standards require that we plan and perform the audit to obtain reasonable assurance about whether the financial statements are free of material misstatement. An audit includes examining, on a test basis, evidence supporting the amounts and disclosures in the financial statements. An audit also includes assessing the accounting principles used and significant estimates made by management, as well as evaluating the overall financial statement presentation. We believe that our audit provides a reasonable basis for our opinion.

In our opinion, the financial statements referred to above present fairly, in all material respects, the financial position of X Company as of December 31, 19XX, and the results of its operations and its cash flows for the year then ended in conformity with generally accepted acounting principles.

Appendix IV includes the cover letter and ballot form sent to the ASB members in January 1988, along with the final ballot draft of the proposed SAS and a marked draft that noted the December meeting changes. As anticipated, the ASB voted to approve the proposed document as a final SAS. The votes received from the 21 ASB members are included in Table 7.1.

Table 7.1 indicates that 13 unqualified favorable votes were received along with five qualified approvals and three dissents. The proposed SAS passed because not all qualified approval votes were qualified for the same issue, thus creating at least 14 positive votes on every issue addressed in the new "mini codification" *SAS 58, Reports on Audited Financial Statements.* The new SAS was considered finalized in April and was printed and released to the AICPA members in May 1988, with an effective date for audit reports issued on or after January 1, 1989.

It is interesting to note that the three dissenters were all from Big Eight accounting firms, while the remaining qualified and unqualified approvals were

Table 7.1. Final ASB Votes

ASB Member	Unqualified Approval	Qualified Approval	Dissent
Jerry Sullivan (Chair), Coopers & Lybrand	X		
Barry Barber, Grant Thornton		X[6]	
John Barna, Peat Marwick Main & Co.			X[8]
Thomas Bintinger, Touch Ross & Co.	X		
James Brown, Crowe, Chizek & Co.		X[1,2]	
Patrick Callahan, Fredrick B. Hill & Co.	X		
James Clancy, Price Waterhouse			X[9]
John Compton, Cherry, Bekbert & Holland		X[4,5]	
Phillip Crawford, Berry, Dunn, McNeil & Parker	X		
Donald Dodson, Gary, Stosch, Walls & Co.	X		
John Ellingsen, Delloite Haskins & Sells	X		
Barbara Gonzales, McElroy Quirk & Co.	X		
Samuel Gunther, Own Account	X		
Richard Johnson, Iowa Auditor of State	X		
Conrad Koppel, Blum Shapiro & Co.		X[1,2,3]	
James Loebbecke, University of Utah	X		
Harold Monk, Davis, Monk, Farnswort & Co.	X		
Donald Neebes, Ernst & Whinney		X[7]	
Robert Roussey, Arthur Andersen & Co.	X		
Robert Temkin, Arthur Young			X[9]
Ernest TenEyck, Laventhol & Horwath	X		
	13	5	3

Notes: [1] Qualified for the handling of reports on uncertainties.

[2] Qualified for the handling of the reference to consistency.

[3] Qualified because of the phrase "free of materially misstated."

[4] Qualified because early application is allowed.

[5] Qualified because of the lack of appropriate guidance on when to use explanatory paragraphs to disclose uncertainties.

[6] Qualified because of the elimination of the "subject to" report wording.

[7] Qualified because of the inclusion of the statement "evaluating the overall financial statement presentation."

[8] Dissent because significant changes have been made to the ED that have not been re-exposed for comment.

[9] Dissent because there is no compelling reason to change the existing audit report and reporting categories.

from a mix of large and small audit firm members. This final vote points to the fact that: (1) similar to findings of Kinney (1986), the ASB was not necessarily dominated by the views of the Big Eight accounting firms to the exclusion of all other views on this issue; and (2) larger CPA firms, in general, may have been less enthusiastic about the potential benefits of a new auditor's report than smaller CPA firms and individual CPAs. However, paradoxically, some of the very strong advocates on the board for a new audit report were from Big Eight accounting firms.

SUMMARY

This chapter has presented the final portion of Phase II of the research project that has attempted to depict the salient influences affecting the ASB during its process of deliberation and final resolution of the 1987 ED. This standard-setting process led to the revised audit report wording embodied in *SAS 58, Reports on Audited Financial Statements*. The process has been discussed chronologically to more accurately depict the steps in developing the final SAS, as well as the timing of the respective influences on the board. Table 7.2 summarizes the major influences that affected the audit report wordings proposed in the 1987 ED. As discussed in this chapter, and clearly illustrated in Table 7.2, the ASB was affected by a variety of influences both from within the profession and from outside. These catalysts caused the TF and the ASB to reconsider earlier positions regarding wording of the auditor's report in route to the final SAS.

Inside influences on the final wording were seen from both the Auditor Communications TF and the ASB members themselves. The TF had a substantial internal influence on the report wording. It analyzed the issues, studied the responses to the ED, and presented an alternate report wording to the board based on the input and insights gleened from the exposure process. The alternate report wording was just "suggested" by the TF because they did not formally have a vote on the board; however, it was noted that the ASB upheld a vast majority of the TF's suggestions. Thus, the TF, even though it was not able to vote, did have a significant influence on the structure and wording of the final audit report.

Additionally, the TF had tremendous impact on how the new report wording would be codified in the SASs by presenting a revised "mini codification" of all relevant existing sections of the codified auditing standards for the board to examine. This arduous "mini codification" project essentially restructured and expanded the existing AU Sec. 509, and was then adopted by the board as the proposed final SAS. Again, the board deliberated on the issues and wordings embodied in this document, however, the board appeared extremely supportive of this document developed by the TF and made relatively few modifications to its wording, and almost none to its overall structure. Thus, the TF played a very important role in developing the actual SAS document that was approved by the ASB in January 1988.

The actions on the part of individual board members were also noted to have influenced the final wording, largely through fine-tuning the recommendations of the TF. These influences came about through insights gained from interactions with individuals and groups both inside and outside the profession, as well as through study and reflection on the related issues involved with changing the audit report wording. These individual insights have not been specifically assessed in this study, however, their presence has been

Table 7.2. Summary of Significant Influences

Time	Influences
February to July 1987	1. TF writes issues paper on referencing internal control in the audit report to address concerns of the Treadway Commission, GAO and Congress, and to document the board's position. 2. Comment letters on the ED analyzed in the last chapter suggest: • retain "independent" and "audited" changes, • retain a reference to management's role in the reporting process, • eliminate "intentionally or unintentionally," • modify "are materially misstated" to sound more positive, • restructure the scope paragraph to enhance readability, • reword the scope paragraph to eliminate any inadvertent indication that the description of an audit is all-inclusive, • eliminate the "appropriateness" reference, • retain "reasonable assurance," • modify the last sentence of the scope paragraph, • retain "in all material respects" addition, • retain "fairly" in the opinion paragraph, • mixed support for deletion of consisting reference, • general support for elimination of subject to report, but retention of a "red flag." 3. Comment letters from Carmichael and Zeff argue to reinstate the phrase "financial position, results of operations, and changes in financial position" to the opinion paragraph. 4. TF aggregates the responses of the comment letters received by the beginning of July and offers a revised report wording to the ASB for consideration in July.
July 1987 Meeting	1. ASB considers and substantially adopts the TF's proposed report. 2. ASB discusses FEI's concern over "representations" in the introductory paragraph, but votes to retain the ED wording. 3. ASB discusses the SEC's position that reference to consistent application of GAAP is a meaningful inclusion in the report. However, the board votes not to reference consistency. 4. Reinstatement of "financial position, results of operations, and changes in financial position" is discussed as a response to the letters of Carmichael and Zeff.
September 1987 Meeting	1. The ASB again discusses the position of the FEI in regard to "representations" of management in the report. The board voted to change "representations" to "responsibility" and to add a statement explicitly stating the responsibility of the auditor—to express an opinion on the financial statements. 2. The ASB again discusses the position of the SEC regarding consistency and upholds their original position. 3. AICPA legal counsel's letter upholding the decision to reinstate "financial position, results of operations, and changes in financial position" is discussed in support of the earlier vote on reinstatement.

(continued)

Table 7.2. (Continued)

	4. TF suggests a "mock up" of AU Sec. 509 incorporating the new report wording.
	5. In response to various comment letters, the board votes to make reference to "uncertainties" in a separate paragraph after the opinion paragraph.
November 1987 Meeting	1. TF presents the board with their "mock up" of Au Sec. 509, which restructures and expands the original section to incorporate all relevant sections of the codification of SASs that relate to audit reports. This document is adopted as the proposed final SAS.
	2. The SEC's position regarding consistency is again discussed. ASB votes to refer to consistency in the audit report only when there has been a change.
	3. Discussion of how to modify the report to refer, if at all, to the FASB's newly required cash flow statement ends unresolved.
	4. In regard to the write-up of guidelines on issuing uncertainty reports, the TF indicates that a large portion of the guidance in the 1985 ED is incorporated in the proposed SAS.
December 1987 Meeting	1. The SEC's position regarding consistency is again presented to the board which votes to modify the standard audit report with a supplemental paragraph following the opinion when there is an inconsistency.
	2. The FASB's position regarding the change from a statement of changes in financial position to a statement of cash flows is discussed, and the board votes to explicitly reference the cash flow statement in the opinion paragraph.
	3. Straw vote taken in support of final SAS.
January 1988	1. ASB votes to approve *SAS 58* requiring a new audit report wording.

appropriately noted and was unmistakable throughout the discussion and resolution of the issues embodied in the new SAS.

The external forces affecting the final report wording came from both the letters of comment received on the ED as well as through interactions with interested outside groups. The comment letters did voice strong concerns on some particular report wordings and overall issues presented in the 1987 ED. These issues were examined in detail in the previous chapter and were also identified by the TF in their examination of the comment letters. Wording issues voiced by large numbers of respondents were addressed by the TF, along with the well-articulated positions of just a few respondents. All respondent concerns identified in the previous chapter were incorporated into the TF's alternative report wording presented to the board in July 1987. Hence, the exposure process of the proposed report rewording was not merely "window dressing" on the part of the ASB, rather, inputs and insights derived through this comment process were actually used to modify the final audit report wording.

Additionally, conversations and liaison meetings with outside interested groups also influenced the board. The anticipation of the Treadway Commission's recommendation was seen to have been the impetus to cause the TF and ASB to perform a considerable amount of work in regard to referencing systems of internal control in the audit report. Their eventual recommendations and the resulting work and conclusions of the TF, however, did not cause the ASB to alter their original position adopted in the 1987 ED. It did, however, cause the AICPA to further address the issue of reporting on internal control and to better document the reasoning behind their position.

Meetings with the FEI and SEC, on the other hand, cuased the ASB to alter the report wording of the ED and some of the respective positions adopted in regard to the ED wording. The FEI eventually persuaded the ASB to alter the wording that discussed management's role in the financial reporting process, while the SEC caused the board to alter its position regarding the reference to consistency in the audit report. The SEC was also noted in Chapter 5 to have influenced the actual ED report wording. Hence, the SEC, as would be expected, was a powerful force in influencing the ASB regarding the adoption of *SAS 58*. These external forces were also noted to have more of an impact later in the finalization process, while the comment letters themselves appeared to more significantly affect the board's earlier deliberations.

In order to assess the impact of the new audit reports required in *SAS 58*, the next chapter will present the recent research that has examined these new reports.

Chapter 8

Research of *SAS 58* Reports

In order to assess the impact of the new audit reports prescribed in *SAS 58*, this chapter will present (similar to Chapter 3), the research to date conducted on these reports. The review, in essence, presents the initial wave of research conducted on the new *SAS 58* reports. Due to the relatively few studies conducted to date, this chapter will not attempt to categorize research endeavors by overall research questions addressed. However, it should be noted that a majority of the research has attempted to assess the effect of the new reports on user understanding and the messages apparently communicated in the new reports. The resulting *SAS 58* reports were intended by the ASB to be better communications of the auditor's work and their responsibility than the former reports. Hence, these assessments are crucial, and are an expected initial outcrop of research activity from an ASB project that directly or indirectly affects all financial statement users.

It should also be noted that the lack of research regarding the capital market reactions to the new reports is not necessarily due to lack of interest in this area, but to an inevitable time lag of financial and audit report information.

EPSTEIN AND GEIGER (1992)

In part an attempt to update our knowledge of the new audit report, this research updates and extends Epstein's earlier study that analyzed what values shareholders place on components of corporate annual reports. Of the 2,300 shareholders surveyed, 246 responded. Germane to this monograph, they found that while in 1973 only 13.3 percent of shareholders found the auditor's report at least "somewhat useful," 29.6 percent responded that way in 1991. Likewise, in 1973, 25.2 percent indicated they read the auditor's report at least "somewhat thoroughly," while in 1991, 30.2 percent indicated such a level of readership. However, the earlier study indicated that only 13.9 percent wanted further explanation of the auditor's report, while the recent study indicates 23.6

percent want more explanation. This last result placed the audit report sixth out of eight annual report items (behind the balance sheet, statement of cash flows, management's discussion and analysis, footnotes, and income statement) in terms of shareholders' desire for more information. However, the auditor's report ranked fourth in difficulty of understanding in both the 1973 and 1991 studies, with a consistent 21.5 percent indicating audit reports were often difficult to understand.

Additionally, the recent study found shareholders are currently expecting very high levels of assurance from auditors that financial statements are free from material misstatement. Forty-seven percent believed auditors should provide "absolute assurance and 51 percent "reasonable assurance" that the financial statements are free from material misstatements as a result of error; while 71 percent believed auditors should provide "absolute assurance" and 26 percent "reasonable assurance" that the financial statements are free from material misstatments as a result of fraud.

Overall, these results indicate that the new report in 1991 is read by more investors and is deemed more useful than the former report. However, shareholders exhibited a considerable desire for more explanation of the new reports. The new reports in *SAS 58* may have caused investors to use audit reports more, but have also appeared to spark a need for further explanation of how to understand the new reports and what they mean, especially in light of shareholders' expected levels of assurance. While this study indicates that *SAS 58* may have achieved some of its goals, it also indicates that more education needs to be provided to investors concerning the new reports.

GEIGER (1992)

This research empirically assesses the deletion of the reference to consistent application of GAAP in the standard unqualified report and the new "modified" unqualified report for consistency exceptions. The study utilized an experiment administered by mail to 242 bank loan officers (14.6% response rate). Bankers were presented case materials for a hypothetical medium-sized retail grocery concern, applying for a $2.2 million loan and operating slightly below industry average. A between-subjects design used seven sets of materials. The first four sets included materials for a company that did not change accounting principles for the period. The only difference across these cases was the wording of the auditor's report: (1) old standard report, (2) new standard report, (3) old standard report without the reference to consistency, and (4) the new standard report with the reference to consistency added. The last three cases involved a company that changed depreciation methods, representing an increase of 8 percent in reported net income. One group of bankers received the old "except for" qualified report, one group received the new "modified" unqualified report, and the third group received the standard *SAS 58* unqualified report. The last group represents the ASB's original position in the 1987 ED regarding reporting on consistency—not to mention it at any time.

The subjects were asked to indicate whether they would or would not grant the loan, and if approved, what interest rate premium above prime they would charge; and if not approved, what interest rate they believed another institution would charge to grant the loan.

Results indicate no difference across the four "no change" groups for the loan decisions. The existence or absence of the consistency reference in either report wording did not affect the decisions of the bankers. However, significant differences were found in the "change" groups. The old qualified report elicited fewer loan decisions than the new consistency report, and if the decision was made to grant the loan, these applicants were charged significantly higher interest rate premiums. In comparing the new standard three-paragraph report to the required four-paragraph consistency report, the companies receiving the new three-paragraph report were charged significantly higher interest rate premiums. Overall, the results support the *SAS 58* handling of consistency, both when there is a change and when principles have been consistently applied.

HATERLY, INNES, AND BROWN (1991)

This study attempts to assess how a United Kingdom derivative of the expanded standard report in *SAS 58* could impact U.K. report reader perceptions. The authors presented 140 part-time MBA students at the University of Edinburgh either the standard U.K. report or an expanded U.K. report based on *SAS 58* wording along with a fictitious company's Directors' Report and financial statements. The students were matched by age and an MBA aptitude test score and then divided into two groups. All materials presented to both groups were identical with the exception of the audit report wording. Subjects were asked to read the materials and indicate their perceptions toward 18 separate phrases regarding aspects of auditor and management responsibility, satisfaction with the audit report, as well as usefulness of the financial statements and aspects of their preparation. A seven-point Likert scale was used to capture the responses.

The results indicate that the expanded report significantly enhanced respondents' perceptions concerning dimensions directly addressed in the audit report (e.g., purpose of an audit clearly communicated, auditor's integrity/ independence, and management's responsibilities) as well as dimensions not directly addressed (e.g., to what extent the company is free from fraud, and to what extent does the audit report enhance the credibility of the financial statements). In fact, 6 out of the 18 items were significantly different between the two groups at the .01 level, and an additional 6 at the .20 level; with almost all items directly addressed by the report being significantly different. Thus, the expanded wording seemed to create not only the desired changes, but also a "halo" effect by changing perceptions toward items not specifically addressed by the report. However, the authors concluded that this "halo" effect would not be beneficial, especially with respect to fraud, if it takes the expectations of the reader too far beyond that intended by the auditors. Thus, they urge that if any expansion is made to the U.K. audit report that it explicitly address fraud as to lessen any potential excessive reader expectations.

HERMANSON, DUNCAN AND CARCELLO (1991)

These researchers in 1989 randomly selected 1,000 members of the American Association of Individual Investors. Each individual was sent a survey instrument containing a copy of either the old or the new standard report and a questionnaire with 11 multiple-choice questions attempting to measure the investor's knowledge of an audit and the auditor-client relationship. Response rates were 60 percent for the old report group and 50 percent for the new report group.

Their results indicate that on 5 of the 11 questions, individuals receiving the new report indicated correct answers significantly more often than those receiving the old report. Conversely, those receiving the old report were superior on only two questions, with no significant difference on the remaining four questions. The results also show that the new report group was superior for the questions concerning the responsibility of management and the auditor, and those dealing with the accuracy of the financial statements. However, on the question dealing with the nature of audit procedures, surprisingly, both groups performed identically.

The authors note that only 6 of the 11 questions were properly answered by 70 percent or more of the new report group. These overall responses indicate what they believe to be a relatively low level of knowledge. Accordingly, the authors offer a suggested modified four-paragraph audit report that amends *SAS 58* to include: (1) specific reference to the auditor's reliance on last year's audit for comparative statements, (2) an explicit statement in the scope paragraph that the financial statements are prepared in accordance with GAAP, and (3) an extra fourth paragraph that indicates an unqualified report implies that auditors are "reasonably confident" that the financial statements are free of material error and that financial statements are subject to inherent limitations of GAAP.

Overall, however, this research evidenced an improvement in communication to users through adoption of *SAS 58*, and attempts to offer suggestions for continued improvement.

HOUGHTON AND MESSIER (1990)

This research was the first in accounting to examine the *proposed* change in audit report wording. Instead of using the final *SAS 58* report wording, this study compares the former report wording to the wording proposed in the 1987 Exposure Draft. Both auditors ($n = 60$) and bankers ($n = 35$) evaluated six types of audit reports for both old and proposed report wordings. A set of 12 semantic differentials were presented for each audit report, as well as similarity/dissimilarity comparisons. These measures were then used to assess the subjects subjective meaning of each report.

The aggregate analysis showed differences between the two groups of subjects as well as differences due to type of report and type of report wording. Of particular interest is the difference between the old and proposed wording across several dimensions of the cognitive structures found among the subjects. Additionally, differences in auditor/banker meaning of the old unqualified report were not found for the ED proposed report wording. Hence, it seems that the proposed wording for the unqualified report would have narrowed the gap in understanding of the standard report meaning. However, results of this study should be interpreted cautiously due to the non-*SAS 58* report used. Indeed, this, or a similar study, needs to be performed with *SAS 58* wording in order to more accurately assess the effect of the newly adopted report on auditor's and user's perceptions and subjective meaning structures.

KELLY AND MOHRWEIS (1989)

In order to determine if the new *SAS 58* report revisions increased user understanding, these researchers examined 50 bankers and 50 investors as to their perceptions regarding the old standard report or the new standard report. Phase I of the study presented half of each group with one of the two reports and asked the subjects to indicate their level of agreement on a 7-point Likert scale, with the following eight statements:___

1. Auditor is unbiased and objective.
2. Financial statements have been audited.
3. Financial statements are responsibilities of management.
4. Purpose of an audit is clearly communicated.
5. Auditor is responsible to detect and correct material errors.
6. Financial statements are 100 percent accurate.
7. Management should be free from responsibility for material errors.
8. Procedures of an audit are clearly delineated.

Phase II of the study then presented each subject with the report form not originally received and asked the subjects to indicate the nature of the change in responsibility of the auditor going from the first to the second report wording.

The results of the first phase indicate that for both groups the new report more clearly delineates the responsibility of management and the auditor, more clearly communicates the purpose of an audit and the procedures of an audit, and that an audit does not ensure 100 percent accuracy of the financial statements. However, no increase in understanding was found in the new report for the belief that an auditor is responsible to detect and correct material errors. Phase II results show that the investors properly perceived no difference in auditor responsibility due to the change in report wording, while the bankers perceived the new report as construing that the auditor's responsibility had decreased.

KNAPP, WALLESTAD, AND ELIKAI (1991)

This related study examines audit partner's assessment of the "substantial doubt" criteria required in *SAS 59*. If there exists substantial doubt that a client will remain viable for at least 12 months from the balance sheet date, *SAS 59* (as well as *SAS 58*) requires a modified audit report that identifies this doubt in an additional paragraph that directs attention to the appropriate footnote disclosures discussing the uncertainty. This study examined 162 audit partners' (38% response rate) assessment of the "substantial doubt" criteria by giving them case materials on a financially distressed client heavily dependent on one customer. They were asked to indicate the minimum likelihood of the failing of the client's major customer that would cause them to issue a going-concern report. Subjects were also asked to indicate on a 0-100 scale their estimate of the likelihood that an audit firm would be sued following the bankruptcy of a client.

Their results indicate that the substantial doubt thresholds were significantly influenced by the auditor's expectation of the likelihood auditors will be sued following a client's bankruptcy and by the size of the client, but not the size of the auditor's firm. They report an inverse relationship between the auditor's perceived litigation risk and their reported substantial doubt threshold. Also, larger clients tended to be subject to lower substantial doubt thresholds than smaller clients. These results indicate that certain contextual variables may affect auditor's substantial doubt judgments and the rendering of going-concern uncertainty reports per *SAS 58* and *59*. However, the authors note that the auditor's substantial doubt thresholds were quite narrow, ranging from 41 percent to 65 percent. They conclude that the contextual effects found in the study may be tempered due to this relative consensus and may not prove to substantially impact the eventual issuance of going-concern reports. Accordingly, they call for more research before definitive conclusions can be reached regarding these audit report decisions.

MILLER, REED, AND STRAWSER (1990)

This study examines the *SAS 58* unqualified audit report in order to determine if the new report is more understandable to users. A survey containing 23 questions addressing the perceived responsibilities of the auditor and management, the scope of the audit, reliability of the financial statements, and the communication effectiveness of the audit report was sent to a random sample of bank loan officers. Each subject was sent either the former unqualified report or the new *SAS 58* unqualified report along with the survey instrument. Sixty-two subjects responded (no response rate given).

Bankers receiving the new audit report had a greater awareness of management's and the auditor's responsibility and believed that the audit report was more useful than those receiving the old report. However, the new report had no apparent effect on the bankers perceptions of the nature or scope of the audit, or on the already high confidence in the reliability of the financial statements. The results also provide some evidence that loan officers from smaller banks had greater improvements in understanding than those from larger banks. They conclude that the ASB has been successful with *SAS 58* in refining certain aspects of communication between auditors and users of financial statements.

MILLER, REED, AND STRAWSER (1991)

Two mail experiments were conducted using bankers and the new audit report forms. The first experiment involved 994 subjects (a 20% response rate) who were sent one of six reports: unqualified, qualified for GAAS limitation, qualified for GAAP departure, disclaimer, review report, and compilation report. Half the reports were signed by a "local CPA" and half were signed by an "international CPA." Subjects responded to 18 perception questions similar to those utilized in their 1990 study.

The second experiment surveyed 410 bankers (a 30% response rate) by giving each subject a set of fictitious financial information for a retail firm applying for a loan accompanied by one of the six reports used in the first experiment. The bankers were asked to rate the applicant's ability to meet future debt service requirements (probability of 0 to 100%) and to decide on the amount of the loan they would grant (from $0 to $5 million). They were then asked to assess the value added by the accountant's report received with the loan packet.

Results of experiment one indicate the subjects clearly distinguished between audit, compilation, and review reports, and that as the auditor involvement declined, the lenders indicated greater concern over the reliability of the financial statements. Also, the reporting of a scope limitation caused the bankers to be more concerned about the integrity of the financial data. The loan officers indicated their belief that management was responsible for the financial statements and demonstrated proper distinctions between the various reports concerning perceptions of scope limitations. However, review reports were rated very similar to audit reports in terms of scope/evidence accumulation, which places higher than desirable levels of confidence in review reports.

Experiment two found that the greatest loans with the least variance were from lenders receiving unqualified reports, and that GAAS qualified and disclaimer reports were viewed as negative signals by the bankers. Surprisingly, however, no differences in perceived ability to service existing debt was found across report types. Finally, no auditor size effects were found in either experiment.

O'CLOCK AND DEVINE (1991)

While not directly assessing the impact of *SAS 58* reports, this related study assesses auditor decision to issue going-concern modified reports (*SAS 58* and *59*) in varying "framed" information contexts as proposed by prosect theory. It was hypothesized that negative framing (e.g., 30% change of failure) of information and probabilities of consequences would cause more report modification decisions than positive framing (e.g., 70% chance of success). One hundred and fifty-eight auditors were presented a case in which they were asked to evaluate the continued viability of a hypothetical client and make a decision with regard to issuing a going-concern uncertainty audit report. The authors also controlled for individual differences in level of audit experience and attitude toward isssuing going-concern opinions.

The results indicate that while experience or attitude were not important in explaining report modifications, framing of information had a significant effect on the auditor's reporting decision. As expected, negatively framed information elicited significantly more going-concern reports than did positively framed information. Implications of this research are that audit report decisions, particularly going concern decisions, may be highly susceptible to being manipulated by the effect of positively or negatively framing the information.

PRINGLE, CRUM, AND SWETZ (1990)

This study examines the new audit report for companies in which there is a going-concern uncertainty. Accounting student subjects were given five sets of financial statements and relevant footnotes accompanied with either *SAS 34* qualified audit reports ("subject-to" qualifications) or new *SAS 59* "modified" unqualified audit reports for uncertainty. Subjects were then asked to rank the five companies from strongest to weakest in terms of relative investment potential. The authors tested for differences in audit report messages by investigating the relative rankings of the five companies.

Their results show no difference in relative company rankings for each set of firms, and also that subjects within each group consistently ranked each company. However, *SAS 34* companies were ranked more consistently than *SAS 59* companies, indicating a possible ambiguous signal in the new reporting format that combines a "clean" opinion with a "red flag" warning.

SPIRES AND WILLIAMS (1990)

The authors discuss potential reasons auditors might have wanted to be or not to be early adopters of *SAS 58* for audit reports issued during the transition period between February 10 to December 31, 1988. Auditors could have viewed the *SAS 58* standard reports as reducing exposure to legal liability due to the new explicit reference to management's responsibility for the financial statements. However, the elimination of the "subject-to" qualification could have been viewed by auditors as not significantly reducing exposure to legal liability. Also, pressure from clients is discussed as a force to encourage auditors to adopt *SAS 58* early in situations that would have required a former qualification. Hence to assess these opposing forces, actual reporting behavior on 722 publicly traded companies issued reports during the transition period was examined.

They found that overall 64 percent of all reports in their transition sample used *SAS 58* reports, and that there were no large differences in relative uses of *SAS 58* reports verses pre-*SAS 58* reports for the standard unqualified and uncertainty reports examined. They conclude that there was no strong evidence that firms were unduly concerned with liability exposure or succumbed to client pressure during the transition period for *SAS 58*.

ZACHRY (1991)

This study surveyed audit practitioners and auditing faculty regarding their views on whether the revisions to the audit report in *SAS 58* will result in a more effective and better understood communication. (No raw response numbers or response rates were provided.) Respondents were asked to give their level of agreement with nine statements regarding the communicative effectiveness of the old and new auditor's report.

In general, the results indicate that both groups held similar impressions of the new reporting requirements. Both groups generally favored the changes in wording embodied in the new report and believed the changes will enhance user understanding of the new report. However, almost half of both groups indicated that they agreed or strongly agreed with the statement: "users of financial statements will not understand the new form of the standard auditor's report." This finding is evidence that the new report, although improved, may not be fully deciferable by all report readers. Additionally, subjects did not believe that the deletion of the consistency reference from the standard report would alter user perceptions, and that the addition of an explanatory paragraph to the audit report describing substantial auditor doubt about the entity's continued existence would be of little aid in helping the auditor limit liability if the entity fails.

SUMMARY

In general, this body of early research on *SAS 58* reports presents a generally favorable impression of the new report's ability to better communicate its intended messages than the former report. In fact, no study found that the new reports were weaker communications than the former report, with the possible exception of Pringle et al.'s (1990) finding of less consistent rankings of distressed firms receiving the new uncertainty modified reports. Overall, the research reviewed generally supports the ASB's decision to adopt the report wordings and reporting categories in *SAS 58*. Nonetheless, several studies have found that the new reports, while improvements, are not flawless. No study, however, has empirically examined possible alternative new report wordings in an attempt to rectify any remaining deficiencies in *SAS 58*. Hermanson et al. (1991) has proposed a modified *SAS 58* report based on their research, but their proposed report was not empirically tested. Similar research, along with replication and extension of the extant studies, is fertile ground for research on the communicative value of the new auditor's report. Additionally, assessing the affect of the new reports on user behavior, the capital markets, and auditor reporting decisions are essential extensions to these initial studies and will unboudtedly provide significant insight into the requirements of *SAS 58*.

Chapter 9

Summary and Conclusions

Chapters 5 through 7 discuss the detailed results of the two interactive research strategies employed in this study and the influences on the ASB in its process of establishing *SAS 58, Reports on Audited Financial Statements.* Chapter 2 has traced the evolution of audit reporting in the United States, and Chapters 3 and 8 discuss the extant research regarding the old and new auditor's reports, respectively. This final chapter is not intended to present an exhaustive summary of the respective research conclusions and results. However, the next section will present some overall comments and the final section will address the implications for practice and research.

OVERALL COMMENTS AND CONCLUSIONS

First, the revised audit report adopted in *SAS 58* indicates that the profession is capable of altering the audit report. Several recent authors analyzing audit reporting in the United States projected that the existing audit report wording would remain unchanged for the foreseeable future (Carmichael and Winters 1982; Estes 1982). These projections were made because of failed attempts by the profession during the past 20 years to alter the report wording. However, the new report wording indicates that:

> The ASB also recognizes, and rightly so, that the auditor's standard report was not etched in stone and that it can, and should, be changed (Landsittel 1987, 84).

In fact, the new report wording is consistent with audit reports prior to the former report adopted in 1948. These earlier reports (see Chapter 2) attempted to more adequately communicate the nature of an audit, and not simply to indicate that an audit was performed and the resulting opinion. The focus on clearly and positively communicating the auditor's responsibility to all readers was a prime motivation for the new report. Research presented in the previous chapter, in general, indicates relative success in increasing understandability and enhancing communicative value of the new report.

Now that the 40-year-old language of the old report has been modified, future changes to the report wording may be more easily made than they were during the 20-year struggle which resulted in the present revision. Because the long-standing "status quo" has been eliminated, change is more likely to occur. In fact, in the discussion of Chapter 7, the ASB was noted to have assumed that a future board may analyze the audit report wording again in the not too distant future. This position was taken in regard to the handling of inconsistent application of GAAP and the report on uncertainties. The 1987 ASB envisioned that the next time the auditor's report was analyzed, all reference to consistent application of GAAP, for example, could be removed from the report. This contention represented a definite posturing by the ASB for the future scrutiny of audit report wording by the profession. It also indicates that the ASB believed that the "evolution" of the auditor's report will undoubtedly continue after the establishment of *SAS 58*.

Second, in regard to the respondents' letters on the ED, each individual appeared to have their own concerns. However, the general reaction to the need for a new audit report was largely positive. Sixty-seven percent of all respondents indicated that a new audit report wording was desirable. Only the SEC registered companies were consistently against a new report. Additionally, an unexpected finding was that the 36 individual CPAs responding to this ED were largely split on the need for a new audit report wording. Prior research and responses to the 1980 ED implied that a large majority of individual CPAs would be in favor of a new report.

The general desire for a new audit report did not mean that the respondents wholeheartedly accepted the ED's proposed wording. Eleven percent of the respondents indicated approval of the report wording as proposed; while 56 percent of the respondents indicated a desire for a new audit report, but offered suggestions for improving the ED report wording. This myriad of suggestions would have been impossible to summarize into one "preferred" audit report based on the response letters alone.

However, some of the concerns and positions noted in the respondents' letters, and included in the analysis of Chapter 6, were: (1) retain "independent" and "audited" changes, (2) retain a reference to management's role in the reporting process, (3) eliminate "intentionally or unintentionally" from further consideration, (4) modify "are materially misstated" to sound more positive, (5) restructure the scope paragraph to enhance its readability and to more accurately state the nature of an audit, (6) reword the scope paragraph to eliminate any inadvertent indication that the description of an audit is all inclusive, (7) eliminate the "appropriateness" reference, (8) retain "reasonable assurance," (9) retain the "in all material respects" addition, (10) retain "fairly" in the opinion paragraph, and (11) general agreement that the auditor's report should not specifically refer to the client's system of internal control. The response letters also indicated mixed support for the elimination of the reference to consistency and marginal agreement with the elimination of the "subject to" report. However, respondents were concerned that the existence of uncertainties should be more adequately highlighted in the new report wording.

It is also important to note that the respondents to the ED from the auditing profession, as well as the ASB, did not view the audit report as a defense mechanism that needed to be tactfully worded to insulate the auditor from potential liability. Both the ASB and the respondents to the ED appeared more concerned with improving auditor communication than with trying to ensure maximum legal protection for the auditor. The issue of legal interpretation of a new report was addressed by these groups; however, the relative importance placed on altering auditor liability because of a new report was minimal.

A major finding of this study was that the concerns of the respondents identified in the analysis of Chapter 6, and summarized above, were also identified and addressed by the TF and the ASB through their in-house analysis of the response letters. More importantly, Chapter 7 demonstrated that the concerns expressed in the response letters actually caused the ASB to modify the ED wording before arriving at the final version in the adopted SAS.

In addition to responding to concerns expressed by several commentors, the board was also responsive to a few individual letters. The well-articulated comment letters of Stephen Zeff and Douglas Carmichael that argued for the reinstatement of "financial position, results of operations and changes in financial position" to the opinion paragraph caused the ASB to reconsider the position in the ED and to eventually reinstate the deleted phrase. These two letters did not simply indicate disagreement with the proposed deletion, but offered a sound and well-articulated argument for their positions. The board's reaction to these two comment letters illustrates that one or a few letters offering well-presented, sound reasoning behind differing positions can significantly impact the ASB. The influence of these two letters also illustrates that the comment letters were actually used by the TF and ASB to gain insight into the potential standards, and not as "votes," per se, on particular issues.

The board's deliberation process and the TF's work have similarly indicated that the letters of comment to the ED were actually used for the purpose espoused by the board—to gain insight into the topic addressed in the ED. This study has documented that the ASB adequately addressed and resolved the concerns expressed in the letters of comment, and did not simply perform a ritual of soliciting comments on the ED as required by the AICPA. The exposure process was seen to have been more than mere "window-dressing" on the part of the ASB which utilized the comments in their process of finalizing the SAS (March and Shapira 1982; Meyer and Rowan 1977).

However, an additional note regarding the comment letters received on this ED was the fact that *none* were received from the financial statement user group (investment analysts, bankers, stockholders, etc.), and few were received from the financial statement preparer community (corporate and not-for-profit management). These zero- and low-response rates are extremely disappointing in that these groups, especially the "users," are the intended beneficiaries of the new audit report. The nonresponse of users is disappointing because a prime reason for altering the former report language was to better communicate with readers of audit reports. Their insights regarding the proposal would have been beneficial to the ASB in its later deliberations. The nonresponse of these two segments points to the fact that the AICPA should consider altering the normal procedures for soliciting outside views when the topic being addressed has a direct impact on groups other than auditors.

The 1987 ED was issued as part of the board's "expectations gap" projects. However, no direct efforts were made to assess the proposed report's impact on readers. Sullivan (1986, 1), in discussing the evolving "expectations gap" EDs, indicated that:

> Until recently, the Auditing Standards Board (ASB) has dealt with subjects that for the most part have been important to auditors . . . Those were subjects of great interest to auditors, but of little interest to those with broader responsibilities for financial reporting or to users of audited financial statements such as investors, creditors and analysts.
>
> Now, however, . . . the ASB has begun several new projects that focus on issues that will have a broader impact on financial reporting than the previous SAS's did.

However, the ASB did not modify its existing standard-setting process to reflect the impact of these 10 "expectations gap" EDs issued in 1987. The ASB should have modified its normal indirect solicitation of outside views regarding these EDs. In 1980 a public hearing was held prior to the release of the 1980 ED proposing a modified audit report. The 1980 respondents included several report users (bankers, financial analysts, etc.) and a higher proportion of financial statement preparers than in 1987 (see Table 6.2). Perhaps public hearings, such as those held in 1980, should be required as part of the standard-setting process when the ASB addresses the auditor's report and related reporting issues (i.e., special reports, etc.). A public hearing may foster heightened interest and awareness among outside groups regarding the issues that affect them. Such a mechanism, coupled with direct solicitation efforts to encourage outside groups to express their views, or possibly with some minimal level of research conducted on these groups (i.e., opinion surveys, etc.) would enhance the ASB's ability to incorporate outside views in the final SASs. An alteration of the process may succeed in better addressing the views of affected groups prior to finalization of the SAS.

Additionally, the ASB should reconsider the philosophy of issuing groups of EDs at the same time. This process, albeit probably more efficient from the board's perspective, may have limited the overall number of respondents on each ED due to an information overload. Also, this "information overload" effect would probably be more pronounced for nonauditing groups, and may have discouraged these relevant views from being expressed concerning the proposed new audit report.

Third, this study has also documented the importance and influence of the Auditor Communications TF in the process of establishing an SAS. The TF chairman and technical manager were seen as the two most prominent and influential members of the TF in its efforts to finalize *SAS 58*. The TF was instrumental in addressing the issues and preparing the wording finally adopted in the ED, including the introduction of the three-paragraph format. The TF was also given sole responsibility for analyzing the written responses to the ED and presenting the respondents' concerns to the board. They were shown to have been responsive to these concerns and presented a revised audit report wording based on the comment letters and their continued discussions. This revised wording was largely adopted in the final report version of *SAS 58*. The TF was also responsible for drafting the final SAS document. Although the ASB discussed the proposed SAS wording and the related issues, they made very few substantive modifications to the draft prepared and presented by the TF. The issues addressed by the board concerning the auditor's report, the resolution of the issues, and the finalization of the SAS were largely and unmistakably affected by the efforts of the TF.

Fourth, this study has also explored and documented the other salient influences on the ASB and how they affected the final SAS report wording. Outside influences such as the Treadway Commission, SEC and FEI affected board discussions, and some eventually affected the final wording of the report.

The Treadway Commission largely influenced the ASB to more thoroughly consider whether auditors should refer to client's system of internal control in their audit report. Although this reassessment of the ASB's position did not result in a change in their original position, the Auditor Communications TF did prepare a 19-page issues paper setting forth preliminary conclusions that were upheld by the ASB.

The FEI influenced the ASB with their persistent interaction both in the form of a formal written response and subsequent meetings with the ASB. This persistence caused the ASB to alter the report wording concerning the role of management in the financial reporting process. It was found that, in the early deliberations concerning the ED, the TF and ASB considered and rejected the FEI's position; however, persistence caused the ASB to reconsider and eventually adopt their position and modify the report wording accordingly.

However, the most influential outside force on the report wording, other than the respondents' letters, was the SEC. This influence stems from their legislated authority to accept or reject auditor reports for entities that are required to be registered with them. Newmann (1981) refers to this as the SEC's "veto power" in accounting and auditing standard-setting. Because the SEC has the authority to reject an alternate report wording, and thus possibly create dual reporting requirements for auditors of SEC and non-SEC registrants, the ASB carefully considered the SEC's positions. Hence, the SEC's position that the report should continue to refer to GAAS caused the ASB to alter the originally proposed ED report wording; and their position regarding auditor attestation on consistent application of GAAP, likewise, caused the ASB to reach a compromise by requiring a separate paragraph in the report if there has been a change. Not surprisingly, the analyses of Chapters 5 and 7 have documented that the SEC had a significant influence on the final audit report wording and the ASB positions eventually finalized in *SAS 58*.

Fifth, this study indicates that outside views did not always correspond with the adopted positions of the ASB. This created situations where a compromise solution was at times enacted by the board. The discussion and conflict-resolution process described in this study is indicative of a political process where not all of the views expressed are identical. Thus, this study depicted the ASB's standard-setting process as a political process that must sometimes address and resolve conflicting positions. The concept of a political process is a marked departure from the "traditional" view that the determination of accounting pronouncements should be a logical theory-based process. Several other researchers have addressed standard-setting in the area of accounting standards and have reached similar conclusions (Horngren 1973; Hussein and Ketz 1980, 1986; Moonitz 1973; Watts and Zimmerman 1979; Zeff 1972, 1978).

This research has also documented that the ASB was not dominated by the opinions of the Big Eight accounting firms. Willingham and Jacobson (1985) have called for research as to whether a select group (i.e., formerly the Big Eight, now the Big Six) exercise control over the AICPA. They indicate that Representative Wyden, during the congressional hearings scrutinizing the accounting profession, charged that within the accounting and auditing professions, "the same people make the rules, interpret them and enforce them" (Willingham and Jacobson 1985, 3), implying that the largest accounting firms dominate the AICPA and the accounting profession. This research has reached a conclusion similar to Kinney's (1986) and that of several earlier researchers regarding the FASB (e.g., Hussein and Ketz 1980; Puro 1985), that the Big Eight accounting firms did not wield ultimate control over the ASB in modifying the audit report wording. All of the dissenting votes (3) on this SAS were from members of the Big Eight accounting firms. The analysis also indicated that, during the course of debate, several non-Big Eight members on the board and on the TF voiced their sincere desire to adopt a new audit report wording. Thus, the Big Eight did not dominate the other members of the ASB regarding the outcome of this new SAS.

As a related aspect of this project, the study has outlined the evolution of the auditor's report in Chapter 2. A review of this evolution indicates that the auditor's report in the United States has undergone considerable change over the last century. This change, in general, has resulted in the auditor's report becoming highly structured and has ultimately resulted in standardized wording as well as reporting categories. It has been argued that the very essence of standardized wording is to religate the auditor's report to being a symbol, because there is no variation between reports (Estes 1982; Seidler 1976). The symbol, once established, takes on its own meaning, regardless of any intended meaning. However, the standardized approach to the auditor's report wording adopted by the profession over 60 years ago, is so enamered that it will likely remain for any foreseeable alterations in the auditor's report.

Finally, this project has also reviewed the extant research to date on the former auditor's reports (Chapter 3), as well as the new auditor's reports (Chapter 8). Several tacts have been employed by auditing researchers to evaluate these reports. Research endeavors have evaluated the readability/understandability of the report, its readership, its effect on capital markets and on user behavior, the auditor's reporting decision, and resultant incremental information content contained in the report. The resultant conclusions of these studies (primarily those in Chapter 3) may or may not extend to the new auditor's report.

The next section will elaborate on the implications identified in this study as well as research needs.

IMPLICATIONS FOR PRACTICE AND FUTURE RESEARCH

Auditing Standards Board

The ASB, as indicated earlier, should consider a modification of the normal exposure process when addressing issues that directly affect outside groups. These outside groups are less likely to respond to an ASB ED issued passively for comment, and should be either directly solicited or actively encouraged to respond to the ED. Additionally, public hearings giving adequate allowance for the opinions of the affected groups would serve to increase the ASB's awareness of these outside positions and may also create increased visibility and interest regarding the issues addressed, thereby creating an atmosphere whereby affected groups outside of the auditing profession would be more likely to respond to the ASB. The ASB's "normal" standard-setting is not being denounced, however, adjustments to the normal process should be made in regard to issues directly affecting groups other than auditors.

Additionally, the ASB should reconsider the issuance of multiple EDs at one time. This practice may contribute to a reduction in the number of respondents to the individual EDs. The ASB should assess the potential for information overload and weigh it against any potential benefit from issuing batches of EDs.

Finally, the Auditor Communications TF had a major influence on the final outcome of *SAS 58*. The TF's influence is not believed to be unique to the auditor's report project. Accordingly, the ASB should carefully appoint TF members, and assign projects to TFs with a keen awareness of their potential influence on not only the final resolution of the topic, but on the entire process of standard-setting.

CPA Firms and Individual CPAs

Practitioners should write comment letters to the ASB. This study found that the ASB did utilize the comments received during the exposure period to alter the final SAS. It was also shown that even a few well-written positions could influence the ASB. The implication of these findings for practitioners, then, is straightforward—write letters because your comments have an impact. For the responses to EDs to have maximum impact they should be logical and articulate. Because the ASB does not view the letters strictly as "votes," it is important to clearly and unequivocally present *and* defend one's insights on the issues. The ASB did appear to be responsive to the concerns expressed by the larger numbers of respondents; however, they appeared most responsive to comment letters that soundly supported their positions (e.g., the letters from Zeff and Carmichael). This study has clearly shown that practitioners should become active in the standard-setting process since the ASB does appear to listen to the concerns of respondents to the EDs.

Non-audit Groups

Likewise, nonaudit groups should also become more active in the auditing standard-setting process, particularly on issues that affect them. This study has shown that the FEI, through continued interaction, did influence the ASB and the final SAS. Their influence shows that groups outside of the auditing profession can affect auditing standards. Accordingly, these outside groups should let their positions be known to the ASB.

Additionally, these outside groups should monitor the activities of the ASB for issues that affect them. It was noted that *no* audit report users responded to the 1987 ED proposing a change in audit report wording. However, the 1980 ED proposing a new audit report elicited responses from this community. Where were the bankers and financial analysts in 1987? Certainly the issue of audit reporting in 1987 affected the same users that responded to the 1980 ED. The ASB cannot take entire responsibility for the lack of response of these user groups in 1987. These groups should not wait for direct solicitation from the ASB. The positions of these users could have made an impact on the outcome of the audit report wording included in the final SAS. However, because no letters of comment were received, or no user organizations contacted the TF or ASB during this period, their silent views had no impact.

Accounting and Auditing Researchers

Similar to practitioners, accounting and auditing researchers should submit letters of comment to the ASB. The two most influential single letters came from individuals involved in research. Because the membership of the ASB is predominately practitioners, responses from academics may provide different insight to the board on topics it addresses.

Also, there are numerous possible extensions and complimentary research projects based on this study. The primary reason for dissatisfaction with the auditor's report was that it poorly communicated the role of the auditor during an audit. Similar to research conducted by Geiger (1992), Hermanson et al. (1991), Houghton and Messier (1990), Kelly and Mohrweis (1989), and Miller et al. (1990), future research should attempt to determine whether the revised report communicates a different message from the report users' perspective, and if so, what that new message is and how it differs from that conveyed by the old report. In fact, Alan Winters, AICPA director of auditing research, in anticipation of the adoption of a new report wording, indicated the following relevant areas in need of research, at the American Accounting Association's National Meeting in August 1987:

- User understanding of audit reports.
- User expectations of audit reports.
- Influence of reports on readers' decisions.
- Influence of reporting standards on what's reported.
- Report modifications or additional communications to enhance reader understanding.

He then went on to indicate the following as some needed specific research projects:

- Effectiveness of reporting consistency exceptions.
- Effect of removing consistency exceptions on user decisions.
- Effect of removing "subject to" reporting on user decisions.
- Effect of removing "subject to" reporting on frequency of uncertainty and going-concern reporting.
- Readability/understanding of a new standard report.
- Effect of a new standard report on the "expectations gap".

These lists of needed projects and the results of this study indicate that the auditor's report is fertile ground for research. Future research, however, should continue to attempt to determine whether the report readers' understanding of the role the auditor has assumed with regard to the financial statements has changed because of the reporting requirements embodied in the new SAS.

The research performed to date on the new audit reports has only begun to address some of these issues. The general findings to date indicate that the new reports are better, but not perfect, communications of the auditor's intended messages. However, very few studies have been performed on only a limited number of audit report types to definitively assess the impact of the new reports and their communication value to various groups.

Additionally, as pointed out by Winters above, future research should attempt to assess how the new reporting standards affect auditor's reporting decisions. Are auditors going to be more apt to offer a new "modified unqualified" report for uncertainties than the old "subject to" qualified report? If so, in what situations or to what clients? Also, how are these new reports interpreted and utilized by financial statement users and financial markets?

Another area of future research is to assess potential new report wordings in order to influence any future report revisions. Although it is difficult to extensively educate through the standard report, some education and rethinking certainly takes place. To this end, future research should evaluate alternative report wordings and models in order to determine what works best and in what circumstances. In this way, future research could serve as a valuable input to the standard-setting process and not simply serve to evaluate wordings and report categories once they have been adopted as has been done in almost all research to date.

Additionally, as in Gul (1990), and Knapp, et al. (1991) future research assessing individuals, whether auditors or users, should also attempt to incorporate individual traits in order to properly ferret out the appropriate cause of any findings concerning various audit reports.

Future research should also attempt to ascertain the impact of these new reports on the capital markets. Results of future studies regarding the new consistency or going-concern reports, for example, should be compared with results from similar studies involving the former audit report wordings. These new reports present a need for replications of existing studies in order to assess the impact of the new report wordings as well as the new report categories and the eliminations of old categories. To date, however, no study has utilized the new reports in a capital markets setting.

Another issue raised in this study, which was also identified in the earlier work of Mutchler (1984, 24), is the interesting question of "whether auditing guidelines should be based on theoretical parity or practical applicability." This study has indicated that "theoretical parity" succumbed to "practical applicability" with regard to reporting on uncertainties and consistent application of GAAP. Future research should also explore this trade-off in conjunction with other auditing standards and guidelines.

Additionally, the content analysis methodology developed in this study can be applied to prior and future issues considered by the ASB, or any other rule-making body that deliberates and solicits outside views on agenda topics. The content analysis methodology is a powerful tool for ascertaining and summarizing messages included in archival communications and is appropriate in a variety of circumstances. Also, a detailed approach to content analysis should be used that attempts to discern as many differences in message content as possible.

This study has also found that each letter of response to the ED did not carry an identical weight. The well-articulated positions of Zeff and Carmichael greatly influenced the board, not necessarily for their approval/disapproval, but primarily for the arguments in support of their positions. Thus, letters advocating similar agreement/disagreement positions may not necessarily carry the same weight due to the presentation of the position and the supporting reasoning, as well as the reputation of the author. Researchers performing content analysis studies should be aware of this potential limitation when assigning all comment letters equal weight. Accordingly, a content analysis enhanced by field observations and interviews, similar to those conducted during this study, may be necessary to properly determine which letters or arguments carried more "weight" than others.

Lastly, Chapter 1 indicated the need for more studies on standard-setting bodies in accounting, in order to more fully understand the standard-setting process. Several researchers have analyzed written responses to the FASB and have assumed a cause/effect relationship for these attempts to influence, without researching their actual impact (Klein 1978; Frazier et al. 1984; Puro 1984). This study has shown that such a simplistic assumption of cause/effect is not necessarily representative of the actual process. The letters were not regarded as votes and simply tabulated. In order to properly assess the causal relationship of written responses, a content analysis approach should be coupled with field observations and interviews with board members and participants. Accordingly, studies examining the standard-setting process should fully incorporate the impact of the staff or TF that aids in establishing the standard. As suggested by Hussein (1981) and documented in this study, to fully understand standard setting, the process should be studied longitudinally, beginning with the identification of the issue and continuing through to the final resolution.

The more longitudinal studies that are performed, the more knowledge will be gained concerning the standard-setting endeavor and the actual interplay of forces that shape the process and final product. This insight, based on a number of studies, would then allow theories of standard-setting that are grounded in actual empirical experience to be formulated. It must also be noted that the standard-setting experience may well be different among the ASB, FASB, GASB, and any other accounting standard-setting body which may require each process to be analyzed separately and may lead to different standard-setting theories.

These suggested extensions and related studies represent a portion of the study's implications for future research. One great strength of an exploratory study is the wealth of relationships and implications for future research it produces. Research contributing to the enhanced awareness of auditors' and report readers' views, concerns and decision behavior, along with increased insight into the relationships between the board and interested outside parties, and the board's decision-making process will be constructive to the development of both practice and future research.

Appendix I

**Respondents to the 1987
ED on the Auditor's Report**

Response Number	Name/Firm	Group*
1	Paul Rosenfield/AICPA Acctg. Standards	6
2	Lorin Carl/Carl & Carlson	3
3	R. L. Daniel, Jr.	4
4	Michael Cummins	4
5	George Botschin	4
6	John Wilson	4
7	Alfred Au	13
8	Joseph A. Bush/Legier & Perron	3
9	James S. Worthington	13
10	Jack L. Curnow	4
11	Henry Dykowsky	4
12	Sterling Stoudenmire	4
13	Willis A. Smith	16
14	J. R. Duputy/Duputy, Montgomery, Inc.	3
15	Conrad A. Koppel/Blum Shapiro & Co.	6
16	Edward J. Silverman/Goldberg Geiser & Co., Ltd.	10
17	Homer Kripke	13
18	Robert S. Waldron	13
19	Holly L. Williams/Broak, Freeman, & Lee	3
20	Kenneth W. Pierce	4
21	Laventhol & Horwath	2
22	Deloitte, Haskins & Sells	1
23	John A. Rasmussen	4
23	Barbara Hutson, Gonzales/McElroy, Quick & Co.	6
25	Crowe, Chizek & Co.	2
26	Peat Marwick Main & Co.	1
27	Barry B. Findley/Findley and Jenkins	3
28	Virginia Society of CPAs	5
29	Gehrig C. Cosgray/Garrison, Mathieson, Cosgray & Falk	3
30	Cherry, Bekaert & Holland	2
31	Robert G. Cronson/Illinois Auditor General	7
32	Dorothy O. Harris/Hedrick & Harris	3
33	Mark L. Roth/Roth & Kubricki	3
34	Jerome F. Prewoznik	4
35	Grant Thornton	2
36	Lee Morton	13
37	Lori Grandstaff	13
38	Jeffery W. Boje	16
39	Lisa Lettenmaier	13
40	Mario deArmas	13
41	Anjie Buland	13
42	James N. Kennedy/Kennedy & Kennedy	3
43	Scott L. Adams	13
44	Sol Spielberg/Spielberg, Herman & Aronin	3
45	David B. Hawkins/Raetz & Hawkins	3

(continued)

Response Number	Name/Firm	Group*
46	Joe Jersild/Zoller, Jersild & Co.	3
47	J. A. Wellman	4
48	Accounting Class/University of Illinois at Urbana	13
49	Robert Lindauer/Greenstein, Logan, & Co.	3
50	Robert K. Hicks/Wood, Singleton & Mackey	3
51	M. K. Willis	4
52	Richard D. Johnson/Iowa State Auditor	7
53	Charles R. Capdepon	4
54	Douglas Carmichael	13
55	Ethel C. Pettigrew/Pettigrew & Co.	3
56	Michael K. Schaefer	4
57	David N. VanDam/Elmore R. Verlander & Co.	3
58	P. D. Rogers	4
59	A. F. Chapin III	4
60	Monte Pipes/Pipes & Rankin	3
61	Joseph A. Sciarrino/Financial Executives Institute	12
62	Michael E. Batts/Forness, Graham & Cottrill	3
63	Robert Scullion/Scullion, Beckman & Co.	3
64	J. Michael Inzina/Hill, Inzina & McGrew	3
65	Joseph A. Hock	4
66	Frank S. Corcell	4
67	Stephen A. Zeff	13
68	A. Clyde Livingston	4
69	Bruce Jefferson/Jefferson & Co.	3
70	Accounting Class/Cleveland State University	13
71	Coopers & Lybrand	1
72	Edward L. Strother/Knight, Vale & Gregory	3
73	Edward L. Schultz/Bertelson Company	3
74	John R. Flynn	4
75	J. G. Eisele/FD & Co.	3
76	Harry W. Child/Child & Smith	3
77	James W. Wilbern/Henderson, Wilkerson & Co.	3
78	Sharon S. Nystuen	4
79	Unknown	16
80	Anthony P. DeStefano	10
81	Richard D. Jergenson/Hansen, Jergenson & Co.	3
82	David W. Dusendschon/Kimberly-Clark	9
83	Ray Michalski/Swearingen & Swearingen	4
84	Randy Tongier/Kansas Legislative Div. of Post Audit	7
85	Arthur Andersen & Co.	1
86	Larry Wolfe/AICPA, PCPS Technical Issues	6
87	Anthony Piccirilli/Rhode Island Auditor General	7
88	Susan B. Stafford/Gaston & Co.	3
89	Steven M. Breshgold	4
90	Roger L. Sample/Sample, Soukup & Bailey	3

(continued)

Response Number	Name/Firm	Group*
91	J. H. Burris/Louisiana Legislative Auditor	7
92	Roger C. Busler	4
93	Arizona Society of CPAs	5
94	National State Auditors Association	7
95	L. R. Scriggins and R. James Gormly/Amer. Bar Assoc.	14
96	W. Scott Weismann/Tannebaum, Bindler & Co.	3
97	New Jersey Society of CPAs	5
98	Patrick J. Carter/Hocker & Carter	3
99	Marshall A. Geiger	13
100	Brian H. U. Denyer	4
101	Rodney L. Scribner/State Auditor of Maine	7
102	Samuel P. Gunther	6
103	Marvin Raymond Brown	4
104	Fredrick W. Deichman/Aetna Life and Casualty	9
105	Larry T. Williams/Charles T. Mitchell Co.	3
106	McElroy, Quirk & Co.	3
107	Unknown	16
108	Richard J. Elder/Moore, Smith, and Dale	3
109	Walter Schuetze/AICPA Auditing Standards. Exec. Comm.	6
110	Jacquelyn L. Hoefer/Kane & Associates	3
111	C. Matthew Lusco/Fed. Fin. Inst. Examination Counsel	8
112	John Benham/Roberts Cherry & Co.	3
113	Legislative Auditor's Office of Montana	7
114	Blum, Shapiro & Co.	3
115	Patrick S. Callahan/Frederick B. Hill & Co.	6
116	Carol Robertson/Swartz, Bresenoff, Yarner & Jacobs	3
117	Charles W. Brown/Brown, Schwab, Berquist & Cook	3
118	Gerald L. Goodman/Surles & Assoc.	3
119	William J. Ihlanfeldt/National Assoc. of Accountants	12
120	Douglas C. Koval/Philip Vogel & Co.	3
121	Marlow C. Hunter/Eads, Hunter & Co.	3
122	Howard M. Siegman	4
123	J. Mutchler, J. Campbell, R. Ziegler, J. Worthington/American Accounting Association	13
124	Nevada Society of CPAs	5
125	Jack Mitchell/AICPA Technical Issues Committee	6
126	K. Becker Rutledge/Kushner, LaGraize & Moore	3
127	Michael A. Stern	4
128	M. F. Sullivan/Shell Oil Company	9
129	E. John Larsen	13
130	Conway B. Moncure	4
131	Louisiana State Society of CPAs	5
132	Eric R. Hofeld	4
133	William V. Allen	4
134	R. James Gormley and Campbell A. Griffin	14

(continued)

Response Number	Name/Firm	Group*
135	Sandra S. Schmidt	4
136	DiSanto, Bertoline & Co.	3
137	Manuel A. Rodriguez	16
138	Wayne Kolins/Seidman & Seidman	2
139	Larry E. Winter	4
140	North Carolina Assn. of CPAs	5
141	Kimberly K. Higgins/Bondi & Co.	3
142	R. L. Leach/Eaton Center	9
143	Linda M. Dodenhoff	4
144	R. R. Kovener/Healthcare Financial Mgmt. Assoc.	12
145	Margrete Kelly/Missouri State Auditor	7
146	Pennsylvania Institute of CPAs	5
147	Colorado Society of CPAs	5
148	Guy M. Wong/Gordon, Odom & Davis	3
149	Franklin C. Pinkelman/Michigan Auditor General	7
150	Connecticut Society of CPAs	5
151	Thomas J. Shedlock/Auditor of Lehigh County, PA	7
152	S. Payne, D. Galloway & C. McCullouge/Washington Public Power Supply CO.	11
153	President's Council on Integrity and Efficiency	8
154	Marvin Lane/Texas Instruments	9
155	John Barber/Botsford General	11
156	Arthur Young & Company	1
157	New York Society of CPAs	5
158	Illinois Society of CPAs	5
159	Edward Regan/State Controller of New York	11
160	Kansas Society of CPAs	5
161	J. Mark Adams/Advisor to Griffith, Anderson, DeLaney & Snoddy	14
162	Kay T. Pohlman/South Carolina State Auditor's Office	7
163	William U. Parfet/The Upjohn Company	9
164	J. Michael Zazulack/Koltun Buckman & Zazulack	3
165	South Carolina Association of CPAs	5
166	Ernst & Whinney	1
167	David McCammon/Ford Motor Company	9
168	Curtis Schleicher/Flegal & Harrison	3
169	Charles A. Werner	13
170	Raymond Johnson	13
171	Price Waterhouse & Co.	1
172	Martin Mand/Dupont	9
173	Ronald Bell/Institute of Internal Auditors	12
174	Charles E. Landes/Spaeth & Batterberry	3
175	Massachusetts Society of CPAs	5
176	Charles Bowsher/Comptroller General of the U.S.	8
177	California Society of CPAs	5
178	Virginia Society of CPAs	5

(continued)

Response Number	Name/Firm	Group*
179	Steven N. Delit	4
180	Orgeon Society of CPAs	5
181	Washington Society of CPAs	5
182	Donald Altieri/Xerox	9
183	H. Liedthe	4

Notes: * *Group Legend:*

1	Big Eight CPA Firms	9	SEC Filing Corporations
2	Next 15 Largest CPA Firms	10	Non-SEC Filing Corporations
3	Smaller CPA Firms	11	Governmental and Not-for-profit Agencies
4	Individual CPAs	12	Organizations Representing Issuers
5	State and Local CPA Societies	13	Academics
6	AICPA Officials and Committees	14	Lawyers and Legal Groups
7	State and Local Municipal Auditors	15	Report Users and User Groups
8	Federal Governmental Audit Agencies	16	Miscellaneous

Appendix II

**Means of Categories Coded in the
Content Analysis: In Total and by Group**

Category	Total	*Group 1	2	3	4	5	6	7	8	9	10	11	12	13	14	15
1	NA	NA	NA	NA	NA	NA	NA	NA	NA	NA	NA	NA	NA	NA	NA	NA
2	NA	NA	NA	NA	NA	NA	NA	NA	NA	NA	NA	NA	NA	NA	NA	NA
3	126	126	102	125	112	153	109	139	160	153	104	150	146	108	146	119
4	1.53	3.00	2.90	1.04	1.51	1.54	1.49	1.08	1.67	1.75	1.13	.917	2.06	1.65	5.58	.850
5	.770	1.00	1.00	.633	.556	1.00	1.00	.917	1.00	1.00	1.00	1.00	1.00	.632	1.00	1.00
6	NA	NA	NA	NA	NA	NA	NA	NA	NA	NA	NA	NA	NA	NA	NA	NA
7	.497	1.00	.600	.388	.472	.611	.125	.667	1.00	.556	.500	.667	1.00	.421	.333	.200
8	.552	1.00	.600	.612	.500	.722	.250	.417	1.00	.556	.000	.667	1.00	.263	.333	.200
9	.448	1.00	.800	.347	.389	.611	.250	.417	1.00	.778	.500	.667	.750	.211	.333	.200
10	.470	.857	.800	.347	.417	.778	.125	.583	1.00	.667	.000	.667	1.00	.316	.000	.200
11	.459	1.00	1.00	.429	.361	.556	.500	.500	.667	.444	.500	.000	1.00	.316	.000	.200
12	.404	1.00	1.00	.286	.389	.444	.375	.250	1.00	.556	.500	.667	.750	.263	.000	.200
13	.410	1.00	.600	.265	.361	.444	.125	.667	1.00	.667	.000	.333	1.00	.368	.000	.200
14	.454	1.00	.800	.265	.361	.611	.375	.667	1.00	.778	.500	.667	1.00	.316	.333	.200
15	.393	1.00	.800	.204	.389	.444	.250	.333	1.00	.889	.000	.333	1.00	.263	.000	.200
16	.022	.286	.000	.020	.028	.000	.000	.000	.000	.000	.000	.000	.000	.000	.000	.000
17	.011	.000	.000	.000	.000	.000	.000	.000	.000	.000	.000	.000	.000	.105	.000	.000
18	.164	.143	.200	.163	.194	.056	.000	.083	.000	.333	.000	.000	.250	.263	.667	.000
19	.022	.000	.200	.020	.028	.056	.000	.000	.000	.000	.000	.000	.000	.000	.000	.000
20	.235	.286	.200	.265	.278	.167	.000	.250	.000	.111	.500	.333	.250	.316	.333	.000
21	.148	.286	.400	.102	.111	.111	.000	.333	.000	.667	.000	.333	.250	.000	.000	.000
22	.082	.000	.400	.020	.028	.056	.000	.333	.000	.444	.000	.333	.250	.000	.000	.000
23	.033	.000	.000	.020	.000	.000	.000	.000	.000	.444	.000	.000	.250	.000	.000	.000
24	.011	.000	.200	.000	.000	.000	.000	.000	.000	.111	.000	.000	.000	.000	.000	.000
25	.224	.429	.400	.204	.222	.222	.000	.250	.000	.333	.500	.333	.250	.211	.333	.000
26	.033	.143	.000	.020	.028	.056	.000	.000	.000	.222	.000	.000	.000	.000	.000	.000

(continued)

| | | Group* | | | | | | | | | | | | | | |
Category	Total	1	2	3	4	5	6	7	8	9	10	11	12	13	14	15
27	.240	.714	.600	.245	.167	.278	.000	.167	.333	.333	.500	.000	.250	.158	.333	.200
28	.022	.000	.000	.020	.000	.056	.250	.000	.000	.000	.000	.000	.000	.000	.000	.000
29	.022	.000	.000	.020	.000	.056	.250	.000	.000	.000	.000	.000	.000	.000	.000	.000
30	.038	.000	.200	.041	.028	.056	.000	.000	.000	.000	.500	.000	.000	.053	.000	.000
31	.011	.000	.000	.000	.056	.000	.000	.000	.000	.000	.000	.000	.000	.000	.000	.000
32	.197	.571	.400	.184	.111	.389	.000	.167	.000	.222	.000	.000	.500	.158	.000	.000
33	.120	.143	.000	.102	.111	.111	.375	.083	.000	.333	.500	.000	.250	.053	.000	.200
34	.000	.000	.000	.000	.000	.000	.000	.000	.000	.000	.000	.000	.000	.053	.000	.000
35	.126	.429	.000	.082	.056	.167	.250	.167	.000	.000	.000	.000	.000	.000	.000	.400
36	.290	.286	.400	.306	.278	.500	.250	.083	.000	.556	.500	.000	.750	.263	.000	.000
37	.060	.143	.200	.082	.056	.056	.125	.083	.000	.000	.000	.000	.000	.105	.000	.000
38	.137	.143	.200	.122	.083	.167	.125	.083	.000	.444	.500	.000	.750	.000	.000	.000
39	.049	.000	.200	.041	.028	.111	.000	.000	.000	.000	.500	.000	.250	.053	.000	.000
40	.120	.286	.200	.122	.083	.222	.125	.083	.000	.111	.500	.000	.500	.053	.000	.000
41	.082	.286	.200	.041	.083	.167	.125	.000	.000	.111	.000	.000	.250	.053	.000	.000
42	.038	.000	.000	.041	.028	.056	.000	.083	.000	.111	.000	.000	.000	.000	.000	.000
43	.071	.000	.400	.041	.111	.000	.000	.000	.000	.000	.000	.000	.000	.053	.000	.200
44	.546	1.00	.600	.490	.278	.944	.750	.833	.333	.556	.500	.667	.750	.211	.333	.200
45	.224	.714	.200	.122	.028	.556	.625	.500	.333	.000	.000	.667	.250	.474	.333	.200
46	.164	.429	.200	.143	.083	.278	.375	.083	.000	.222	.500	.000	.250	.105	.000	.000
47	.071	.286	.000	.061	.028	.056	.000	.000	.000	.222	.000	.000	.500	.105	.000	.000
48	.126	.143	.400	.143	.056	.167	.000	.250	.000	.000	.500	.333	.250	.158	.000	.000
49	.153	.286	.000	.122	.056	.278	.125	.417	.000	.111	.500	.333	.000	.158	.000	.200
50	.011	.000	.000	.000	.000	.000	.000	.083	.000	.000	.500	.000	.000	.053	.000	.000
51	.230	.429	.400	.245	.139	.389	.500	.083	.000	.111	.500	.000	.000	.211	.333	.200
52	.131	.286	.000	.163	.167	.056	.000	.083	.000	.556	.000	.000	.250	.000	.000	.000

(continued)

Category	Total	*Group 1	2	3	4	5	6	7	8	9	10	11	12	13	14	15
53	.005	.000	.200	.000	.000	.000	.000	.000	.000	.000	.000	.000	.000	.000	.000	.000
54	.077	.286	.000	.061	.028	.056	.375	.083	.000	.000	.500	.000	.000	.053	.333	.000
55	.137	.286	.400	.122	.111	.167	.250	.083	.000	.111	.500	.000	.000	.158	.000	.000
56	.077	.143	.000	.102	.028	.222	.000	.000	.000	.000	.500	.000	.000	.053	.333	.200
57	.077	.000	.200	.082	.083	.111	.125	.000	.000	.111	.000	.333	.000	.000	.000	.200
58	.186	.429	.200	.163	.139	.278	.125	.250	.333	.000	.500	.000	.250	.263	.333	.000
59	.104	.286	.000	.143	.111	.056	.000	.000	.000	.444	.000	.000	.000	.000	.000	.000
60	.071	.286	.000	.041	.028	.222	.000	.083	.333	.000	.000	.000	.000	.053	.333	.000
61	.208	.429	.400	.163	.139	.333	.250	.333	.000	.111	.500	.000	.000	.211	.333	.200
62	.131	.286	.000	.163	.167	.056	.000	.083	.000	.444	.000	.000	.250	.053	.000	.000
63	.148	.286	.200	.143	.139	.222	.250	.167	.000	.111	.500	.000	.000	.053	.333	.200
64	.169	.429	.200	.184	.139	.167	.000	.250	.000	.444	.000	.000	.250	.053	.000	.200
65	.153	.429	.200	.163	.167	.167	.125	.167	.000	.111	.500	.000	.000	.053	.333	.000
66	.164	.286	.200	.163	.111	.222	.125	.250	.000	.444	.000	.000	.250	.053	.333	.000
67	.038	.286	.000	.000	.083	.056	.125	.000	.000	.000	.000	.000	.000	.000	.000	.200
68	.142	.000	.400	.143	.139	.222	.250	.167	.000	.111	.500	.000	.500	.105	.000	.000
69	.208	.714	.200	.204	.194	.167	.250	.000	.000	.444	.500	.000	.250	.105	.333	.000
70	.093	.571	.200	.041	.083	.111	.250	.000	.000	.000	.000	.000	.250	.053	.000	.200
71	.142	.286	.400	.143	.111	.222	.250	.083	.000	.111	.500	.000	.250	.053	.333	.000
72	.180	.429	.200	.224	.194	.111	.000	.083	.000	.444	.500	.000	.250	.053	.333	.000
73	.044	.143	.200	.020	.056	.056	.000	.000	.000	.000	.500	.000	.000	.105	.000	.200
74	.175	.286	.400	.163	.167	.278	.250	.167	.000	.111	.500	.000	.500	.053	.333	.000
75	.137	.429	.000	.163	.111	.056	.125	.000	.000	.444	.500	.000	.000	.053	.000	.200
76	.164	.286	.400	.184	.167	.222	.250	.083	.000	.111	.500	.000	.250	.105	.333	.000
77	.142	.429	.000	.143	.111	.111	.125	.083	.000	.444	.000	.000	.000	.105	.000	.200
78	.027	.000	.000	.020	.028	.000	.000	.000	.000	.000	.500	.000	.250	.053	.333	.000
79	.066	.143	.000	.041	.083	.111	.000	.000	.000	.111	.000	.000	.000	.053	.333	.200
80	.098	.286	.400	.041	.056	.222	.000	.083	.000	.444	.500	.000	.000	.000	.000	.000

(continued)

Category	Total	1	2	3	4	5	6	7	8	9	10	11	12	13	14	15
81	.142	.286	.200	.163	.111	.167	.125	.333	.000	.000	.000	.333	.000	.053	.333	.000
82	.055	.143	.400	.020	.028	.111	.000	.000	.000	.000	.500	.000	.000	.053	.333	.000
83	.224	.571	.400	.184	.222	.278	.000	.167	.000	.556	.500	.000	.250	.105	.333	.200
84	.016	.000	.000	.000	.000	.111	.000	.000	.333	.000	.000	.000	.000	.000	.000	.000
85	.219	.429	.400	.204	.194	.278	.000	.167	.000	.556	.500	.000	.250	.105	.333	.200
86	.038	.286	.200	.000	.028	.056	.000	.000	.333	.000	.000	.000	.000	.053	.000	.000
87	.005	.000	.000	.000	.000	.000	.000	.000	.000	.000	.000	.000	.000	.053	.000	.000
88	.005	.143	.000	.000	.000	.000	.000	.000	.000	.000	.000	.000	.000	.000	.000	.000
89	.000	.000	.000	.000	.000	.000	.000	.000	.000	.000	.000	.000	.000	.000	.000	.000
90	.208	.571	.400	.184	.222	.222	.000	.083	.000	.556	.500	.000	.250	.053	.333	.200
91	.016	.000	.000	.000	.000	.056	.000	.083	.000	.000	.000	.000	.000	.053	.000	.000
92	.175	.429	.600	.102	.194	.167	.000	.250	.000	.333	.500	.000	.250	.105	.333	.000
93	.060	.000	.000	.082	.083	.000	.000	.083	.000	.222	.000	.000	.000	.053	.000	.000
94	.104	.429	.600	.122	.083	.000	.000	.167	.000	.000	.500	.000	.000	.053	.000	.000
95	.120	.143	.000	.041	.194	.167	.000	.000	.000	.222	.500	.000	.500	.158	.333	.000
96	.038	.000	.000	.000	.056	.000	.000	.000	.000	.222	.000	.000	.250	.105	.000	.000
97	.033	.000	.000	.041	.056	.111	.000	.000	.000	.000	.000	.000	.000	.000	.000	.000
98	.044	.143	.000	.020	.056	.111	.000	.000	.000	.000	.500	.000	.000	.000	.333	.000
99	.033	.000	.000	.020	.056	.000	.000	.000	.000	.000	.500	.000	.250	.053	.000	.000
100	.120	.286	.400	.143	.111	.056	.000	.167	.000	.000	.500	.000	.000	.105	.333	.000
101	.060	.143	.000	.000	.083	.000	.000	.000	.000	.333	.000	.000	.500	.105	.000	.000
102	.175	.571	.400	.143	.167	.056	.000	.167	.000	.222	.500	.000	.500	.211	.333	.000
103	.005	.000	.000	.000	.028	.000	.000	.000	.000	.000	.000	.000	.000	.000	.000	.000
104	.197	.571	.400	.163	.222	.167	.125	.000	.000	.000	.500	.000	.000	.263	.333	.000
105	.137	.429	.000	.082	.139	.000	.125	.250	.333	.667	.000	.333	.000	.105	.333	.000
106	.016	.000	.000	.041	.028	.000	.000	.083	.000	.000	.000	.000	.000	.000	.000	.000
107	.273	.429	.400	.224	.194	.500	.375	.417	.333	.333	.000	.000	.500	.158	.000	.200

Group

(continued)

| | | Group* | | | | | | | | | | | | | | |
Category	Total	1	2	3	4	5	6	7	8	9	10	11	12	13	14	15
108	.093	.286	.400	.102	.111	.000	.000	.083	.000	.000	.500	.000	.000	.053	.333	.000
109	.022	.000	.200	.000	.056	.000	.000	.000	.000	.000	.000	.000	.000	.053	.000	.000
110	.044	.143	.400	.000	.083	.056	.000	.000	.000	.000	.000	.000	.000	.053	.000	.000
111	.251	1.00	.800	.102	.139	.389	.375	.083	.333	.444	.500	.333	.500	.158	.667	.000
112	.131	.714	.400	.061	.083	.167	.375	.000	.000	.111	.000	.333	.000	.105	.333	.000
113	.087	.286	.400	.041	.056	.056	.000	.083	.333	.333	.000	.000	.500	.000	.000	.000
114	.055	.571	.200	.020	.028	.056	.000	.000	.000	.000	.000	.000	.000	.053	.000	.000
115	.142	.286	.200	.061	.111	.278	.250	.083	.333	.333	.000	.333	.500	.053	.333	.000
116	.104	.286	.200	.041	.083	.167	.125	.083	.333	.111	.000	.000	.500	.053	.333	.000
117	.060	.286	.000	.020	.056	.222	.125	.083	.333	.000	.000	.000	.000	.053	.333	.000
118	.016	.000	.200	.020	.000	.056	.000	.000	.000	.000	.000	.000	.000	.000	.000	.000
119	.055	.286	.200	.020	.028	.111	.125	.000	.333	.000	.000	.333	.000	.053	.000	.000
120	.044	.143	.000	.000	.056	.056	.000	.083	.000	.111	.000	.000	.000	.158	.333	.000
121	.060	.286	.400	.020	.056	.000	.000	.000	.333	.000	.000	.000	.000	.000	.000	.000
122	.027	.286	.400	.020	.000	.000	.000	.000	.000	.000	.000	.000	.000	.000	.000	.000
123	.060	.000	.400	.041	.056	.111	.000	.083	.000	.000	.000	.000	.000	.105	.000	.000
124	.022	.143	.000	.041	.028	.000	.000	.000	.000	.000	.000	.000	.000	.000	.000	.200
125	.208	.286	.200	.163	.417	.111	.000	.167	.000	.556	.000	.000	.250	.053	.000	.600
126	.667	.714	.800	.694	.500	.833	.625	.500	.667	.444	.500	1.00	.750	.842	1.00	.200
127	.126	.000	.000	.143	.083	.056	.375	.333	.333	.000	.500	.000	.000	.105	.000	.400
128	.109	.143	.000	.122	.194	.056	.000	.000	.333	.000	.000	.000	.000	.105	.000	.000
129	.492	.286	.800	.510	.250	.722	.625	.500	.000	.444	.500	1.00	.750	.579	1.00	.200
130	.066	.286	.000	.061	.056	.056	.000	.000	.333	.000	.000	.000	.000	.158	.000	.000
131	.115	.143	.200	.061	.222	.000	.000	.167	.000	.444	.000	.000	.250	.053	.000	.000
132	.016	.000	.000	.020	.056	.000	.000	.000	.000	.000	.000	.000	.000	.000	.000	.000
133	.311	.714	.400	.306	.139	.333	.250	.333	.333	.111	.000	.333	.250	.526	.667	.400
134	.158	.286	.200	.143	.278	.056	.000	.083	.000	.556	.000	.000	.250	.053	.000	.000

(continued)

Category	Total	Group*														
		1	2	3	4	5	6	7	8	9	10	11	12	13	14	15
135	.093	.286	.200	.122	.167	.000	.000	.000	.333	.000	.000	.000	.250	.000	.000	.000
136	.011	.143	.000	.000	.000	.000	.000	.000	.000	.000	.000	.000	.000	.053	.000	.000
137	.011	.000	.000	.020	.000	.000	.000	.000	.000	.000	.000	.000	.250	.000	.000	.000
138	.126	.286	.200	.102	.167	.056	.000	.083	.667	.444	.000	.667	.250	.053	.000	.200
139	.372	.714	.600	.347	.278	.444	.250	.333	.333	.333	.000	.667	.250	.368	.667	.400
140	.399	.429	.600	.429	.250	.611	.250	.333	.333	.333	.000	.000	.500	.421	.667	.400
141	.191	.571	.200	.163	.278	.111	.000	.083	.000	.556	.000	.000	.250	.053	.000	.200
142	.022	.000	.200	.020	.028	.000	.000	.000	.000	.333	.000	.000	.000	.053	.000	.000
143	.115	.429	.200	.061	.083	.167	.125	.000	.333	.333	.000	.000	.500	.053	.000	.000
144	.038	.143	.000	.000	.000	.000	.000	.000	.000	.556	.000	.000	.250	.000	.000	.000
145	.033	.000	.600	.041	.028	.000	.000	.000	.000	.000	.000	.000	.000	.000	.333	.200
146	.033	.143	.000	.041	.000	.056	.000	.000	.000	.000	.000	.000	.000	.000	.000	.000
147	.158	.000	.400	.143	.222	.167	.250	.000	.000	.111	.500	.000	.000	.263	.000	.000
148	.022	.000	.000	.000	.028	.000	.125	.000	.000	.000	.000	.000	.000	.105	.000	.000
149	.077	.000	.200	.102	.111	.111	.000	.000	.000	.000	.500	.000	.000	.053	.000	.000
150	.000	.000	.000	.000	.000	.000	.000	.000	.000	.000	.000	.000	.000	.000	.000	.000
151	.000	.000	.000	.000	.000	.000	.000	.000	.000	.000	.000	.000	.000	.000	.000	.000
152	.087	.143	.200	.143	.139	.000	.000	.000	.000	.000	.500	.000	.000	.053	.000	.000
153	.011	.000	.000	.020	.000	.000	.000	.000	.000	.000	.000	.000	.000	.053	.000	.000
154	.082	.000	.400	.102	.028	.111	.000	.000	.333	.000	.000	.000	.000	.211	.000	.000
155	.077	.429	.000	.061	.028	.000	.000	.083	.333	.111	.000	.000	.000	.158	.000	.200
156	.016	.000	.000	.020	.028	.000	.000	.000	.000	.000	.000	.000	.000	.053	.000	.000
157	.055	.000	.200	.102	.083	.000	.000	.000	.000	.000	.500	.000	.000	.000	.000	.000
158	.016	.000	.000	.000	.028	.000	.000	.000	.000	.000	.000	.000	.000	.105	.000	.000
159	.049	.000	.200	.061	.083	.000	.000	.000	.000	.000	.500	.000	.000	.053	.000	.000
160	.011	.000	.000	.000	.000	.000	.000	.000	.000	.000	.000	.000	.000	.053	.000	.200
161	.142	.286	.200	.041	.111	.278	.000	.083	.000	.333	.000	.000	.250	.263	.000	.400

(continued)

Category	Total								Group*							
		1	2	3	4	5	6	7	8	9	10	11	12	13	14	15
162	.000	.000	.000	.000	.000	.000	.000	.000	.000	.000	.000	.000	.000	.000	.000	.000
163	.109	.429	.200	.082	.083	.222	.250	.000	.000	.000	.500	.000	.000	.105	.000	.000
164	.093	.143	.600	.020	.028	.222	.250	.083	.333	.000	.000	.000	.250	.053	.333	.000
165	.049	.000	.000	.041	.000	.000	.000	.000	.333	.111	.000	.000	.000	.158	.333	.200
166	.005	.000	.000	.000	.000	.000	.000	.000	.000	.000	.000	.000	.000	.053	.667	.000
167	.049	.286	.000	.000	.028	.000	.000	.000	.000	.222	.000	.000	.000	.105	.333	.000
168	.016	.143	.000	.020	.000	.000	.000	.000	.000	.000	.000	.000	.000	.000	.333	.000
169	.027	.000	.200	.000	.000	.056	.125	.000	.000	.222	.000	.000	.000	.000	.333	.000
170	.131	.000	.200	.061	.111	.111	.125	.167	.667	.111	.000	.000	.500	.211	.667	.000
171	.219	.571	.200	.102	.167	.333	.375	.083	.667	.333	.000	.000	.500	.316	.333	.000
172	.000	.000	.000	.000	.000	.000	.000	.000	.000	.000	.000	.000	.000	.000	.000	.000
173	.005	.000	.000	.000	.000	.000	.000	.000	.000	.000	.000	.000	.000	.053	.000	.000
174	.011	.143	.000	.000	.028	.000	.125	.000	.000	.111	.000	.000	.000	.053	.000	.000
175	.027	.000	.000	.000	.028	.000	.000	.000	.000	.111	.000	.000	.000	.105	.333	.000
176	.038	.143	.000	.000	.111	.167	.750	.000	.000	.111	.000	.000	.000	.211	.333	.000
177	.148	.857	.400	.041	.000	.111	.000	.000	.333	.000	.000	.000	.250	.000	.000	.000
178	.033	.286	.200	.020	.000	.056	.000	.000	.000	.000	.000	.000	.000	.000	.000	.000
179	.027	.429	.200	.000	.000	.056	.000	.000	.000	.000	.000	.000	.000	.000	.000	.000
180	.016	.000	.000	.020	.000	.000	.000	.000	.333	.000	.000	.000	.000	.000	.000	.000
181	.011	.000	.000	.020	.000	.000	.000	.000	.000	.111	.000	.000	.000	.000	.000	.000
182	.016	.000	.000	.020	.000	.000	.000	.000	.000	.111	.000	.000	.000	.053	.000	.000

Notes: * Group Legend:

1 Big Eight CPA Firms
2 Next 15 Largest CPA Firms
3 Smaller CPA Firms
4 Individual CPAs
5 State and Local CPA Societies
6 AICPA Officials and Committees
7 State and Local Municipal Auditors
8 Federal Governmental Audit Agencies
9 SEC Filing Corporations
10 Non-SEC Filing Corporations
11 Governmental and Not-for-profit Agencies
12 Organizations Representing Issuers
13 Academics
14 Lawyers and Legal Groups
15 Report Users and User Groups
16 Miscellaneous

Appendix III

Table of Contents for the Auditor Communications
Task Force Composite of Comment Letters

The Auditor's Standard Report
Table of Contents

Appendix IV

Final Ballot Sent to Auditing Standards Board Members

AICPA

American Institute of Certified Public Accountants
1211 Avenue of the Americas, New York NY 10036-8775 (212) 575-6200 Telex 70-3396
Telecopier (212) 575-3846

Page 1 of 2
File Reference No. 2347

January 11, 1988

TO THE AUDITING STANDARDS BOARD

Enclosed is the draft on "Reports on Audited Financial Statements" for balloting as a Statement of Auditing Standards. As you know, the Planning Subcommittee will meet on January 26 and 27, 1988, to review any substantive issues identified in the voting process. Therefore, please return your ballot to Mimi Blanco NO LATER THAN January 22, 1988.

Sincerely,

Dan M. Guy
Vice President, Auditing

Enclosure

Page 2 of 2
File Reference No. 2347

BALLOT FOR FINAL APPROVAL
PROPOSED STATEMENT ON AUDITING STANDARDS
REPORTS ON AUDITED FINANCIAL STATEMENTS

_____ 1. I approve publication of the Statement.

_____ 2. I approve publication of the Statement with qualification, and request that my qualifcation be recorded if the Statement is published.

_____ 3. I dissent to publication of the Statement and request that my dissent be recorded if the Statement is published.

(If your ballot records a dissent or qualified approval, please send a brief statement with respect thereto for publication.)

Without further qualification of my approval, I make the following suggestion for changes in form. _____
_____
_____
_____
_____

Name _____ Date _____

The Auditing Standards Division is regarded as free, at the discretion of the V.P., Auditing and with the approval of the Chairman of the Board, to make minor changes to the text not affecting its substance which may be suggested by Board members. However, if members suggest changes in substance and only approve the issue subject to such changes being made, the suggestions will be treated wither as dissents or as cause for resubmission of the document, with the substantive suggestions, to the entire membership of the board.

*   *   *   *   *   *   *

(Please return to Mimi Blanco, Technical Manager, Auditing Standards Division, American Institute of Certified Public Accountants, 1211 Avenue of the Americas, New York, NY 10036, NO LATER THAN January 22, 1988).

References

Abdel-khalik, A.R., P.R. Graul, and J.D. Newton. 1985. Eliminating "subject-to" audit qualifications and bankers' assessment of risk. Working paper, University of Florida.

Alderman, C.W. 1977. The role of uncertainty qualifications: Evidence to support the tentative conclusions of the Cohen Commission. *The Journal of Accountancy* (November): 97-100.

_____. 1979. An empirical analysis of the impact of uncertainty qualifications on the market risk components. *Accounting and Business Research* (Autumn): 258-266.

Altman, E.I. 1982. Accounting implications of failure prediction models. *Journal of Accounting, Auditing and Finance* (Fall): 4-19.

Altman, E.I., and T.P. McGough. 1974. Evaluation of a company as a going-concern. *Journal of Accountancy* (December): 59-67.

Ameen, E.D., K. Chan, and D.M. Guffey. 1992. Information content of qualified audit opinions: An extension to over-the-counter firms. Unpublished Manuscript, Louisiana State University.

American Institute of Accountants (AIA). 1939. *Statements on Auditing Procedure No. 1*, Extensions of auditing procedure, October.

_____. 1948. *Statements on Auditing Procedure No. 24*, Revision in short-form accountant's report or certificate, October.

_____. 1962. *Statements on Auditing Procedure No. 62*, Qualifications and disclaimers, September.

American Institute of Certified Public Accountants. 1978. *Commission on Auditors' Responsibilities: Report, Conclusions, and Recommendations.* New York: AICPA.

_____. 1980, September 19. *Proposed Statement on Auditing Standards. The Auditor's Standard Report, Exposure Draft,* New York: AICPA.

————. 1982. *A Users Guide to Understanding Audits and Auditors' Reports.* New York: AICPA.

————. 1986. *Codification of Statement on Auditing Standards 1 to 47.* New York: AICPA.

————. 1987a, February 14. *Proposed Statement on Auditing Standards. The Auditor's Standard Report, Exposure Draft.* New York: AICPA.

————. 1987b. *Auditing Standards Division,* Summary of Operating Policies. New York: AICPA.

————. 1987c. *The Communication of the Auditor's Responsibilities for Systems of Internal Control When Conducting an Examination in Accordance with Generally Accepted Auditing Standards, Issues Paper.* New York: AICPA.

————. 1988a. *Statement On Auditing Standards No. 58,* Reports on auditied financial statements. New York: AICPA.

————. 1988b. *Statement on Auditing Standards No. 59,* The auditor's consideration of an entity's ability to continue as a going concern. New York: AICPA.

————. 1989a. *Statement on Auditing Standards No. 62,* Special reports. New York: AICPA.

————. 1989b. *Understanding Audits and the Auditor's Report.* New York: AICPA.

————. 1991. *Codification of Statement on Auditing Standards 1-65.* New York: AICPA.

Aranoff, T.D. 1975. *The Auditor's Standard Report.* Background paper, AICPA, New York.

Arthur Andersen & Co. 1974. *Public Accounting in Transition: American Shareowners View the Role of Independent Accountants and the Corporate Reporting Controversy.* Chicago: Arthur Andersen & Co.

Ashton, R.H., J.J. Willingham, and R.K. Elliott. 1987. An empirical analysis of audit delay. *Journal of Accounting Research* (Autumn): 275-292.

Augenbraun, B.S. 1980. Proposed audit report-A lawyer's view. *CPA Journal* (November): 15-19.

Bailey, K.E. III, J.H. Bylinski, and M.D. Shields. 1983. Effects of audit report wording changes on the perceived message. *Journal of Accounting Research* (Autumn): 355-370.

Bailey, W.T. 1982. An appraisal of research design used to investigate the information content of audit reports. *The Accounting Review* (January): 141-146.

Ball, R., R.G. Walker, and G.P. Whitehead. 1979. Audit qualifications and share prices. *Abacus* (June): 23-34.

Banks, D.W., and W.R. Kinney, Jr. 1982. Loss contingency reports and stock prices: An empirical study. *Journal of Accounting Research* (Spring): 240-254.

Barnett, A.H. 1976. Communication in auditing: An examination of investors' understanding of the auditor's report. Unpublished D.B.A. dissertation, Texas Tech University.

Baskin, E.F. 1972. The communicative effectiveness of consistency exceptions. *Accounting Review* (January): 38-51.

Beaver, W.H. 1981. *Financial Reporting: An Accounting Revolution.* Englewood Cliffs, NJ: Prentice-Hall.

Beck, G.W. 1973. The role of the auditor in modern society: An empirical appraisal. *Accounting and Business Research* (Spring): 117-122.

Bell, T.B., and R.H. Tabor. 1991. Empirical analysis of audit uncertainty qualifications. *Journal of Accounting Research* (Autumn): 350-370.

Berelson, B. 1952. *Content Analysis in Communications Research.* Hafner Publishing Company.

Bremser, W.G. 1975. The earnings characteristics of firms reporting discretionary accounting changes. *Accounting Review* (July): 563-573.

Brenner, V.C. 1971. Are annual reports being read—An empirical study. *The National Public Accountant* (November): 16-21.

Briloff, A.J. 1966. Old myths and new realities in accountancy. *The Accounting Review* (July): 484-495.

Brown, P.R. 1981. A descriptive analysis of select input bases of the Financial Accounting Standards Board. *Journal of Accounting Research* 19(Spring): 232-246.

Brown, R. G. 1962. Changing audit objectives and techniques. *The Accounting Review* (October): 696-703.

Buckley, J.W., M.H. Buckley, and H.F. Chiang. 1976. *Research Methodology & Business Decisions.* New York: National Association of Accountants.

Campbell, J.E., and J.F. Mutchler. 1988. The 'expectations gap' and going-concern uncertainties. *Accounting Horizons* (March): 42-49.

Carmichael, D.R. 1978. The auditor's reporting obligation, *Auditing Research Monograph No. 1.* New York: AICPA.

Carmichael, D.R., and A.J. Winters. 1982. The evolution of audit reporting. Pp. 1-20 in *Symposium VI: Proceedings of the 1982 Touche Ross/ University of Kansas Symposium on Auditing Problems*, edited by D.R. Nichols and H.F. Stettler. Lawrence, Kansas: University of Kansas.

Chandler, R. 1984. Forget the jargon, let's communicate. *Accountancy* (March): 105-106.

Chen, K.C.W., and B.K. Church. 1992. Default on debt obligations and the issuance of going-concern opinions. *Auditing: A Journal of Practice & Theory* (Fall): 30-49.

Chewing, G., K. Pany, and S. Wheeler. 1989. Auditor reporting decisions involving accounting principle changes: Some evidence on materiality thresholds. *Journal of Accounting Research* (Spring): 78-96.

————. 1992. Inter-firm differences in propensities to modify audit opinions for "immaterial" pre-SAS No. 58 consistency exceptions. Unpublished manuscript, Florida State University.

Chow, C.W. 1982. The demand for external auditing: Size, debt and ownership influences. *The Accountign Review* (April): 272-291.

Chow, C.W., and S.J. Rice. 1982a. Qualified audit opinions and share prices—An investigation. *Auditing: A Journal of Practice and Theory* (Winter): 35-51.

————. 1982b. Qualified audit opinions and auditor switching. *The Accounting Review* (April): 326-335.

Cochrane, G. 1950. The auditor's report: Its evolution in the U.S.A. *The Accountant* (November): 448-460.

Cook looks ahead based on past agenda. 1986, November 12. *The CPA Letter*, p. 1.

Cushing, B.E. 1974. Accounting changes: The impact of APB Opinion No. 20. *Journal of Accountancy* (November): 54-62.

Cushing, B.E., and E.B. Deakin. 1974. Firms making accounting changes: A comment. *Accounting Review* (January): 104-111.

Davis, R.R. 1982. An empirical evaluation of auditors' "subject-to" opinions. *Auditing: A Journal of Practice and Theory* (Fall): 13-32.

Dillard, J.F., and D.L. Jensen. 1983. The auditor's report: An analysis of opinion. *The Accounting Review* (October): 787-798.

Dillard, J.F., R.J. Murdock, and J.K. Shank. 1978. CPAs' attitudes toward 'subject-to' opinions. *The CPA Journal* (August): 43-47.

Dodd, P., N. Dopuch, R.W. Holthausen, and R.W. Leftwich. 1984. Qualified audit opinions and stock prices. *Journal of Accounting and Economics* (April): 3-38.

Dopuch, N., R.W. Holthausen, and R.W. Leftwich. 1986. Abnormal stock returns associated with media disclosures of "subject-to" qualified audit opinions. *Journal of Accounting and Economics* (June): 93-117.

————. 1987. Predicting audit qualifications with financial and market variables. *Accounting Review* (July): 431-455.

Editorial: Public reaction to audit reports. 1947. *Journal of Accounting* (July): 3-4.

Elliott, J.A. 1982. "Subject-to" audit opinions and abnormal security returns: Outcomes and ambiguities. *Journal of Accounting Research* (Autumn): 617-638.

Emory, W.C. 1985. Business Research Methods, 3rd. ed. Homewood, IL: Richard D. Irwin.

Epstein, M.J. 1975. *The Usefulness of Annual Reports to Corporate Shareholders*. Los Angeles: Bureau of Business and Economic Research, California State University.

Epstein, M.J., and M. Geiger. 1992. Use and usefulness of the auditors' report. Working paper, University of Rhode Island.

Estes, R. 1982. *The Auditor's Report and Investor Behavior* Lexington, MA: D.C. Heath Co.

Estes, R., and M. Reimer. 1977. A study of the effect of qualified auditors' opinions on bankers' lending decisions. *Accounting and Business Research* (Autumn): 250-259.

_____. 1979. An experimental study of the differential effect of standard and qualified auditor's opinions on investors' price decisions. *Accounting and Business Research* (Spring): 157-62.

Federal Reseve Bulletin. 1917, April 1. *Uniform Accounting: A Tentative Proposal.* Submitted by the Federal Reserve Board.

Feroz, E.H. 1987. Financial accounting standards setting: A social science perspective. *Advances in Accounting* 5: 3-14.

Fess, P.E., and R.E. Ziegler. 1977. Readership of the audit report. *CPA Journal* (June): 5-6.

Fiebelkorn, G.A., Jr. 1977. The role of the certified public accountant in the accounting communication process as perceived by sophisticated users', with an empirical analysis of factors affecting management credibility and certified public accountant credibility. Ph.D. dissertation, Georgia State University.

Fields, L.P., and M.S. Wilkins. 1991. The information content of withdrawn audit qualifications: New evidence on the value of "subject-to" opinions. *Auditing: A Journal of Practice and Theory* (Fall): 62-69.

Financial Accounting Standards Board. 1987. *Statement of Financial Accounting Standards No. 95*, Statement of Cash Flows. Stamford, CT: FASB.

Firth, M. 1978. Qualified audit reports: Their impact on investment decision. *The Accounting Review* (July): 642-650.

_____. 1979. Qualified audit reports and bank lending decisions. *Journal of Bank Research* (Winter): 237-241.

Flesher, T.K., and D.L. Flesher. 1980. The development of the auditor's report in the United States. Working paper series number 45, Academy of Accounting Historians, 58-70.

Foster, G. 1986. *Financial Statement Analysis*, 2nd ed. Englewood Cliffs, NJ: Prentice-Hall.

Frazier, K.B., R.W. Ingram, and B.M. Tennyson. 1984. A methodology for analysis of narrative accounting disclosures. *Journal of Accounting Research* (Spring): 318-331.

Frishkoff, P. 1970. An empirical investigation of the concept of materiality in accounting. Pp. 116-129 in *Empirical Research in Accounting: Selected Studies.* Chicago: University of Chicago.

Frishkoff, P., and R. Rogowski. 1978. Disclaimers of audit opinion. *Management Accounting* (May): 52-57.

Frost, C.A. 1991. Loss contingency reports and stock prices: A replication and extension of Banks and Kinney. *Journal of Accounting Research* (Spring): 157-169.

――――. 1992. Uncertainty-qualified audit reports and future earnings. Working paper, Washington University, 1992.

Garsomke, H.P., and S. Choi. 1992. The association between auditor's uncertainty opinions and business failures. *Advances in Accounting* 10: 45-60.

Geiger, M.A. 1992. Audit disclosure of consistency: An analysis of loan officer reaction to SAS No. 58. *Advances in Accounting* 10: 77-90.

Gorton, D.E. 1991. The SEC decision not to support SFAS 19: A case study of the effect of lobbying on standard setting. *Accounting Horizons* (March): 29-41.

Gosman, M.L. 1973. Characteristics of firms making accounting changes. *Accounting Review* (January): 1-11.

Gul, F.A. 1990. Qualified audit reports, field dependence cognitive style, and their effects on decision making. *Accounting and Finance* (November): 15-27.

Hatherly, D., J. Innes, and T. Brown. 1991. The expanded audit report—An empirical investigation. *Accounting and Business Research* (Autumn): 311-19.

Hermanson, R.H., P.H. Duncan, and J.V. Carcello. 1991. Does the new audit report improve communication with investors? *The Ohio CPA Journal* (May-June): 32-37.

Hicks, J.D. 1960. *Republican Ascendency 1921-1933*. New York: Harper and Row.

Holsti, O.R. 1969. *Content Analysis for the Social Sciences and Humanities*. Boston, MA: Addison-Wesley.

Hopwood, W., J. McKeown, and J. Mutchler. 1989. A test of the incremental explanatory power of opinions qualified for consistency and uncertainty. *Accounting Review* (January): 28-48.

Horngren, C. 1973. The marketing of accounting standards. *Journal of Accountancy* (October): 61-66.

Houghton, K.A. 1983. Audit reports: Their impact on the loan decision process and outcome: An experiment. *Accounting and Business Research* (Winter): 15-20.

――――. 1987. True and fair view: An empirical study of connotative meaning. *Accounting, Organizations and Society*, 12(2): 143-52.

Houghton, K.A., and W.F. Messier, Jr. 1990. The wording of audit reports: Its impact on the meaning of the message communicated. Working paper, The University of Melbourne.

Hussein, M.E. 1981. The innovative process in financial accounting standards setting. *Accounting, Organizations and Society* 6(1): 27-37.

Hussein, M.E., and J.E. Ketz. 1980. Ruling elites of the FASB: A study of the big eight. *Journal of Accounting, Auditing and Finance* (Summer): 354-367.

———. 1986. Politics of accounting standard-setting: A critical analysis. Working paper, The Pennsylvania State University.

———. 1987. Politics of accounting standard-setting: A critical analysis. Working paper, The Pennsylvania State University.

Jackson, H.J. 1926. Audit certificates and report. *The Accounting Review* (September): 45-63.

Johnson, D.A., and K. Pany. 1984. Forecasts, auditor review, and bank loan decisions. *Journal of Accounting Research* (Autumn): 731-743.

Johnson, D.A., K. Pany, and R. White. 1983. Audit reports and the loan decision: Actions and perceptions. *Auditing: A Journal of Practice & Theory* (Spring): 38-51.

Journal of Accountancy. 1981, April. Late developments, p. 3.

Keller, S.B., and L.F. Davidson. 1983. An assessment of individual investor reaction to certain qualified audit opinions. *Auditing: A Journal of Practice and Theory* (Fall): 1-22.

Kelly, A.S., and L.C. Mohrweis. 1989. Bankers' and investors' perceptions of the auditor's role in financial statement reporting: The impact of SAS No. 58. *Auditing: A Journal of Practice and Theory* (Fall): 87-97.

Kida, T. 1980. An investigation into auditors' continuity and related qualification judgments. *Journal of Accounting Research* (Autumn): 506-523.

Kidder, M. 1981. *Research Methods in Social Relations,* 4th ed. New York: Holt, Rinehart and Winston.

Kinney, W.R. 1986. Auditing technology and preferences for auditing standards. *Journal of Accounting and Economics* (March): 73-89.

Klein, L.A. 1978. The influence of outside parties on the Financial Accounting Standards Board: An analysis of responses to the exposure draft on segment reporting. Unpublished dissertation, The Pennsylvania State University.

Knapp, M.C., D.A. Wallestad, and F.M. Elikai. 1991. Inconsistent interpretation of auditing standards and the resulting statement users: The case of SAS 59. Working paper, the University of Oklahoma (July).

Knoll, M. 1976. Auditor's report—Societies expectations v. realities. *Accounting and Business Research* (Summer): 182-200.

Krippendorff, K. *Content Analysis: An Introduction to Its Methodology* Beverly Hills, CA: Sage.

Landsittel, D.L. 1987. The auditor's standard report: The last word or in need of change? *Journal of Accountancy* (February): 80-84.

Lee, T.A., and D.P. Tweedie. 1975. Accounting information: An investigation of private shareholder usage. *Accounting and Business Research* (Autumn): 280-291.

——. 1977. *The Private Shareholder and the Corporate Report.* London: The Institute of Chartered Accountants in England and Wales.

Libby, R. 1979a. Bankers' and auditors' perceptions of the message communicated by the audit report. *Journal of Accounting Research* (Supplement): 99-122.

——. 1979b. The impact of uncertainty reporting on the loan decision. *Journal of Accounting Research* (Supplement): 35-57.

Loudder, M.L., I.K. Khurana, R.B. Sawyers, C. Cordery, C. Johnson, J. Lowe, and R. Wunderle. 1992. The information content of audit qualifications. *Auditing: A Journal of Practice & Theory* (Spring): 69-82.

Louis Harris and Associates, Inc. 1986. *A Survey of Perceptions, Knowledge, and Attitudes Toward CPAs and The Accounting Profession.* Prepared for the American Institute of Certified Public Accountants.

Lynn, S.A., and M.A. Gaffney. 1990. Auditor perceptions of municipal audit report messages. *Research in Governmental and Nonprofit Accounting* (Spring): 101-125.

March, J.G., and Z. Shapira. 1982. Behavioral decision theory and organizational decision theory. Pp. 95-115 in *Decision Making: An Interdisciplinary Inquiry.* Boston, MA: Kent Publishing.

May, G.S., and D.K. Schneider. 1988. Reporting accounting changes: Are stricter guidelines needed. *Accounting Horizons* (September): 68-74.

McKeown, J.C., J.F. Mutchler, and W. Hopwood. 1991. Towards an explanation of auditor failure to modify the audit opinions of bankrupt companies. *Auditing: A Journal of Practice & Theory* (Supplement): 1-13.

Mednick, R. 1986. The auditor's role in society: A new approach to solving the perception gap. *Journal of Accountancy* (February): 70-74.

Menon, K., and K.B. Schwartz. 1987. An empirical investigation of audit qualification decisions in the presence of going concern uncertainties. *Contemporary Accounting Research* (Spring): 302-315.

Merino, B.D., and M.D. Neimark. 1982. Disclosure regulation and public policy: A sociohistorical reappraisal. *Journal of Accounting and Public Policy* (Fall): 33-57.

Meyer, J.W., and B. Rowan. 1977. Institutionalized organizations: Formal structure as myth and ceremony. *American Journal of Sociology* (Spring): 340-360.

Miller, J.R., S.A. Reed, and R.H. Strawser. 1990. The new auditor's report: Will it close the expectations gap in communications. *The CPA Journal* (May): 68-72.

——. 1991. An examination of the effects of type of audit opinion, level of accounting service and CPA firm size on banker perceptions and lending actions. Working paper, Texas A&M University.

Mitchell, J.S. 1983. The auditor's standard report. Unpublished masters paper, Pennsylvania State University.

Mittelstaedt, H.F., P.R. Regier, E.G. Chewning, and K. Pany. 1992. Do consistency modifications provide information to equity markets? *Auditing: A Journal of Practice & Theory* (Spring): 83-98.

Moonitz, M. 1973. *Obtaining Agreement on Standards in the Accounting Profession*, Studies in Accounting Research No. 8. Sarasota, FL: American Accounting Association.

Morris, M.H., and W.D. Nichols. 1988. Consistency exceptions: materiality judgments and audit firm structure. *Accounting Review* (April): 237-254.

Mutchler, J.F. 1984. Auditor's perceptions of the going-concern opinion decision. *Auditing: A Journal of Practice and Theory* (Spring): 17-30.

————. 1985. A multivariate analysis of auditor's going-concern opinion decision. *Journal of Accounting Research* (Autumn): 668-682.

————. 1986. Empirical evidence regarding the auditor's going-concern opinion decision. *Auditing: A Journal of Practice and Theory* (Fall): 148-163.

Mutchler, J.F., and D.D. Williams. 1990. The relationship between audit technology, client risk profiles, and the going-concern opinion decision. *Auditing: A Journal of Practice & Theory* (Fall): 39-54.

Nair, R.D., and L.E. Rittenberg. 1987. Messages perceived from audit, review, and compilation reports: Extension to more diverse groups. *Auditing: A Journal of Practice and Theory* (Fall): 15-38.

Neumann, F. 1968. The auditing standard of consistency. Pp. 1-17 in *Empirical Research in Accounting: Selected Studies*. Chicago: University of Chicago.

————. 1969. The incidence and nature of consistency exceptions. *Accounting Review* (July): 546-554.

Newmann, D.P. 1981. The SEC's influence on accounting standards: The power of the veto. *Journal of Accounting Research* (Supplement): 134-156.

Nogler, G.E., and K.B. Schwartz. 1989. Financial reporting and auditor's opinions on voluntary liquidations. *Accounting Horizons* (September): 12-20.

O'Clock, P., and K. Devine. 1991. An investigation of the effect of framed information and consequences on the auditor's report modification decision with respect to going concern. Unpublished manuscript, Mankato State University.

Pany, K., and D.A. Johnson. 1985. The death (perhaps timely) of an audit report: Some empirical results. *Advances in Accounting* 2: 247-259.

Pany, K., and C.H. Smith. 1982. Auditor association with quarterly financial information: An empirical test. *Journal of Accounting Research* (Autumn): 472-481.

Peat, Marwick, Mitchell and Co. 1983. *How the Profession is Viewed by Those It Serves*. New York: Peat, Marwick, Mitchell & Co.

Pearson, M.A., J.H. Lindgren, and B.L. Myers. 1979. A preliminary analysis of AudSEC voting patterns. *Journal of Accounting, Auditing & Finance* (Winter): 122-134.

Phillips, B.S. 1971. *Social Research Strategy and Tactics*, 2nd ed. New York: MacMillan.

Pringle, L.M., R.P. Crum, and R.J. Swetz. 1990. Do SAS No. 59 format changes affect the outcome and quality of investment decisions. *Accounting Horizons* (September): 68-75.

Puro, M. 1984. Audit firm lobbying before the financial accounting standards board: An empirical study. *Journal of Accounting Research* (Spring): 624-646.

———. 1985. Do large accounting firms collude in the standards-setting process? *Journal of Accounting, Auditing & Finance* (Spring): 165-177.

Radoff, P.L. 1975. *Court decisions on auditors' liability: The role of GAAP and GAAS*. Background paper, American Institute of CPAs (September).

Report of the National Commission on Fraudulent Financial Reporting. 1987, October.

Richardson, A. P. 1931. Editorial. *Journal of Accountancy* (July): 1-12.

Robertson, J.C. 1988. Analysts' reaction to auditors' messages in qualified reports. *Accounting Horizons* (June): 82-89.

Rosenfield, P., and L. Lorensen. 1974. Auditors' responsibilities and the audit report. *Journal of Accountancy* (September): 73-83.

Sale, D.C. 1981. The auditors' responsibilities: The gathering storm. *Journal of Accountancy* (January): 76-86.

Seidler, L.J. 1976. Symbolism and communication in the auditor's report. Pp. 32-44 in *Symposium III: Proceedings of the 1976 Touche Ross/University of Kansas Symposium on Auditing Problems*, edited by H. Stettler. University of Kansas.

Shank, J.K., J.F. Dillard, and J.H. Bylinski. 1979. What do "subject to" auditors' opinions mean to investors? *Financial Analysts Journal* (January/February): 41-45.

Shank, J. K., J.F. Dillard, and R.J. Murdock. 1978. Lending officers' attitudes toward 'subject to' audit opinions. *The Journal of Commercial Bank Lending* (March): 31-45.

———. 1979. How financial executives regard "subject to" opinions. *Financial Executive* (November): 28-35.

Spires, E.E., and D.D. Williams. 1990. Auditor's adoptions of SAS 58 audit reports. *Accounting Horizons* (September): 76-82.

Stobie, B. 1978. The audit report: A valuable product or a useless anachrinism? *The South African Chartered Accountant* (February): 49-57.

Sullivan, J.D. 1986. Closing the expectations gap. *The Auditor's Report*. Sarasota, FL: American Accounting Association (Summer), pp. 1-3.

Sullivan, J.D. 1987. *Letter to Auditor Communications Task Force.* New York: AICPA.

Tinker, A.M., B.D. Merino, and M.D. Neimark. 1982. The normative origins of positive theories: Ideology and accounting thought. *Accounting, Organizations and Society*, (7)2: 167-200.

U.S. Congress. 1985. Hearings before the Subcommittee on Oversight and Investigations and the Committee on Energy and Commerce, Ninety-ninth Congress, 1st Session (February 20 and March 6).

Wall Street Journal. 1985, February 19. Rep. Dingell to take aim at accountants, sec in hearings on profession's role as watchdog, p. 4.

Wallace, W.A. 1984. Auditing research: Where are we now. *Accounting Research Convocation.* The University of Alabama.

Warren, C.S. 1977. Characteristics of firms reporting consistency exceptions—a cross sectional analysis. *Accounting Review* (January): 150-161.

Watts, R.L., and J.L. Zimmerman. 1979. The demand for and supply of accounting theories: The market for excuses. *The Accounting Review* (April): 273-304.

Whittred, G.P. 1980. Audit qualification and the timeliness of corporate annual reports. *The Accounting Review* (October): 563-577.

Wilkerson, J.E. 1987. Selecting experimental and comparison samples for use in studies of auditor reporting decisions. *Journal of Accounting Research* (Spring): 161-167.

Willingham, J.J., and P.D. Jacobson. 1985. A research response to the Dingell hearings. *The Auditor's Report.* Sarasota, FL: American Accounting Association (Fall): 1-3.

Winters, A.J. 1975. Bankers perceptions of unaudited financial statements. *The CPA Journal* (August): 29-33.

Zachry, B. 1991. Who understands audit reports? *The Woman CPA* (Spring): 9-11.

Zeff, S. 1972. *Forging Accounting Principles in Five Countries: A History and an Analysis of Trends.* Houston: Stupis Publishing Company.

_____. 1978. The rise of economic consequences. *Journal of Accountancy* (December): 45-63.

AUTHOR INDEX

SUBJECT INDEX